Praise for *Who We're Reading V*

"When a work of fiction touches someone, it becomes contagious, swimming into new worlds through the lives and spirits of its readers; when a work of fiction is translated, it is reborn. There is something intensely human in this miraculous process, though that something is often lost in the larger currents that surround it. This book shows us, in all their warmth and sincerity, and through their own earnest words, the people who make translations possible."　　　　　　　　　—SAYAKA MURATA,
author of *Convenience Store Woman*

"An astonishingly thorough and illuminating look at the way that Murakami became recognized, and at all the people—translators in particular—who made it possible by the decisions they made. Karashima's book is a hands-on and very frank look at the social construction of a literary reputation."　　　—BRIAN EVENSON,
author of *Song for the Unraveling of the World* and
*Raymond Carver's What We Talk About
When We Talk About Love*

"The result of years of research and countless interviews, *Who We're Reading When We're Reading Murakami* offers an engaging, thought-provoking behind-the-scenes look at the people whose enthusiasm, dedication, and vision paved the way for Haruki Murakami's emergence as one of the world's great contemporary writers. This book will make you see literature, and translation, in a whole new light."　　　　　　—MICHAEL EMMERICH,
translator and author of *The Tale of Genji:
Translation, Canonization, and World Literature*

"Karashima, a Japanese novelist and translator, has conducted a profound riff on the art of translation in considering the work of Haruki Murakami, and how it differs in English from its original publications in Japanese. Like William H. Gass's book, *Reading Rilke*, this will probably become a must read for translators and fans of Murakami alike."
—JOHN FREEMAN,
author of *Dictionary of the Undoing*

"Murakami fans will particularly revel in Karashima's comprehensive coverage, but anyone curious about the alchemy and sheer amount of work that goes into making a single author's success will be entranced by this fascinating work."
—*Publishers Weekly* (starred review)

"A lively account of the many people involved in bringing Haruki Murakami's writings to English-speaking readers . . . A fascinating glimpse into the inner workings of publishing."
—*Kirkus Reviews*

"A fascinatingly detailed account that enables the reader to gradually grasp how winding and tricky the trail bends from one culture to another, and how dependent individual literary success is on the creative and logistical whims of a selected team of enablers . . . A book not so much about 村上春樹, the Japanese writer, but rather about 'Haruki Murakami,' the English variant of his moniker, and also not-so-coincidentally the brand name that has spread throughout the whole globe . . . About how international bridges are built, one sympathetic brick at a time." —*nihongobookreview*

Who We're Reading When We're Reading Murakami

Mura

Soft Skull New York

Who We're Reading When We're Reading

kami

David Karashima

First Soft Skull edition: 2020

Library of Congress Cataloging-in-Publication Data

Names: Karashima, David James, author.
Title: Who we're reading when we're reading Murakami / David Karashima.
Description: First Soft Skull edition. | New York : Soft Skull, 2020. |
Includes bibliographical references.
Identifiers: LCCN 2020010744 | ISBN 9781593765897 (paperback) |
ISBN 9781593765903 (ebook)
Subjects: LCSH: Murakami, Haruki, 1949-—Criticism and interpretation. |
Murakami, Haruki, 1949-—Relations with editors. | Murakami, Haruki,
1949-—Translations—History and criticism. | Literature publishing—
Japan—History—20th century.
Classification: LCC PL856.U673 Z7555 2020 | DDC 895.63/5—dc23
LC record available at https://lccn.loc.gov/2020010744

Cover design & Soft Skull art direction by salu.io
Book design by Jordan Koluch

Published by Soft Skull Press
1140 Broadway, Suite 704
New York, NY 10001
www.softskull.com

Printed in the United States of America
1 3 5 7 9 10 8 6 4 2

For M, H, and T

Contents

Contents

Contents

Who We're Reading When We're Reading Murakami

Preface

A writer friend once said to me that if non-Japanese readers know anything about Japan, they usually know just two things: manga and Murakami. But what—or who—is it that these non-Japanese readers of Murakami know? While Murakami's books have now been published in more than fifty languages and have sold millions of copies globally, it is easy to forget that the works that a great many of his readers—devotees, fans, critics, and detractors alike—have come to know are also creations of his translators, editors, and publishers around the world. This book explores the Murakami phenomenon from a very particular angle, traveling back in time to tell the stories of the colorful cast of characters who first contributed to publishing Murakami's work in English, which in turn laid the foundation for the author's subsequent global reach.

In the early stages of my research I had a pretty good sense of what I wanted to say. The more people I got to talk to and the more documents I managed to excavate, however, the more convinced I became that any point I was hoping to make might be best communicated through the voices of the many people who played key roles in the making of the author we know as Haruki Murakami. So this book—which is an adaptation of a book first published in Japanese in 2018—has come to be largely about their efforts and recollections. It seems somehow fitting that I am able to share this tale about translation with readers of English through a process of translation and adaptation.

DAVID KARASHIMA
March 24, 2020

Pinball, 1973 and Hear the Wind Sing

The first three novels I read by Murakami ...
were all translated by Alfred Birnbaum.
When I finished the books, I was mildly
curious to know more about Murakami;
I was *desperate* to know more about
Birnbaum.

—WENDY LESSER, *Why I Read*[1]

The Making of a "Bohemian" Translator

Alfred Birnbaum lives in a narrow two-story house near Ino-kashira Park in west Tokyo with his wife, Thi, and their two cats, Koko and Chacha. The structure had been an abandoned boardinghouse when he purchased it around ten years ago; he has since transformed it into a unique, charming, self-designed home. The living room, which is on the second floor, rises to an open-beam ceiling. A wood-burning fireplace has been situated in a corner overlooking train tracks that connect two popular hubs of the city, Kichijōji and Shibuya. When a train stops at the crossing, Birnbaum walks over to the window and waves at the people in the train. Nobody glances in his direction.

There are fewer books lining the bookshelf than you might expect in the house of a literary translator. Birnbaum explains that while he is almost never away from an open book, he has been on the move for most of his life, so once he's done with a book he leaves it behind or gives it away. Anyway, this house does not have the kind of space that can afford walls of books. This is Tokyo, after all. The ones that have managed to stay on his shelf include *The Book of Dave* and *Dr. Mukti and Other Tales of Woe*, by Will Self ("An excellent writer, great sense of humor"); Zadie Smith's *NW* ("Can't remember if I read that"); Thomas Pynchon's *Bleeding Edge* ("A gift"); and a range of novels in Spanish, including those by Julio Cortázar and Jorge Luis Borges ("Those I read many times").

He seems to have no books by Haruki Murakami. When I point this out, Birnbaum shrugs. "They still send them to me . . . don't think they sent me the latest yet . . . but the others should be somewhere."[2]

Packed into the shelves next to the books are artworks he has created on a specialty printer at Kobe Design University, where he briefly served as a visiting professor. There are long handscroll prints collaged from photographs. On the walls are masks Birnbaum has collected from his travels throughout Mexico and Asia.

Birnbaum met his wife in 1990 when he first visited Yangon, in Myanmar. They married in 1998 in a ceremony in Yangon attended by friends from around the world; Murakami was one of the guests. For the next several years, the couple moved with the seasons, spending their winters in Myanmar, where the hot air suited Birnbaum; summers in Seattle, when the rains ceased; and the spring and fall in Japan. But when the Burmese government, in a moment of bureaucratic confusion, blacklisted him and refused to renew his visa, he found himself suddenly unable to go "home." He was eventually allowed re-entry to the country, and he now visits regularly, though not as often as before.

When Birnbaum decided to buy a place in Tokyo, he could not find a single bank willing to give a foreigner and freelance translator a loan, so he began looking for a place he could purchase in cash. He put together enough money to buy this property, standing on a small plot of land by the train tracks, for which no other buyer had emerged. A handyman who takes pride in doing things himself, he knocked down the walls, put in new stairs, and reworked the ceilings. More than ten years on, he is still working on the house. The latest project is a hinoki bath he has squeezed into a two-mat space on the first floor. The fig tree he planted soon after moving in has reached the roof and last year produced several kilograms of fruit. Birnbaum still travels out of Japan every few months, but he finally feels, he says, like he has "settled down."[3]

Alfred Birnbaum's home, west Tokyo

Escapes

Birnbaum first came to Japan in 1960, when he was five years old. His father, Henry Birnbaum, had been tasked with establishing the Tokyo office of the National Science Foundation, and moved the family—his wife, Nancy, and his sons, Bob and Alfred—from their home in Wheaton, Maryland.

As far as Birnbaum can recall, there were no other foreigners living in Kagomachi, in north Tokyo, where his family settled. He attended the Nishimachi International School in central Tokyo, and spoke English both at home and in school, but he was quick to pick up Japanese from the housekeeper and the neighborhood kids. He recalls watching television in Japanese, though he does not recall specific programs. He also remembers spending a lot of time alone drawing.

Birnbaum's family moved countries every few years. After Tokyo, they spent three years in the States, including a year in Honolulu, where Henry Birnbaum was vice chancellor of the newly founded East-West Center on the grounds of the University of Hawaii at Manoa.[4] But in these early years of grade school he had very little contact with the Japanese language. Many of his classmates at the Iolani School, a private preparatory academy, were of Asian descent, but English was their common language. It didn't occur to him to use Japanese even with his Japanese American classmates. Birnbaum says that, having lived in Japan, it "felt natural" to be surrounded by Asians. If anything, he "felt a little out of place" when he was "only surrounded by white people."[5]

When he was in middle school, Birnbaum's family moved to Mexico City. He remembers being affected by "the feel of the place, the ambience and people, the color and life in the streets, the food and folk art . . . I was focused on drawing and obsessed with Dalí and surrealism. We traveled all over Mexico and everything seemed like a grand strange wonderful chaotic dream painted large, a complete contrast to the dull banality of the suburban U.S. In retrospect, my knowledge of Latin America was very shallow and superficial, a riot of exuberance to match my wannabe rebellious teenage posturing. Kind of embarrassing, to think back now."[6]

The Birnbaum family. Left to right: Alfred, Henry, Nancy, Bob

The family returned to Tokyo when Birnbaum was in high school, and he enrolled in the American School in Japan. He spent most of his free time in the art studio, and at home he would read Latin American authors—García Márquez in Gregory Rabassa's translations first, then Borges and Cortázar—to transport himself back to Mexico.

Did his early interest in these writers influence which works he would decide to translate later? While Birnbaum does not make that connection, it is true that the two Japanese writers he has introduced to the Anglophone world—Haruki Murakami and Natsuki Ikezawa—have both been compared to "magic realist" writers from Latin America.[7]

After graduating from high school in Japan, Birnbaum, dissuaded from art as a career, attended the University of Texas at Austin to pursue his "second interest," Latin American literature.[8] The Latin American Institute had been established at UT in 1940 and had just moved to a new building in 1970. The school owned the second-largest archive of materials related to Latin America in the country, after the Hispanic Division of the Library of Congress.[9] The fact that Austin was only a four- to five-hour drive from the border with Mexico was another attraction. When Murakami was invited to the same university in 1994 as part of a five-day author tour, he wrote about falling in love with the city, with its greenery, its many cats, and the river running through it; he even wrote that it "might not be a bad place to spend the rest of my life."[10] But when Birnbaum had arrived in the city as a student twenty years earlier, he had the opposite reaction. Whether it was Japan or Mexico, he had always managed to find a place for himself. But in Texas he experienced "terrible culture shock." Austin was a liberal oasis, a city unlike any other in Texas, and his roommate had assured him that he was going to "love Texas," but Birnbaum never got used to the place. He thinks, in retrospect, that the issue may have been not where he was but what he was doing. He was still having trouble letting go of the idea of becoming an artist.

In the end, Birnbaum escaped Texas to the University of Southern California. His father had recently taken a job at the university, where he would eventually be named associate provost, which meant that Birnbaum would not have to pay tuition. He took the opportunity to change his major to East Asian studies.

"When I was in Japan I didn't want to be there and tried to avoid everything Japanese," he says. "Didn't even read Japanese literature. But once I left Japan, the country started to interest me. I always find myself being drawn to things and places far away. So every time I moved, my interests would shift too. I suppose it just means I'm always trying to escape myself."[11]

As far as Birnbaum can remember, there were no Japanese literature specialists at USC when he was there. He came across short stories by Kyōka Izumi and Motojirō Kajii while working at the school's East Asian Studies Center, and he began translating them "to kill time." These stories had the same fantastic and visually stimulating elements that had attracted him to Latin American writers. The outsider perspective was also appealing. "I considered myself an outsider wherever I went, so that must have been an attraction."[12]

The Waseda Years

For his junior year in college, Birnbaum opted to study abroad—in Tokyo, at Waseda University, from which Haruki Murakami had graduated half a year earlier. It was the fall of 1975, Japan's economy was stirring, and the Western world was beginning to take notice. Most of the foreign students Birnbaum encountered at Waseda were "MBA types who saw business opportunities in Japan."[13] Birnbaum spent time with like-minded friends—among them Keith Holeman, who would go on to direct films, and Beth Nishihara, who was taking part in the activities of the Asbestos Studio led by the dancer Tatsumi Hijikata.

Waseda currently has around 8,000 international students, but foreign students were a rarity in the seventies. Almost every day, when walking through the campus, Birnbaum was approached by someone wanting to practice English conversation with him. Birnbaum quickly grew tired of this. With Holeman, a student from the U.S. like himself, he created a short film as part of a class assignment in which the cause of a character's mysterious death turns out to be karōshi—death by overwork—from having accepted endless requests to provide free English conversation lessons.

The film, received with mild amusement by the other students, was an early manifestation of Birnbaum's sense of humor, which has a kindly absurd edge, and which seems to creep into his translations. In any case, Birnbaum was learning to deal with the constant gaze under which foreigners in Japan often found themselves.

Birnbaum returned to USC in the fall of 1976 to finish college, but a year later he was back in Tokyo—at Waseda—on a Ministry of Education scholarship. He focused on Japanese art history, and once his research year was up, he applied for official admission to Waseda's graduate school to continue his studies. He prepared assiduously for the exam—which was in Japanese—and was accepted to the program.

Birnbaum entered graduate school in April 1978. At the same time, Haruki Murakami had begun writing what would become his first published book, *Kaze no uta o kike (Hear the Wind Sing)*.[14] While Murakami was sitting at his kitchen table struggling to put words to paper, Birnbaum found himself struggling too. His new official status as a grad student meant he was subject to unspoken rules and obligations—none of which had been required of him when he was a one-year fellow (essentially a guest) of the Ministry of Education. When his professor asked him to change his research topic "to Nara period sculpture or whatever it was that [the professor] was researching at the time," Birnbaum took umbrage and left Waseda.[15] Years later, he would go on to a master's program at the University of London's School of Oriental and African Studies and, for a short period, to teach creative writing back at Waseda, but he says that he never again considered taking up residence within academia.

Birnbaum doubts that he would have become the translator he is if he had followed the conventional academic path. "It's difficult," he says, "for an academic to become a good writer."[16]

Becoming a Translator

After dropping out of Waseda, Birnbaum moved to the U.S., where he took a position at the Visual Arts Center, an outreach program of Antioch College, in Columbia, Maryland, teaching painting and calligraphy. It wasn't long before he began feeling restless, finding the suburban environs of the college uninteresting and confining. After several years, Birnbaum moved back to Japan—Kyoto this time—and married Yumi, whom he'd met at USC when she was an undergraduate exchange student. He enrolled at Urasenke, one of the three main schools of tea in Kyoto. After some time, owing to his ability to speak and read Japanese, he was asked to translate short articles for the school's publication, *Chanoyu Quarterly*, which introduced chadō—the way of tea—to foreigners. He gladly accepted because it would help pay his bills. "The editorial team at *Chanoyu Quarterly* was a group of misfits. And as a misfit myself, I fit in perfectly."[17]

Kyoto had been a positive reentry to Japan, but soon his work at the quarterly began to feel constricting, the city over-mannered. Birnbaum moved back to Tokyo and eventually separated from his wife. He gradually began to take on longer translation projects while "dabbling in video art." His work at *Chanoyu Quarterly* had opened opportunities for translating art and architecture books for Kodansha International, the English-language subsidiary of Kodansha Inc., one of the three largest publishing houses in Japan. The books he translated included *Yoshitoshi: The Splendid Decadent*, by Shin'ichi Segi, and *Traditional Japanese Furniture: A Definitive Guide*, by Kazuko Koizumi. But even then, Birnbaum had no intention of becoming a translator. "It just never occurred to me to pursue a career of any kind."[18]

Birnbaum Discovers Murakami

It was around this time that a friend recommended he read a short story collection by a young author named Haruki Murakami. Comprising seven stories that had appeared in various magazines between April 1980 and December 1982, *Chūgoku yuki no surō bōto* (*A Slow Boat to China*) had been published in the spring of 1983.

Birnbaum was immediately drawn to Murakami's writing, especially its humor, something he found to be rare in Japanese literature.[19] As soon as he finished reading the stories, he sat down at his typewriter and proceeded to translate several.

In the spring of 1984, Birnbaum visited the Kodansha International office in Tokyo to meet with the editor who was overseeing the nonfiction Birnbaum was translating. Kodansha International, established in 1963, focused on books that introduced Japanese culture to foreigners. In addition to books on fine art, martial arts, crafts, food, and business, it also published biographies and criticism by Western scholars of Japanese literature.

KI, as Kodansha International was known, was also one of the leading publishers of Japanese literature in English translation. In the 1970s it published Japanese classics of the early and mid-twentieth century, including Sōseki Natsume's *Botchan*, Yasunari Kawabata's *The Lake*, Yukio Mishima's *Sun and Steel*, and Kenzaburō Ōe's *The Silent Cry*. In the 1980s it went on to publish more contemporary works, like Ryū Murakami's *Almost Transparent Blue* and Yūko Tsushima's *Child of Fortune*.

Ryū Murakami and Haruki Murakami—no relation—had both made their debuts by winning the Gunzō New Writers' Prize, in 1976 and 1979 respectively. At the time, they were often referred to as "Double Murakami," and in 1981, Kodansha had published a book-length conversation between them under the title *Wōku donto ran* (*Walk Don't Run*).[20] Birnbaum was hopeful that Kodansha International would show interest in "the other Murakami."[21]

Near the end of his meeting with the editor, Birnbaum pulled out his translation of "Nyū Yōku tankō no higeki" ("New York Mining Disaster"), from Murakami's story collection. He also expressed his interest in translating *Hitsuji o meguru bōken* (*A Wild Sheep Chase*), a novel that had first appeared in *Gunzō*, the literary journal in which Murakami had made his debut.

As Murakami has recounted in a 1991 interview, *Hitsuji o meguru bōken* (*A Wild Sheep Chase*) had gotten a "cold reception" at first.[22] He was told by the editors at *Gunzō* that it was too long, and recalls that "it wasn't easy getting them to accept the piece for publication."[23] But in the end, the novel appeared in full in the August 1982 issue of the journal and was published as its own hardcover book by Kodansha several months later. That December it was awarded the Noma New Writer's Prize and, according to Murakami, sold around 150,000 copies.[24]

For Birnbaum, the attention the book had gotten was vindication of his interest. "I think what was remarkable about *Sheep*, both the attraction and the challenge, was that unlike almost all Japanese writing that is either extremely realistic (and mired down in minute details that obscure a broader or deeper vision) or extremely fantastic (like slapstick manga or robot-monster inanities) with no middle ground, it cut a fine balance between everyday tedium and fantasy; it kept the surrealism well within the realm of possibility, if not the plausible. And in that regard it was amazingly unique (especially at the time) and showed both perfect restraint and daring command in equal measures. Very different from anyone else in Japan, definitely more akin to US/UK novelists—which of course is why he was attacked by critics here. The total antithesis of heavy-handed dour pain-in-your-face voices like Kenzaburō Ōe, Kōbō Abe, Jūrō Kara, and Kenji Nakagami. I don't know if that makes sense, but *Sheep* was really nicely understated."[25]

The KI editor whom Birnbaum had been working with specialized in nonfiction, so she introduced him to one of her colleagues. The new editor took Birnbaum's "New York Mining Disaster" and told him he would read it. When Birnbaum visited the office several weeks later, however, the same editor told him that from a business standpoint *Sheep* was too long. Birnbaum remembers being handed copies of Murakami's first two novellas—*Kaze no uta o kike* (*Hear the Wind Sing*) and *1973-nen no pinbōru* (*Pinball, 1973*)—instead. He did not totally buy the explanation that publishing *Sheep* was less financially viable than publishing the novellas, but he also didn't feel that he was in any position to disagree with the editor; he was, after all, a freelancer trying to carve out a living on the fringes of the Japanese art and literary worlds.

Birnbaum started flipping through the books on the train ride home, and once he finished reading, he began translating *1973-nen no pinbōru* (*Pinball, 1973*). He had chosen the title over *Kaze no uta o kike* (*Hear the Wind Sing*), Murakami's debut, because he thought it was "the better book." He tells me that he might have started with *Kaze no uta o kike* if he had been offered a two-book contract, but at the time it was far from clear that he would have the chance to translate a second book. "I think the surreal parts of *Pinball* appealed to me," he adds. "The scene where the protagonist converses with the pinball machine was very much my kind of humor."[26]

In a few months, Birnbaum produced what he felt was a "reasonably faithful" translation. His interactions with the editor on the manuscript were "minimal."[27] Back then it never occurred to him to deviate from the original. "I was still a nobody and there wasn't anybody I could turn to for advice. I just had to trust my instincts."[28]

The "Immature" Novellas

Birnbaum assumed that the manuscript he handed KI would be released as a hardcover, like Ryū Murakami's *Almost Transparent Blue*. But the copy of the book that arrived in his mailbox in the fall of 1985 was a slim, pocket-sized paperback.

Pinball, 1973 was published as part of the Kodansha English Library series, which was aimed at English-language learners in

Japan and at the time included books like *A Knock on the Door*, a collection of stories by the prolific flash-fiction writer Shin'ichi Hoshi, as well as *Totto-chan: The Little Girl at the Window*, a bestselling memoir by the television celebrity Tetsuko Kuroyanagi. The cover of *Pinball, 1973* used an illustration commissioned for the original Japanese version, and at the back of the book were grammatical notes prepared by a high school English teacher.

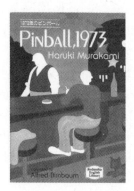

Pinball, 1973, Kodansha English Library, 1985

KI's hardcover books were distributed in the English-speaking world by overseas distributors. The Kodansha English Library series, on the other hand, was only distributed domestically. The first English translation of Murakami's work never made it out of Japan.

Pinball, 1973 had been edited by Jules Young, who had moved to Japan in the mid-sixties and worked for KI for more than twenty years, starting in 1969. Young, who now lives in Bangkok, says that his edits "didn't try to cater to the Japanese readership" and that he "relied on the Japanese editor who prepared the notes to explain any confusions." He tells me that if there had been plans to release the translation outside of Japan, he "would have made some changes, just to inform someone not familiar with Japan and its culture."[29]

Birnbaum says that Young had suggested the title *Pinball, 1973*. (A "literal" translation of the Japanese title would have been something like *The Pinball[s] of 1973*.) When I ask Young, he initially tells me that he does not remember anything about the title, but then writes to me later: "Thinking about it further, I remember that the comma in the Pinball title seemed to accentuate the time frame of the story. Without the comma it was a bit bland."[30]

Although Birnbaum was disappointed that *Pinball, 1973* had been published only in Japan, he accepted the offer to translate Murakami's other novella, partly "to keep open the possibility of translating *Sheep* in the future." He does not remember discussing the translation of either book with Murakami directly. "We were both overseas a lot . . . They were only for distribution in Japan and I don't think Murakami was all that interested in them."[31]

When I ask Murakami about this, he agrees. He tells me when the first two books were being translated, he had "kind of lost interest" in them because he was "already invested in writing longer works."[32] In a 2004 interview in *The Paris Review*, he describes the novellas as "immature."[33]

Hear the Wind Sing, Kodansha English Library, 1987

Even years after Murakami's work started to reach a wider readership abroad, translations of the two early novellas remained hidden from readers outside Japan. In 2015, more than thirty years after their original publication, they were released as a single volume in new translations by Ted Goossen (who chose to keep Young and Birnbaum's titles).

I'm afraid that it might be a sensitive issue, but I ask Murakami about the decision to finally publish new English translations of his first two novellas. He does not seem at all bothered by the question. In fact, none of the questions I was worried about asking seem to faze him. We are in his Aoyama office in Tokyo and he is taking sips of coffee from a mug with the cover of Raymond Chandler's *The Big Sleep* printed on it.

"It wasn't as if I was against the idea," he says to me in Japanese. "I just felt that the books wouldn't be all that interesting to read anymore. But there were so many requests that I finally relented. In Japan people have been reading my books in the order they were published, but outside Japan [the publication order] is all over the place. It seemed inevitable that some were going to read these two books as if they were my latest works. I was concerned that those readers would think, 'What's this?' Also, I had created these two books by borrowing from American authors like Vonnegut and Brautigan that I had admired as a student. There's a part of me that finds that a little embarrassing now."[34]

When Birnbaum first began translating Murakami, he was a young freelance translator with no institutional affiliation. He created translations of "New York Mining Disaster" and later *Pinball, 1973* and various short stories despite the fact that there was no guarantee that they would be published. When I ask Birnbaum how he supported himself while he worked on the translations, he shrugs and says that he "led a simple life" and that his "costs were minimal." Birnbaum seems almost to thrive on getting by on a limited budget. He tells me that as a graduate student, during the month or so before his scholarship money was paid into his bank account, he subsisted on free bread crusts from the local bakery and twenty-yen packs of fermented soybeans from the supermarket. "My job," he tells me, "is to not spend money."[35]

Even today, he maintains this lifestyle. When I'm at his house, we always talk in the kitchen, with Birnbaum standing over the stove and me sitting at the kitchen counter with my laptop. Many of the cooking utensils, pots, and pans on the kitchen counter were purchased at the local flea market for a handful of coins. Our chats end in the late afternoon, when it's time for him to make his rounds of the local supermarkets in search of the day's bargains. Birnbaum and his wife rarely eat out. Once, when a literary festival in the U.K. offered to fly him business class, Birnbaum surprised the organizers by politely asking them to change his ticket so that he could sit in economy. This inclination to keep things simple may be one reason Murakami referred to Birnbaum in his interview with *The Paris Review* as a "bohemian":

> Alfred is a kind of bohemian; I don't know where he is right now. He's married to a woman from Myanmar, and she's an activist. Sometimes they get captured by the government. He's that kind of person. He's kind of free as a translator; he changes the prose sometimes. That's his style.[36]

The *Paris Review* interview was translated into Japanese and compiled with other selected interviews in a 2010 book titled *Yume o miru tame ni maiasa boku wa mezameru no desu* (*I Wake Up Every Morning Just to Dream*). In this Japanese translation the same passage has been edited:

> Alfred is the bohemian type. He translates quite freely. He sometimes rewrites the prose. That's his style.

Birnbaum tells me he has no idea why certain parts of the interview were deleted, but that he had been "shocked" when he first saw the comments in *The Paris Review*. "Murakami must have gotten us mixed up with the couple in 'The Second Bakery Attack,'" he says. "With fiction writers there's always a blurring of fiction and reality."[37]

Europe Calling

In February 1987, *Hear the Wind Sing*—translated by Birnbaum and again edited by Jules Young—was published as part of the Kodansha English Library series. Soon after, KI finally offered Birnbaum a contract for the book that would become *A Wild Sheep Chase*.

Birnbaum isn't sure why KI changed its mind about the book it had originally deemed too long. He says it may have had to do, at least partly, with the brisk sales of *Pinball, 1973* and *Hear the Wind Sing*. It may also have been a reflection of KI's ambition to find more success in the U.S. market. Either way, Birnbaum accepted the job and started working toward a December 1987 deadline.[38]

While Birnbaum was working on his translation, a new novel by Murakami, *Noruwei no mori* (*Norwegian Wood*), became a massive bestseller in Japan. Released in September 1987 in two hardcover volumes—one with a green cover and the other red—the book took off during the Christmas shopping season. By January 1988 it had sold a combined total of 800,000 copies, and by the end of that year this number had exploded to 3.55 million.[39] By 2009, sales of the book in Japan alone had surpassed 10 million copies.[40]

Birnbaum read *Noruwei no mori* only after KI asked him to translate it. He found it to be "missing the humor and surreal aspects I like" and "a bit sentimental," but agreed to take on the translation.[41] In a published conversation with Motoyuki Shibata, a translator of American literature and professor emeritus of Tokyo University, Murakami jokingly suggests that Birnbaum had translated *Norwegian Wood* purely "to make a living."[42] When I ask Birnbaum about this he says, "Sure, earning a living was a big part of it."[43]

Once Birnbaum had managed to put away some savings, and to complete his stint as a curator of two video art events in Tokyo, he packed up his belongings, left them with a friend, and boarded a plane to Spain. He had a gig in hand to cover Europe for a new magazine, launched by the Japanese publishing house Shinchōsha. He sublet an apartment in Barcelona and used it as a base from which to travel around Europe. In Birnbaum's view, however, the editorial team seemed to have very little interest in any perspectives unrelated to trends in Japan. Birnbaum kept sending feature proposals to Tokyo, all of which were rejected. Even so, it was an exciting time to be in Europe and to "witness the world changing right in front of [him]" as the Iron Curtain fell.[44]

The first issue of *03: TOKYO Calling* was published in December 1989. It focused on New York and its cover was a photo of Spike Lee (who had just directed *Do the Right Thing*). Other features included a joint interview of Gary Fisketjon—who would eventually become Murakami's editor—and Jay McInerney, whose *Bright Lights, Big City* had become a bestseller in a Japanese translation by the novelist Gen'ichirō Takahashi. McInerney would interview Murakami in New York several years later.[45]

Birnbaum was disappointed that the magazine was placing such a strong emphasis on New York. He wasn't a fan of the city, although his father's family was from there and he had occasionally visited over the years. So what if it was the self-appointed center of the universe? He felt that the art world there "was too much of a game for showmen, a real estate market requiring salesmanship" and that the city was generally not "a place for introverts or pseudo-intellectuals like myself."[46] "The Japanese are always looking toward America," he tells me. "They need to get over this addiction."[47]

While seeking out projects and writing for *03: TOKYO Calling*, Birnbaum continued working on his Murakami translations, completing a draft of *A Wild Sheep Chase*. He submitted the manuscript to KI. Several months passed, and then an editor he'd never heard of before got in touch. His name was Elmer Luke.

A Wild Sheep Chase

I want to thank the passionate editors at Kodansha International—in particular Elmer Luke. This Hawaii-born, Chinese-American editor, who may be small in stature but is full of vitality, initially sold my work to the American market with great enthusiasm. Elmer started the engine.

—HARUKI MURAKAMI, foreword to
*Zō no shōmetsu: tanpen senshū
1980–1991* (*The Elephant Vanishes*)[1]

Elmer Luke "Starts the Engine"

Since the late 1990s—for over a decade—Elmer Luke had split his time between Tokyo and New York City, "never really living in either place." But exactly one week before the March 11, 2011, triple disaster in Japan—the earthquake that led to the tsunami that led to the meltdown at the Fukushima Daiichi nuclear power plant—he and his partner, Robert Seward, a just-retired professor of media and politics at Meiji Gakuin University, cleared out their apartment in Nishi Nippori, and returned to their apartment in New York. They'd purchased a house upstate, hoping to maintain a city-and-country existence, but soon enough found the arrangement "not the easiest, especially the four-hour drive." When out of the blue, unsolicited, someone expressed interest in buying their city apartment, they did not refuse. "It was unexpectedly freeing." Luke and Seward now live the year round in Cooperstown, New York.[2]

The property they bought had belonged to a descendant of the writer James Fenimore Cooper, whose father had founded the town. In the basement of one of the small houses on the lot, Luke and Seward found a full set of Cooper's novels among three bottles of aged wine, which "probably aren't any good." In their garden they grow Japanese cucumbers, edamame, shiso, kabocha, and fava beans. While Seward works on his dyes and pottery in the atelier behind the garden, Luke sits in their second-floor study, working only on books "of genuine interest" to him.[3] On the shelves in Luke's study are the books he has edited over the years, many of them English translations of Japanese literature: Masahiko Shimada's *Dream Messenger*, translated by Philip Gabriel; Hiromi Kawakami's *Manazuru*, translated by Michael Emmerich; and Alfred Birnbaum's translations of Haruki Murakami's *A Wild Sheep Chase*, *Hard-Boiled Wonderland and the End of the World*, and *Dance Dance Dance*. There are also two novels that I translated: Hisaki Matsuura's *Triangle* and Shinji Ishii's *Kutze, Stepp'n on Wheat.*

Elmer Luke's home, Cooperstown, New York

Luke was born in Honolulu in 1948, the fifth child and first son of Hawaii-born Chinese American parents. His mother's family had immigrated from Canton Province in the late nineteenth century and his father's family arrived, "probably," in the early twentieth.[4]

Luke left Hawaii for the first time when he went to the 1964 World's Fair in New York, spending the summer at his eldest sister's house on Long Island. But it was only when he moved to the Midwest for college that he came to realize that "Hawaii was an island."

"In Hawaii you can't escape your boundaries, the ocean surrounds you, literally, so you can't escape your family, immediate and extended, your history, yourself—even who you were in elementary, middle, and high school. I love the ocean, and the land—the mountains and valley—is beautiful, but the place is somehow choking. I don't think I would ever consider living there again."[5]

When Luke enrolled at the University of Illinois in 1966, he found himself in a massive dorm. He was—as far as he recalls—the only nonwhite student out of two thousand men. Coming from multicultural Hawaii, Luke had "a stark realization of racial difference not experienced before."[6]

"I remember this feeling of not wanting to stand out, wanting to blend in," he tells me in an email. We talk in person many times in Tokyo, New York, and London, but continue to correspond by email and speak every so often on the phone once I start writing this book. "And if I did stand out, which was inevitable, I suppose, I did not want to be viewed as Asian ('Oriental' in those days)—an Asian who had this identity as Asian and only had Asian friends. I mean, I imagined I was bigger than that. An actually very messy identity thing since I was categorizing other Asians on campus not as individual human beings, but as Asians. Which was, in a way, how I imagined I was being categorized by white students."[7]

Luke started as premed but found that organic chemistry "didn't agree" with him, and he eventually declared his major in English literature and rhetoric.[8] He enrolled in a creative writing class led by the writer Paul Friedman and began writing fiction. "Took me weeks and weeks before I handed in my first story, and I was stunned, when I read it to the class, which is what we had to do, that people actually thought it was good. I mean, stunned.

"Friedman was, for me, an excellent teacher. I remember he would circle things in the stories I submitted and I would ask him what was the problem. He'd say, no problem, I just wondered why you did it, why it was that way. I never forgot that. I mean, that a writer needed to be conscious of every word he writes. That's what I try to do when I'm editing, make sure that the writer is aware of the why behind every written word."[9]

Luke began to imagine an academic career. "In those days, for a PhD, you needed two foreign languages—now one will do." Along with Russian (which he had started in high school), he signed up for Mandarin. He'd had eight years of Cantonese Chinese school in Hawaii, but he'd never learned proper grammar, so "it wasn't a free ride, but it was not a struggle . . . If you think about the times—the late sixties, the Cold War, et cetera—I would have been perfect for the CIA! Though of course I never went near them."[10]

Luke got involved in political movements on campus and went to protests against the Vietnam War in Washington, D.C. In his senior year, the first year of the draft, his birthday was picked 71st out of 366, meaning it was almost certain that he'd be drafted. He filed for conscientious objector status. In spite of this, he soon received notice to report for a physical. On the early morning chartered bus to Chicago, where the physical would take place, Luke found that every student had a plan for getting out of the draft. Luke himself had fasted and lost enough weight to be ineligible. He fasted on the two other occasions he was summoned for a physical, and each time he was found to be underweight, and so was able to avoid going to Vietnam. (His conscientious objector application had been placed on hold.) These experiences as a student in the sixties and seventies would later become a shared topic of discussion between Murakami and himself.

After college, Luke pursued a graduate degree in Chinese literature at the University of Michigan. It wasn't just his interest in the subject that kept him in the Midwest. He had spent time at a summer institute at Indiana University, where "a woman I met" (who would become his wife) and his assigned roommate were both from the University of Michigan, and Luke had hoped that they could "keep the commune thing going."

At the University of Michigan, Luke briefly made the acquaintance of Edward Seidensticker, known for his translations of *The Tale of Genji* as well as the works of Yasunari Kawabata and Jun'ichirō Tanizaki. Luke thought that Seidensticker's translations were "works of very fine writing in themselves . . . There's a reason, when Kawabata won the Nobel, he offered to share it with Seidensticker. I didn't know him well at Ann Arbor. I was a graduate assistant to another professor [of Chinese] in the department [of Far Eastern Languages and Literatures], and we'd acknowledge each other as we passed by in the hall. My brush with his fame came when I was answering the department's phones during lunch hour and a call came in for him from the National Book Foundation . . . Turned out it was for his winning the National Book Award for his translation of Kawabata's *Sound of the Mountain*."

If Luke had been thinking strictly in terms of securing a position in academia, the practical thing to do would have been to continue with East Asian studies, an emerging field where he had a comparative advantage (already being able to read Chinese characters). But Luke didn't want to be cast as an "Asian studying Asia." Deciding that he didn't have the passion to commit himself to a field he had "pursued in part for the scholarship money," Luke dropped out of the program, got married, and returned to Hawaii with his wife. He was hired as a writer for a state Department of Education project and, when that ended, as a janitor while his wife completed her degree at the University of Hawaii. Eventually he reapplied to graduate school, this time in American studies at the University of Hawaii, which had established one of the first American studies departments in the country.[11]

Kyoto to New York (By Way of Cambridge, New Mexico, and Philadelphia)

In 1974, a year after completing his master's degree, Luke moved to Japan with his wife, who had been awarded a fellowship to study in Kyoto.

I ask Luke how his parents felt about him moving to Japan. Luke's father had been too old to be drafted in World

War II, but his father's younger brother was killed in France, and the family had vivid memories of Pearl Harbor. "My father recounted hearing the bombs dropping early on December 7—though he, like many people, thought it was military maneuvers. He climbed the slope near our house to take a look at all the action going on. Only later, though soon enough, I'd think, did they learn it was an attack. But growing up, I did not hear any anti-Japanese sentiment. I did hear stories about nightly blackouts, where the family had to cover up windows with black paper so no light could be seen from planes above, and I did hear about air-raid alarms when the family would hurry into the gully next to the house to hide and take shelter. They were stories about fear, cowering, but less about hating the enemy."[12]

Still, Luke did have some concern about how his parents would react to his moving to Japan. "Japan has a very mixed history with the Chinese, the same way with Koreans. I was not brought up to love Japan. But my parents' reaction was all positive and encouraging, surprising me . . . Years later, my parents went on an Asian tour. They loved Japan, found China backward, Hong Kong unruly."[13]

It was the first time Luke had lived abroad. "While then-wife was doing research (we were now living separately) I was working part-time as an English editor (what else?) for CDI (Communication Design Institute), a think tank whose director was Hidetoshi Katō, who's still alive, a sociologist who studied in the US, where he met my mentor, Reuel Denney . . . When Reuel learned I was going to Kyoto, he suggested to Kato that perhaps he could use my services . . . The gig was grounding during a very ungrounded time in life. Little did I know that Japan would prove to be so much of the ground in my life.

"(I am rambling, but your questions induce that): I hadn't planned that Susan (that's the wife) and I would live separately. I was unprepared for living on my own in Kyoto. But when you're breaking up, things get either/or polarized—I answered an ad to live in a room in the apartment of a physician whose wife and two young kids had preceded him in going to the States for a fellowship . . . being a young neurologist, he was almost never there. From Friday morning, when he went to work, until Monday evening, he was gone completely. It was terrible. I'd never felt so alone. On weekends I'd take the train and go downtown to Kawaramachi just to be in bump-physical contact with the masses on the sidewalk—but when you're breaking up, it's something you have to go through—even as this aloneness may have been extreme. As an Asian I was absorbed into the flow of the street, but I did not know the language, knew no one, could speak to no one. I had a lot of conversations with myself. Got to know myself better."[14]

Luke returned to Hawaii and completed his doctoral coursework and, on the introduction of Reuel Denney, went to Harvard to work on his dissertation on Gore Vidal with the playwright William Alfred. "Vidal caught my eye—early on he wrote of gay stuff, with innuendo and frankness and nastiness too, his historical fiction you couldn't put down, and his nonfiction ranged wide and fluidly and wisely. But as his years stretched on, he grew tiresome (to me), revealing among other things a self-righteousness and, after all, a sexual reactionariness that was a disappointment—he became sad and boring."[15]

Luke also continued to write fiction. He would exchange stories with another student who was doing his PhD at Harvard at the time. Tim Parks—who abandoned his doctoral work at Harvard after a year and a half but went on to become an author, translator, and scholar—recalls that they would "read each other's fiction aloud and give each other a few pages. It was all paper then. I can't recall anything coming of those pieces. It was a kind of apprenticeship, for me at least. Elmer was attractively different from most of the grad school students. A little older than the others perhaps, determinedly cheerful, ironic, sharp, and witty. We had exciting conversations. And we came from totally different backgrounds. So it was fun."

I ask Parks if he had any inkling at the time that Elmer would go on to become an editor rather than a writer or academic. "We're talking about a time when I was twenty-two, twenty-three. I just didn't think in terms of, is this guy going to be a writer or editor or what. Elmer was fun to be around. He'd been married, he was in a relationship with a man. It was all very adult and new to me . . . Elmer was very knowledgeable about contemporary American literature, poetry as well, which I knew little about, but was eager to understand. Reading it didn't do much for me and I felt someone like Elmer could help me 'get it.' In general, he was into really writing and reading stuff that was being written now, whereas most of the students were still in a 'let's study the past' mode. Academics. Elmer saw literature as really part of our lives, now. Something to be done. And that was encouraging for a guy like me, trying to write. And he was willing to read. I guess these were the qualities of an editor, but I never thought of that."[16]

In the meantime, Luke found himself making very little progress on his dissertation on Vidal. Eventually he decided to give up on finishing his PhD. He had a new plan: to move to New York and get a job in publishing. "It may have been a reflection of the times, where suddenly, it seemed, Asians were emerging more visibly in technology, finance, sciences, advertisements, popular culture too. They had haircuts I never had! An Asian in the US who had college loans would not think of going into publishing since the start-up pay was plainly terrible; they'd go into medicine, law, science, finance . . . I had no loans, by the way, made it through school with jobs that waived tuition and then had assistantships and fellowships, so didn't have that urgency—or was naive enough not to have it."[17]

Before moving to New York, Luke decided that he would first drive to New Mexico to see one Robert Seward, whom he had met in San Francisco, and who had begun a job as assistant professor of political science at the University of New Mexico. In four days, Luke drove cross-country in his "beat-up, rusting" Volkswagen Beetle. The idea had been to leave the car with Seward and fly back to New York. But Luke "just ended up never leaving." Instead he got a job with the Institute of Public Law, editing civil procedure, and then concentrated on renovating an old Victorian house they'd bought. He also continued to write short stories ("a manageable form") in the evenings on an IBM Selectric that Seward had bought him. One story was published in *Canto:*

Review of the Arts alongside nine other authors, including John Updike.[18]

Luke did eventually leave New Mexico, but only when Seward accepted a position at the University of Pennsylvania. "That was amusing—denied tenure at New Mexico, goes on to Ivy League school." In Philadelphia, Luke worked as a freelance editor for university presses and eventually got a job editing statistics papers at an institute at the Wharton School, a job where "there was no creativity but there was rigor." Luke speculates that this may have had some influence on the way he later demanded "understanding and clarity" even when he was editing fiction. He also continued to send stories to magazines and "got positive responses but no bites," and would eventually give up his own writing, deciding that he had the ability to "improve somebody else's work but not my own."[19]

When Seward was offered a job by New York University, the two moved to New York. Luke was thrilled to finally find himself there. After serving as a reader for agents, publishing houses, and book clubs ("another way to be exploited and I happily did it"), he finally managed to land an editorial assistant job with a publisher. "I was much older than the usual editorial assistant . . . I suppose I did think I was better than what I was doing, but I did it—and met people and learned how things worked."

Luke was eager to publish books that would be recognized by the literary community in New York. "And in my ambition, I didn't want to be identified professionally as being an editor who was, again, Asian who did Asian books, though the first original title I published was *Japanese Business Etiquette*."[20]

Luke bounced around a number of publishers: Pinnacle, Warner, Atheneum, where he worked on "a biography of Laurence Olivier, a book on running, a biography of Gordon of Khartoum, etc." While he was "pleased to have done them," they were not the kind of books he had imagined himself publishing. "The great irony is that I struggled in New York—Asians in publishing were few and far between then (I think I counted six); there were very few nonwhites in the business, so of course nonwhites stood out, were not neutrally viewed. Different expectations, different prejudices, different. One felt one should not stand out, or had to stand out brilliantly if at all."[21]

Back to Japan

In 1987, Seward was once again offered a position in another city—a professorship at Meiji Gakuin University in Tokyo and Yokohama. Until then, Luke had gone wherever Seward's academic career had taken him, but he "wasn't jazzed" about going to Japan. "For one, I had bad Japan memories (ex-wife left me in Kyoto), but for another, professionally I was focusing more on the West—dreaming about publishing good fiction and nonfiction, having a career that was not Asia-focused."[22]

Luke was afraid that moving to Japan would derail his career. It wasn't even clear if he would be able to find a job in publishing. But once he started looking around, he heard of an opening at the Tokyo office of Kodansha International.

Luke's interview was arranged by Tetsu Shirai. Murakami

refers to Shirai in one of his essays as "the President of Kodansha America, and the type of person who didn't bother with the typical Japanese way of doing things and allowed the American staff the freedom to do the work they needed to do."[23] (Shirai was actually the executive vice president.) Shirai had started out in sales in Kodansha's headquarters in Tokyo and had used the study abroad program offered by the company to take courses in marketing at George Washington University in Washington, D.C. He took charge of Kodansha's New York office in 1983, a post he would hold until the fall of 1991.

Kodansha International had been looking for someone who could run the editorial department in Tokyo and help their books break into the U.S. market. The company already had a handful of skilled editors, mostly from the U.K., but none had experience working in U.S. publishing. Shirai was tasked with identifying candidates in New York, and Luke was one of them.[24] Shirai recalls that Luke "had yet to establish his career as an editor, but he was full of vitality, and I could really sense his desire to work in Japan and his confidence that he could make a contribution."[25]

For the director position, KI ultimately decided to hire Leslie Pockell, an editor who had worked at St. Martin's and Doubleday, but called Luke and asked him if he might be interested in working in Tokyo under Pockell. The proposed compensation package "wasn't anything to complain about either," Luke says. "Colleagues [at Kodansha International] and I never compared, but my frame of reference was New York, and KI was a plus, and got to be more of a plus as endaka [a strong yen] took hold. I think the exchange rate was 130 to 135 yen to the dollar when I began at KI. When I left, it was just above 100. Big difference on that basis alone."[26]

Elmer Luke in Tokyo, 1988

Luke Discovers Murakami

Luke and Seward decided to share a house in Kamakura, south of Tokyo, with Michitarō Tada, a scholar of French literature, and his wife, Chieko. "The Kamakura house was a large property, deep in the valley and up on a hillside, with a big Japanese garden (I planted a small vegetable garden too) and a pretty nice unobstructed view looking toward the sea (which I don't think we could see, though). (Our cat was outdoors a lot, in fact was outdoors when we were at work.) It was an old house that'd been long unoccupied, built for a wealthy family. It was uninsulated (frigid in winter), and could have used better construction, and was a bit too 'close to nature' with mukade [centipedes], shiro ari [termites], nomi [fleas] (in summer, in the tatami), and kabi [mold] such as I'd never seen (long hairy green stuff growing on shoes). But it was enormous, as I said, and good for having people over."[27]

Elmer Luke's cat, Lili'uokalani

The commute from Kamakura to Tokyo was just under two hours one way. Luke was late to work "almost every day," but also tended to stay late "like a proper salaryman. I even did the whole thing of wearing suits to work every day. To surrender yourself to your surroundings. That was still important back then." When he left the company several years later, Luke was handed a memo by a woman in human resources indicating "the exact number of days I hadn't been late ... which weren't many."[28]

His second time around in Japan was better, but the sense of alienation was still there. "I'd never lived as part of a majority before, and suddenly I was passing as Japanese, as one of the majority, and while that spared me stares or rudeness, it had another kind of alienated-minority effect ... I'm thinking that—maybe, big maybe—this sense of alienation was part of the bond established with Haruki and Yōko [Murakami's wife], who felt a similar sense (though different, of course)."[29]

At KI Luke worked on craft and architecture books, a collection of short stories by Harumi Setouchi, and a reissue of the classic *The Book of Tea*. "I must have done a reasonable enough job, because Pockell then handed me Birnbaum's translation of *Hitsuji o meguru bōken* (*A Wild Sheep Chase*)."[30]

Minato Asakawa, executive vice president of KI's Tokyo office at the time, tells me that he had been of the opinion that Murakami should be translated and edited by people who "shared the 'pop' feelings in his writings."[31] On the other hand, Stephen Shaw, who had already been working for KI for more than twenty years then, remembers that he had been "put off" by some of Murakami's early work in English—"his early work seemed so static, as if the needle got stuck on a long-playing record of quiet jazz"—and "rather grandly, handed over the job to Elmer."[32]

Luke, for his part, says that he does not recall being passed the job from Shaw. "His decision must have preceded my arrival. I do know that Asakawa told me that he and Les (as co-editorial directors) had discussed and thought that there'd be a good fit between Haruki and me, our being the same age and of kindred sensibility (sort of)."

Luke also suggests that there was some tension between the old-timers in Tokyo and new editors who had come from New York. "I don't know what they [the old-timers] were told, but in a way we were given special consideration . . . There might have been the sense that we knew more, could provide a lift. We didn't, not about the kaisha [company] anyway, and of course, we were beaten down immediately!"[33]

When I ask Shaw how the other editors responded to the arrival of the New York editors, he responds, "Not hostilely at all. But it was immediately apparent that their New York publishing habits were ill-suited to Tokyo. And neither of them spoke much Japanese, which hampered their efforts."[34]

While Luke had never read Murakami, he was not unfamiliar with the name. The literary critic Norihiro Katō, to whom Luke had been introduced in Montreal in the early eighties, had recommended him highly. Katō, who died in 2019, recalled Luke coming to visit him soon after his arrival in Tokyo to start his job, to ask him for some names of promising young contemporary Japanese writers. "Topping the list was Haruki Murakami, followed by Gen'ichirō Takahashi. I explained their work in quite some detail. If I remember correctly, some others on the list included Ryū Murakami, Kenji Nakagami, Yoshikichi Furui, and Yumiko Kurahashi, but I wasn't sure that these writers would reach a wide readership in translation."

Katō had written relatively long pieces of criticism on both *Hitsuji o meguru bōken* (*A Wild Sheep Chase*) and *Sekai no owari to hādoboirudo wandārando* (*Hard-Boiled Wonderland and the End of the World*) and felt confident that these two works would be well received in the U.S. "On the other hand, I thought that *Noruwei no mori* (*Norwegian Wood*) was too sentimental and would not be received well outside Japan. I clearly turned out to be wrong about that, but until I witnessed the warm reception of Jay Rubin's translation of the book, I was pessimistic about its possibilities—maybe Asia, I thought, but not Europe."[35]

As with the first two Murakami titles, *A Wild Sheep Chase* had been slotted for publication as part of the Kodansha English Library series. But, according to Luke, the team at KI—including Pockell, Asakawa, and himself—had "roundly agreed" that "this was bigger than eigo bunko [Kodansha English Library series]." Luke also says that "Birnbaum's translation blew me away—it was witty, word-playful, ironic, creative." Luke was convinced that he, working with Birnbaum, could "make every sentence sing" and appeal to a wider audience than any before. "It was a great story, thrilling actually, the unfolding, the digressions, the woman's ear, the Sheepman, the Mafioso, the Rat, the resolution. It really was like nothing I'd read in any literature."

I ask Luke if his early experiences in Japan somehow helped him better relate to the protagonist in Murakami's fiction. "I think this narrative theme of Haruki's—sensitive, un-macho, lonely, newly single male on a journey of (re)discovery—is something that is the basis of his wild popularity," Luke responds. "And the Sheepman here is the agent—foreign, spiritual, magical—that contributes, empowers, affirms his sense of self. So, yeah, for sure there was a resonance."[36]

Updating *Sheep*

When Luke started editing *A Wild Sheep Chase*, Birnbaum was still traveling around Europe from his base in Barcelona. The two first met when Birnbaum returned to Japan for a short visit. "Alfred was staying at his friend's place and he asked if I'd like to come there," says Luke. "He was very polite and even offered me tea and manju."[37]

When I mention this to Birnbaum, who had initially said that he had no memory of their first meeting, he says, "Ah, I remember now. It was at the office slash home of a designer friend of mine. But I certainly don't remember serving him manju."[38]

How did Luke approach editing the book? One of the most significant changes—as has been noted by Jay Rubin, Minami Aoyama, and other scholars—is that the published translation leaves out dates from chapter and section headings that would set the novel in the seventies. For example, Part 1, which was "1970/11/25" in the Japanese original, is rendered "A Prelude." Part 2, "July 1978," is translated "July, Eight Years Later." And Part 3, "September 1978," becomes "September, Two Months Later." Similarly, in Part 5, the chapter whose literal translation would have been "The Rat's First Letter (Postmarked December 21, 1977)" is "The Rat's First Letter (Postmarked December 21st, One Year Ago)," and "The Rat's Second Letter (Postmarked May, 1978)" is "The Rat's Second Letter (Postmarked May, This Year)."

Dates have also been omitted from the body of the English text. "I met her in autumn nine years ago, when I was twenty and she was seventeen" was, in the original Japanese, "I met her in the autumn of 1969, when I was twenty and she was seventeen," and the final sentence of Part 1—"July, eight years later, she was dead at twenty-six"—has been changed from "July 1979, she was dead at twenty-six."

One paragraph in the first chapter of the English translation begins, "I still remember that eerie afternoon. The twenty-fifth of November." A literal translation of the original would be "I still remember clearly that strange afternoon of November 25, 1970." This refers to the day that the Japanese novelist Yukio Mishima publicly committed ritual suicide after failing to inspire a coup d'état to restore power to the emperor. The passage on the following page of the book, where Mishima is mentioned in passing, is retained in the English translation:

> It was two in the afternoon, and Yukio Mishima's picture kept flashing on the lounge TV. The volume control was broken so we could hardly make out what was being said, but it didn't matter to us one way or the other.[39]

Readers outside of Japan may not recognize the reference to Mishima's suicide even with the mention of the year. Without the year, however, it seems virtually impossible to make the connection, especially because it was not all that unusual for Mishima, who also starred in films, to be on television.

The book is updated in more subtle ways as well. The title of chapter 24, which is "Iwashi no tanjo" in the Japanese original and translates literally to "The Birth of Sardine," is, in Birnbaum's translation, "One for the Kipper" in English. "Iwashi" is the name given to the protagonist's cat by a limo driver, because the protagonist is "treating him like a herring after all."[40] In *Haruki Murakami and the Music of Words*, Jay Rubin has suggested that, given that the action was set in 1978, the novel "should not have contained—and does not in the original—this allusion to the famous movie line 'Make it one for the Gipper,' which flourished during the Reagan years after 1980."[41] Reagan had used the phrase as a political slogan throughout his tenure as president, including in his speech at the Republican National Conference in 1988 as he was about to leave office, in which he encouraged his vice president George H. W. Bush to "win one for the Gipper."[42]

Jay Rubin notes that these changes were made to improve the appeal of the book for "an international readership," but when I ask Luke what might be meant by that, he replies that it would have been more precise to say that they had "American—particularly New York American—readers in mind."[43] Both Birnbaum and Luke tell me that they felt that America was looking for a "contemporary" author and work. It was something that Murakami also noticed when he visited New York soon after the translation came out. Asked in an interview for *Asahi Shimbun*, one of the major dailies in Japan, what the publishing professionals he had met in New York seemed to be interested in, Murakami responded:

> They wanted to know how young people in Japan today think and live. In America there is zero knowledge about these things. People read Jun'ichirō Tanizaki and Yasunari Kawabata, but the Japanese lifestyle has completely changed in the past twenty-five to thirty years. The novels translated into English, however, are from before that time, and they don't give you a sense of life [in Japan] today. Though that may not be the only thing of value, I do think that there is room for more contemporary works to be translated.[44]

When *Hitsuji o meguru bōken* (*A Wild Sheep Chase*) was initially published in Japan in 1982, the action set in the seventies was less than a decade old. When the book was being prepared for publication in English in 1989, it had been seven years since the book was first published in Japanese, and close to twenty years since the period in which the book was set. The efforts to make the book more contemporary may have been a way to compensate for this time lag as well as to expand the potential readership beyond traditional fans of Japanese literature.

In the latest Kindle version of the book, the date has been

reinstated in the first chapter, so that it is no longer called "A Prelude" but "Part One: November 25, 1970."[45] When I ask Lexy Bloom, Murakami's current editor at Knopf, about this change, she tells me that despite some searching she is unable to pinpoint when or why it was made.[46] When I tell Luke about the change and ask him if he would put the dates back if he were in a position to edit the book now, he tells me that "the situation, including his [Murakami's] popularity, is completely different now. It's hard to say without rereading the book, but I guess I might leave them in."[47] When I ask Murakami for his opinion, he looks puzzled. It's clear to me that he is unaware of the change or had forgotten about it.[48]

Of Sheep and Men

Generating attention for a new book published by a small publisher is never easy. It can be especially tricky when the book is a translation of a novel by an unknown writer. Luke began to work with the Kodansha International USA office in New York to position Murakami as an exciting new voice from Japan. Kodansha International USA would eventually change its name to Kodansha America and take on an editorial function, but at the time it was primarily charged with the sale and promotion of books produced by KI in Tokyo. "We gathered people from all kinds of places toward that end," says Tetsu Shirai.[49]

The business manager, Stephanie Levi, had arrived from

Chase Manhattan Bank. Her father's work had taken her to To-kyo in the sixties, when she was aged seven to thirteen. Having also spent her year abroad studying at the International Christian University, Levi was fluent in Japanese. Her husband, author Jonathan Levi, had helped relaunch the U.K. literary magazine *Granta* in 1979 with Bill Buford, and was the magazine's U.S. editor at the time. Later, once Murakami got over his dislike of public events, Jonathan Levi would occasionally join him onstage for a conversation or reading.

Marketing director Gillian Jolis had worked at Simon & Schuster and the Free Press before joining KI. She makes a brief appearance in one of Murakami's essays, in which he visits various publishing professionals in the Hamptons. In the piece, Jolis tells Murakami that John Irving had put his house up for sale and suggests, "Why don't you buy it, Mr. Murakami?"[50]

The publicist for KI-USA was Anne Cheng. Born in Tai-wan, Cheng had moved to the U.S. when she was twelve. After studying English literature at Princeton and creative writing at Stanford, she had started working in publishing. Before coming to KI she had been at the educational pub-lisher McGraw-Hill, and after leaving KI she went back to graduate school. She is now a professor of English literature at Princeton University. "It was while I was working at Kodan-sha, working with a lot of great literature (including the works of Haruki Murakami), that I realized I needed to go back to graduate school because there were books I was reading that I wanted to write about."[51]

At the KI-USA offices in New York.
Left to right: Gillian Jolis, Anne Cheng, Tetsu Shirai

The first decision made by the KI/KI-USA team—Jolis and Cheng in New York, Les Pockell and Luke in Tokyo—was to push back *Sheep*'s publication by a year to fall 1989. The team then discussed the need for a title that "would appeal to a Western audience." Some ideas included *An Adventure Surrounding Sheep* (a more or less direct translation from the Japanese) and *Of Sheep and Men* (a nod to John Steinbeck's *Of Mice and Men*), but in the end, the team agreed on *A Wild Sheep Chase*, proposed by Birnbaum.[52]

Birnbaum says that *Of Sheep and Men* was one of his suggestions but was "more of a joke than a real working title . . . *A Wild*

Sheep Chase, on the other hand, was obviously a play on the common, now dated expression 'a wild goose chase,' which does convey something of the convoluted quirks of the plot. Surprisingly, to me at least, no one ever seems to comment on that."[53]

Mike Molasky, a professor at Waseda University, was living in Japan when Birnbaum was working on the translation. He recalls seeing Birnbaum, whom he had known well at the time, on the Marunouchi subway line one day, lugging a large computer (according to Birnbaum, a "totally non-portable Macintosh Portable"). When Molasky asked him what he was doing with the massive machine, Birnbaum explained that he was translating a book by Haruki Murakami. Then he added, "I decided to call it *A Wild Sheep Chase*. Don't you think it's a much better title than the original?"[54]

Of Copy and Capital

Kodansha International budgeted $46,000 for the promotion of *A Wild Sheep Chase*. This money was spent on advance reading copies and postcards, ads in *The New York Times*, including one in the Sunday *Book Review*, and a co-op ad in the *San Francisco Chronicle*.[55]

The advance reading copies featured the cover design by Shigeo Okamoto, who had also designed the cover of Murakami's short story collection *Kaiten mokuba no deddo hīto* (*Dead Heat on a Merry-Go-Round*), published in Japan in 1985. When I ask Murakami about the cover, he says that he was not involved in the process and that he "left it all to Elmer." "In Japan . . . I make very detailed requests including the style of the font. But in America I'm hands-off," he says. "The one request I do make is to avoid 'oriental' designs."[56]

The advance reading copy of *A Wild Sheep Chase*

Birnbaum's name was featured on the front cover of the book. Luke says that it was KI's policy to recognize the translator's work in this way and that it was probably something started by Stephen Shaw. When I ask Shaw about this, he responds that the decision was "(a) encouraged by the prominence that one or two translators in Europe such as Constance Garnett (for Dostoevsky) were given, and (b) by being puzzled when there was no reference to a translator at all, as if it was an Immaculate Conception."[57]

The description on the jacket flap of *A Wild Sheep Chase* emphasized the "originality" and "novelty" of the voice ("a voice the likes of which no Western reader of Japanese fiction will have encountered before"), the contemporariness of the work and author ("The time is now. The setting is Japan—minus the kimono and the impenetrable mystique of an exotic, distant culture"), and the fact that the book was Murakami's debut in English ("Haruki Murakami's dazzling debut in the West").

In the spring of 1989, Gillian Jolis and Leslie Pockell (who was visiting New York) met with the Book-of-the-Month Club and the Literary Guild in the hopes that they would pick up *A Wild Sheep Chase*.

"Book clubs were a big deal," Luke says. "They had a built-in readership—mostly suburban, perhaps, less so in the cities where bookstores thrived (as they once did)—and members trusted the book club to select the kind of book they wanted or should want to read. So a book's being picked up by a book club was indication of its appeal, salability, and the buyers (the staff who placed the orders) at bookstores and chains paid attention when that happened."[58]

The Literary Guild chose *A Wild Sheep Chase* as one of its selections. It was still unusual for book clubs to select works in translation at the time; *Asahi Shimbun* gave this as an example of the U.S. becoming more open to new Japanese literature.[59]

A couple of weeks after publication, a large ad ran in *The New York Times Book Review*, calling *A Wild Sheep Chase* "The American Debut of Japan's Premier Contemporary Writer" and using phrases such as "marvelously engaging," "gripping plot," "comic," "fresh, brave" from responses to the early copies that had been sent out to reviewers.

Ad in *The New York Times*

The KI team was feeling the benefits of the strong Japanese economy (the Nikkei recorded an all-time high of 38,915.87 at the end of 1989)[60] and, more specifically, the backing of their parent company, Kodansha. "If this was five, ten years later," Luke says, "I don't know if there would have been the environment to invest so much money and manpower into the project."[61] Cheng said it was a benefit that extended to all of KI-USA's projects; it meant that the publisher could be "dedicated to quality rather than simply the bottom line . . . So we could do gorgeous art books that are $300 apiece and tailored for libraries and other projects of love like that."[62]

Needless to say, a large promotional budget does not guarantee the success of a book. Being relatively new and small, KI had fewer connections and less prestige than its more established rivals; it may have been flush with economic capital, but its social and symbolic capital was limited. Luke, for instance, was forty years old when he joined KI. Given that he had "stumbled into" the profession, he didn't have the same networks and influence that an editor of similar age would after working in the field for a couple of decades. The team had to find ways to borrow the networks and prestige of individuals and institutions already established in the U.S.[63]

Luke met many of the journalists who would go on to write about Murakami's work at the Foreign Correspondents Club of Japan. He says that this eventually led to an Associated Press article calling Murakami a member of Japan's literary "Brat Pack" and "perhaps the biggest sensation in Japanese publishing in recent years."[64]

The writer Robert Whiting also played a role in helping Luke and KI expand their media contacts. Whiting had been receiving attention for *You Gotta Have Wa*, his second book on Japanese professional baseball, which had been published in the summer of 1989 and was a Book-of-the-Month Club selection and nominated for the Pulitzer Prize later that same year. In June 1989, he had taken part in a three-week-long promotional tour in the U.S. and was interviewed "35 times in two and a half weeks."[65]

Luke and Whiting were both living in Kamakura at the time, and Luke had read and commented on the manuscript of *You Gotta Have Wa* before publication. (Luke's name appears in the acknowledgments.) They were also planning to work together on a memoir of the Yomiuri Giants star Warren Cromartie (published by Kodansha America in 1991 under the title *Slugging It Out in Japan: An American Major Leaguer in the Tokyo Outfield*).

Whiting tells me that Luke was "a very good editor . . . I remember I submitted a manuscript that used Cromartie's voice, as it was recorded during our interviews. The result was that the manuscript was flat. Elmer said so, quite emphatically. I had to go back and rewrite the whole thing creating a more reader-friendly version of Cromartie's speaking style, part fictional . . . I had a falling-out with Cromartie during the interview process. I would show up at his apartment sometimes and he would just be gone, no explanation, nothing. So towards the end I got fed up and quit. Elmer patched that up and even did one final interview himself with Cromartie and had a very frank discussion about racial discrimination, which proved to be a good addition to the book."

When I ask Whiting about the publication of *A Wild Sheep Chase*, he tells me that he does not remember any details. "I just remember Elmer was very enthusiastic about Murakami."[66]

The Murakamis Go to New York

On May 10, 1989, Luke sent Murakami a fax reporting on the sale of paperback rights to *A Wild Sheep Chase* (to Plume for $55,000)[67] and asking him to take part in the promotional activities that were scheduled in New York that fall. Murakami declined. Several months later, Luke and Murakami met in person for the first time in Tokyo (together with another editor from KI), and on August 14, just three days before a copy of *A Wild Sheep Chase* arrived at the Murakamis' home, Luke again asked Murakami to join him in New York. Murakami once again declined. On September 24, Luke asked again, saying that Birnbaum had become unable to attend, and that they had also managed to arrange an interview with *The New York Times*. Murakami finally relented.[68]

Murakami and his wife, Yōko, landed in New York on October 21, and Luke and Shirai picked them up at the airport. Shirai remembers handing Murakami a copy of that day's *New York Times* folded open to a story in the Arts section about him and *A Wild Sheep Chase*. The headline, "Young and Slangy Mix of the U.S. and Japan," was followed by a tagline: "A best-selling novelist makes his American debut with a quest story."[69] "Of course, it was something that had been in the works," Shirai tells me, "but I was surprised by how well the timing worked out."[70]

Shirai and Luke had chosen a hotel on the Upper East Side, thinking Murakami, an avid runner, would like to be near Central Park. Ten years later, Murakami would write in an essay for the women's magazine *an an* that, while he preferred the Village and SoHo with its many bookshops and secondhand record stores, he ended up staying uptown in New York because "the appeal of running in Central Park in the morning is too great."[71]

Of the boutique hotels close to Central Park, the team at KI decided on the Stanhope Hotel. Luke says that he suggested the Stanhope, "which might seem odd (uptown, old-world-ish, maybe even stuffy, not hip or cool)," because it was the setting for *The Hotel New Hampshire* by John Irving.[72] When Murakami had visited the U.S. in 1984 at the invitation of the Department of Defense, he had interviewed Irving while jogging through Central Park with him. Two years later he had also translated Irving's debut novel, *Setting Free the Bears*, into Japanese.

Murakami spent eleven days promoting his book in New York. Many of the interviews were conducted in KI-USA's new office, which had a large poster of the cover of *A Wild Sheep Chase* on one of its walls. Cheng says that her most vivid memory of working on the book was "me trying to get this huge, glossy, bigger than life, poster reproduction of the book cover—that startling peacock blue background and the sheep in the foreground—to hang in our beautiful glass offices, next to the fresh ikebana arrangement that Mr. Shirai ordered for the entryway every week. There were a bunch of logistic and mundane details, but when the poster (almost five feet tall) was finally hung up, it was breathtaking and felt like a symbolic tribute to a book that was also larger than life."[73]

KI-USA/Kodansha America's offices, New York

At the time, Murakami was already known for avoiding media attention. But during his time in New York, he agreed to an interview with *Asahi Shimbun/Aera* in which he told the reporter that he wanted to publish English translations of three of his novels, *Sekai no owari to hādoboirudo wandārando* (*Hard-Boiled Wonderland and the End of the World*), *Noruwei no mori* (*Norwegian Wood*), and *Dansu dansu dansu* (*Dance Dance Dance*), "at the rate of one book every year" as well as "short stories in magazines."[74]

In addition to individual interviews, Cheng thinks that there may also have been a book party at the Helmsley Palace Hotel. "I may not be getting the details right ... I seem to remember—please double check with Mr. Shirai—we had a row of seven sushi chefs making exquisite fresh sushi to order. It was a wonderful event."[75]

Shirai has no recollection of the Helmsley Palace event, but tells me it may simply have been that he hadn't attended and that Stephanie Levi would have a better idea.[76] Levi says that she does remember a big party at the Helmsley Palace, but isn't sure either whether it was for *A Wild Sheep Chase* or not.[77] When I ask Luke about this, he laughs. "No way! Really? Would be amazing if it were true. True, they could have had it and I wasn't there. I mean, the Helmsley Palace was a pretty big deal back then. If Gillian were alive, she'd be the one to know. The Seven Sushi Chefs. Sounds like a parody of a Japanese film."[78]

A private party was also held at the Levis' apartment, attended by the Murakamis, Kodansha staff, and researchers from Columbia, as well as the editor Gary Fisketjon and the literary agent Andrew Wylie, who, according to Jonathan Levi, were "the only two Americans [he] knew who had heard of Murakami" and who were "both very keen to work with him."[79] One guest recalls coming back into the living room after being given a tour of the Levis' apartment to find Andrew Wylie still talking to Murakami. The Murakamis left a short while later, saying they had plans to go to a jazz club.[80]

Luke also accompanied the Murakamis on visits to book-stores. *A Wild Sheep Chase*, he says, was prominently displayed in Three Lives, "a terrific independent store in Greenwich Village that was my favorite—and that, many years later, would host midnight opening parties on publication dates of Murakami books." Luke says that Murakami may have signed books, but that no public events were planned.[81] It would be another couple of years before Murakami would do his first ever public event with Jay McInerney at the PEN America Center.[82]

"Haruki was excited, though guardedly, not effusively, in his Haruki way . . . We [KI] were careful about overdosing him with publicity, and he was a bit shy about availing himself, but he was willing to participate. Not as guarded as he is now."[83]

In the afterword of his 1990 collection of travel writing, *Tōi taiko* (*Far-off Drums*), Murakami shared his impressions of the New York trip, writing that although it had been some time since he had last visited the city, he "did not feel especially out of sorts," and that while he would never want to live in New York, the fact that people were direct "in some ways made it less uncomfortable than Tokyo."[84] Nearly thirty years later, Murakami tells me that he "remembers the response in New York being especially big." When I show him the *New York Times* review with his photo on it, he laughs and says, "I was a lot younger back then."[85]

15

Books of The Times

Young and Slangy Mix Of the U.S. and Japan

By HERBERT MITGANG

A best-selling novelist makes his American debut with a quest story.

A Wild Sheep Chase
By Haruki Murakami
Translated by Alfred Birnbaum. 299 pages. Kodansha International $18.95.

Review/Dance

A Traditional Form From India

By JACK ANDERSON

Minneapolis Museum Director to Retire

Concert Programs Changed

Nilsson to Give Master Class

Entertainment Events

Music

Dance

THEATER DIRECTORY

BROADWAY

OFF-BROADWAY

This Sunday in The New York Times Magazine

- Peter Guber and Jon Peters: two Hollywood producers "as powerful as any studio."

- Hong Kong: caught between a retreating British master and a looming Chinese menace.

- Hot topic: "The End of History?"—A controversial essay by Francis Fukuyama.

Plus

- The Magazine's famous life style features, challenging puzzles and prestigious advertising—all combining to enrich your life.

The New York Times Magazine

Advertisers: Call (212) 556-1203 for full information about The New York Times Magazine... The Right Space.

Without a Kimono in Sight

The *New York Times* review that appeared on the day of the Murakamis' arrival in the city had been written by Herbert Mitgang, who had been at the paper since immediately after the Second World War.[86] He had just published *Dangerous Dossiers: Exposing the Secret War Against America's Greatest Authors* and had also reviewed Robert Whiting's *You Gotta Have Wa* several months earlier.[87]

Mitgang wrote that *A Wild Sheep Chase* was a "bold new advance in a category of international fiction that could be called the trans-Pacific novel." He continued:

> This isn't the traditional fiction of Kōbō Abe ("The Woman in the Dunes"), Yukio Mishima ("The Sailor Who Fell From Grace With the Sea") or Japan's only Nobel laureate in literature, Yasunari Kawabata ("Snow Country"). Mr. Murakami's style and imagination are closer to that of Kurt Vonnegut, Raymond Carver and John Irving.[88]

Mitgang also emphasized that "there isn't a kimono to be found in 'A Wild Sheep Chase.'" Actually, a kimono does appear in the novel, when the protagonist visits the Boss's residence and an "elderly maid in kimono entered the room, set down a glass of grape juice, and left without a word." But there is a chance that Mitgang was influenced by the description on the book jacket: "The setting is Japan—minus the kimono."[89]

Mitgang concludes by stating, "What makes 'A Wild Sheep Chase' so appealing is the author's ability to strike common chords between the modern Japanese and American middle classes, especially the younger generation, and to do so in stylish, swinging language. Mr. Murakami's novel is a welcome debut by a talented writer who should be discovered by readers on this end of the Pacific." After Mitgang's review appeared, *Yomiuri Shimbun*—the Japanese broadsheet with the largest circulation in the world—published an article headlined "US Newspaper New York Times Lauds Haruki Murakami."[90]

Mitgang's was the first of many reviews that placed Murakami in contrast to the "Big Three" postwar writers in Japan. In *The Washington Post*, novelist/journalist Alan Ryan wrote, "Readers who treasure the refined sensibilities of Kawabata and Tanizaki, the grand but precisely etched visions of Mishima, or even the dark formalities of Kōbō Abe, are in for a surprise when they read Murakami," and went on to say that he was not surprised to learn that Murakami had translated authors such as F. Scott Fitzgerald, Paul Theroux, Raymond Carver, and John Irving. Ryan also suggests that "Murakami echoes the state of mind of the ordinary Japanese, caught between a fading old world and a new one still being invented, willing to find magic but uncertain where to look."[91]

Not everyone was thrilled by Murakami's arrival on American shores. One of the least enthusiastic reviews was by another Japanese novelist. Foumiko Kometani had received the Akutagawa Prize (an award for emerging writers that Murakami was short-listed for twice but never won) in 1986 for *Sugikoshi no matsuri* (translated into English by the author as *The Passover*). In her *Los Angeles Times* review, "Help! His Best Friend Is Turning Into a Sheep!" Kometani criticized the narrative voice of *A Wild Sheep Chase* for "sound[ing] more like a black Raymond Carver or a recycled Raymond Chandler or some new ghetto private eye than a contemporary Japanese novelist" and suggested that his readers in Japan are "people who have taken their places sheep-like on the conveyor belt of Japanese society as salaried men and housewives, but still like to harbor images of themselves as cool and hip and laid-back, sophisticated and aware, and, yes, above all, Western."

Kometani was a translator herself (she translated not only her own novel into English but also her husband's nonfiction books into Japanese), and her otherwise scathing review is kind to the translator: "Not that Alfred Birnbaum's excellent translation has not gotten Murakami's sentences down exactly right."[92]

Many of the other reviewers were also complimentary about the translation. In *The New York Times*, Mitgang noted that "the novel is racily translated from the Japanese by Alfred Birnbaum."[93] Ann Arensberg went further in *The New York Times Book Review*: "Without question, [Murakami] has help from Alfred Birnbaum, who seems more like his spiritual twin than merely his translator."[94] When I ask Birnbaum what his initial reaction had been on reading these positive reviews, he says, "Disbelief, but I more keenly remember one bad review that cited 'Birnbaum's tin ear.'"[95] (I was unable to locate this particular review, but the review in *The Washington Post* stated, "Alfred Birnbaum's translation constantly jars with its odd sentence structures, punning chapter titles, colloquial Americanisms, Britishisms, and at least one Boston-ism.")[96] One review seemed almost to predict what lay in store for Murakami. In *The New Yorker*, novelist and poet Brad Leithauser wrote that the book "lingers in the mind with the special glow that attends an improbable success" and that "[i]t is difficult not to regard *A Wild Sheep Chase* as an event larger even than its considerable virtues merit . . . Many years have elapsed, after all, since any Japanese novelist was enthusiastically taken up by the American reading public—and this may soon be Murakami's destiny."[97]

Leithauser, who has published eight novels and six poetry collections with Knopf and is currently a professor at Johns Hopkins, had lived in Kyoto in the early eighties. He tells me in an email that he "wasn't terribly surprised" by Murakami's success. "It seemed clear to me from the first that he was bringing something new to Japanese literature. There's a peculiar lightness in what he's doing that should not be confused with any lack of seriousness . . . I think to Western eyes Japanese literature is apt to seem light in another sense—in its sparsity. This is certainly true of Kawabata. And this sparsity is for me one of the great appeals of Japanese literature. But I'm talking here of a different kind of lightness, an antic and lyrical and sunny quality. I tend to love writers who have this quality. Calvino [one such writer] is much more articulate than I'm being in his essay on lightness versus heaviness. I'm thinking he [Calvino] would have admired him [Murakami]."[98]

The U.K. Calling

According to a memo that the Kodansha America office in New York sent the Kodansha International office in Tokyo, *A Wild*

Sheep Chase sold 8,500 copies in addition to the 3,000 copies sold to the Literary Guild.[99]

These numbers seem perfectly respectable for a debut work in translation; KI's first print run usually ranged between 3,000 and 5,000 copies.[100] But given the announced print run of 25,000 copies (and second printing of 3,000 copies before publication),[101] as well as the significant resources that had gone into promoting the book, Luke suggests that the "actual numbers may have been a disappointment."[102] Kuniaki Ura, who was a marketing manager at KI-USA at the time and currently runs his own publishing company in Tokyo, also recalls that while sales were solid compared with other KI titles, they were far from spectacular when compared with other books being published in the U.S.[103]

But perhaps the exact number of copies sold is not as important as the level of critical attention the publishing team had achieved. "It was an opening. A pretty good opening," Luke tells me during one of our Skype sessions.[104]

When I bring up *A Wild Sheep Chase* to Murakami during our interview in his Aoyama office, he tells me that he remembers the distribution and sales being "poor" but the critical reception being "very good." He says, "Lots of places picked up the book. *The New Yorker* published a long review by John Updike, which made me really happy."[105] (In fact, the review for *The New Yorker* was by Brad Leithauser. Updike wrote a long review of *Kafka on the Shore* for the magazine in 2005.)[106]

This moderate success in New York also created new opportunities in Europe. Just a month after publication in the U.S., rights had been sold to the U.K., France, Germany, the Netherlands, Spain, and Italy, and interest had been expressed by publishers in Israel, Russia, Sweden, and Catalonia.[107]

U.K. rights had been obtained for Hamish Hamilton by Clare Alexander, who is now chair of the literary agency Aitken Alexander Associates. Her memory of how she first came across the book is unclear. "Either Kodansha offered me the rights, or I do remember reading a good review in *Publishers Weekly*, either before I had read it or after—I can't remember. I may have requested it after reading the review. In any case I remember loving its energy, wit, and originality. I loved the way it was told in a Chandler-like voice (at that time, Hamish Hamilton were also Chandler's publishers, by the way) mixed up with an antic Japanese sensibility that made for a fresh take on a traditional form."[108]

On Christmas Day 1989, *The Washington Post* published an extended interview with Murakami. Fred Hiatt, the paper's Tokyo correspondent, emphasized the coming paperback and translations across Europe and wrote, "Murakami may be the first Japanese writer since the days of Mishima and Kawabata to break through to the general reading public outside Japan."[109]

The response in countries that had bought the rights to publish translations, however, was relatively quiet. "My memory is that the book was not successful in the U.K. market," Alexander says. "But it did mean that Hamish Hamilton became Murakami's option publisher, and of course his international career began to take off and he became a bestseller thereafter."[110]

Andrew Franklin, who headed Hamish Hamilton at the time (and who now runs Profile Books), also recalls that the book did not do particularly well for them. "We published the books because they were fun, quirky, original and enjoyable. There was no understanding that he would go on and become an enormous bestseller . . . I am afraid I have no memory of how the books did except that they didn't do anything special."[111]

In 1989, Kazuo Ishiguro won the Booker Prize for *The Remains of the Day*. When I ask Murakami about Ishiguro, he tells me that he has long been a fan of the Japanese British author's books. "What most impresses me about him is how he changes his style with each work. That's completely different from the way I work. I'm the type to gradually develop and evolve my style . . . But we are similar in that we both place a great importance on style."[112]

I ask Alexander if she remembers there being any attempt to bring the two authors together in those early years. "If only we had been that smart," she responds. "With hindsight, perhaps the combination of a Japanese sensibility with Western storytelling had a cultural moment then—the one being an American-style first-person crime narrative, the other being the very English first-person story of a great house in the lead up to the Second World War."[113]

When I put the same question to Franklin, he also says that he is pretty sure there was no such attempt. "That would be an odd thing to do: just because both writers are Japanese that is not the most salient fact about the way they write or what they write. Both are global writers."[114]

When I check with Luke, who accompanied the Murakamis to the U.K. for a promotional tour in 1990, he responds, "I believe the Hamish Hamilton publicist tried to arrange some kind of conversation onstage between Haruki and Ish, but Ish's handlers declined (Haruki was an unknown, not on Ish's level was the sense I got) and the time may not have been right as Haruki was very nervous—and probably would have demurred—being on stage (that was then) and having to contend with an English-speaking audience even if there would have been an interpreter (which he doesn't need now)."[115]

Becoming a *"New Yorker* Author"

The year after *A Wild Sheep Chase* was published, *The New Yorker* published a story by Murakami. "TV People," translated by Birnbaum, appeared in the magazine's September 10, 1990, issue. In the foreword to the Japanese edition of his story collection *The Elephant Vanishes*, Murakami writes that it was an event "as incredible as walking on the moon" that made him "happier than any literary prize could."[116] He also writes in his essay "Going Abroad. A New Frontier":

[T]he prestige and influence of *The New Yorker* is so great that it's a little difficult to understand in terms of Japanese magazines. When you tell people in America that your novel sold a million copies in Japan or that you won a certain award, people aren't all that impressed. But when they find out that you've had a few stories in *The New Yorker* they start treating you completely differently.[117]

At the time, the editor of *The New Yorker* was Robert Gottlieb, who had left his position as editor-in-chief and publisher of Knopf to become editor of the magazine in February 1987. Gottlieb replaced William Shawn, who had been at the magazine for more than fifty years and its editor for thirty-five.[118]

In a 1997 essay, Murakami describes his first meeting with Gottlieb:

> Once when I visited the office of an editor at *The New Yorker*, I noticed that there were half a dozen copies of the English translation of Jun'ichirō Tanizaki's *Sasameyuki* [*The Makioka Sisters*] on the bookshelf behind his desk. When I asked him, "Why do you have so many copies of the same book?" he smiled and said, "So as to make everyone who visits here ask that very question. That way I get the chance to explain what a wonderful book it is. And if people get interested in the book I can gift them a copy. Would you like one?"
>
> "No thank you," I said laughing. "I have a copy of the Japanese original at home."
>
> "Right, of course, you're Japanese."[119]

When I mention this to Gottlieb he tells me that he remembers this first "and most likely last" meeting with Murakami almost thirty years ago, but does not recall the exchange about *The Makioka Sisters*. He also tells me that, given that Tanizaki is his favorite Japanese author, and he had been "obsessed" with *The Makioka Sisters*, it was entirely possible that he'd had a few copies of the book in his office.[120]

Gottlieb had first come across Murakami's fiction when Donald Keene, the scholar and translator of Japanese literature, had asked him to serve on a jury for the Japan-U.S. Friendship Commission Prize for the Translation of Japanese Literature. *Pinball, 1973* was one of the translations being considered and had "piqued everyone's interest."[121] So when *A Wild Sheep Chase* was published in the fall of 1989, Gottlieb commissioned the Brad Leithauser review.

What was it about Murakami's work that appealed to Gottlieb? "Difficult to say exactly what, but Murakami's work was original, full of energy, and very contemporary." Gottlieb says that while there are many contemporary works of Japanese literature in English translation today, there were hardly any at the time and Japan was "hot, hot, hot."[122]

During the last couple of years of Gottlieb's five-and-a-half-year stint at the magazine, he published four of Murakami's stories. The first two, "TV People" (September 10, 1990) and "The Windup Bird and Tuesday's Women" (November 26, 1990), were translated by Alfred Birnbaum, and the other two, "The Elephant Vanishes" (November 18, 1991) and "Sleep" (March 30, 1992), by Jay Rubin.

In a 1994 interview in *The Paris Review*, Gottlieb suggests that a magazine "is in a sense an emanation of its chief editor—of his impulses and views and, to use a disgusting word, vision." He proposes that a magazine editor has more power than a book editor and says, "The editors I worked with at *The New Yorker* were not essentially procuring editors—they were working editors. Only the editor had the authority to buy a piece."[123]

Given this authority, Gottlieb may have been pivotal to Murakami's career. (In his memoir, Gottlieb mentions three fiction writers whom he "added to the mix" at *The New Yorker*: Anne Tyler, Margaret Atwood, and Murakami.)[124] It seems far from certain that Gottlieb's predecessor, William Shawn, who was said to be reluctant to "seem trendy,"[125] or his successor, Tina Brown, under whose editorship the number of pages devoted to fiction initially fell sharply,[126] would have pushed Murakami with the same level of enthusiasm.

What does seem clear is that, as with his New York debut, Murakami's "*New Yorker* debut" was helped by Birnbaum and Luke. Birnbaum first prepared the translation of "TV People" for an anthology he was editing, *Monkey Brain Sushi: New Tastes in Japanese Fiction*, which was published by KI less than a year after the story's publication in *The New Yorker*.[127]

While the pair were working on the anthology, Gottlieb had visited Japan in order to take part in the judging of another prize, the Noma Award for the Translation of Japanese Literature, newly established by Kodansha. Gottlieb tells me that he doesn't recall the winner of the prize, but that he had felt a great responsibility, because the committee appeared to give the opinion of the two foreign guests, himself and Donald Keene, greater weight than its other members.[128] (It included Kenzaburō Ōe, who would be awarded the Nobel Prize a few years later.)[129]

In his memoir, Gottlieb does recall an episode from the dinner that followed the selection committee meeting:

The high point of the evening on which the adjudication took place came after dinner as we were all being ushered into our separate limousines and the owner of the restaurant presented each of us with a farewell gift as he bowed us out: a pair of Christian Dior black socks. Why? Being mere Westerners, we'll never know.[130]

It was during this visit, when Gottlieb was being shown around Tokyo by Kodansha, that Luke had met with Gottlieb and given him Birnbaum's translation of "TV People."[131] The story was published in the magazine a few months later.

Luke says it was "personally gratifying" to see a story he edited published in a magazine he had been reading for many years. "Though they were not my written words, I'd worked on every single one of them, sounded them out, worried them to death. And because Alfred, who ordinarily would have been the writer who worked out any questions with *The New Yorker* editor, was traveling extensively and not easily reachable by phone or fax, I took on that role."[132]

Birnbaum, on the other hand, says, "I never held *The New Yorker* in awe or 'pinnacle' reverence—I didn't grow up with issues of the magazine around the house—so I don't remember being wowed by the prospect of publication."[133]

Murakami tells me that he had initially been "doubtful" about being published successfully in the U.S., "but then Elmer helped get my short stories published in *The New Yorker* and I began to think that things might work out after all. Without Elmer's efforts I don't think my work would have been published in *The New Yorker*. So in that sense I'm really grateful to him."[134]

Luke sent Gottlieb an early copy of *Monkey Brain Sushi* just before the book came out in May 1991, and Gottlieb responded with a short note.

> Many thanks for MONKEY BRAIN SUSHI. What a title! I'll settle down with it one of these nights, and if any particular writer excites my interest (for the magazine) I'll give a shout.

> Of course I'm looking forward to the new Murakami (remember: I'm apparently the only living person who wasn't embarrassed by "Norwegian Wood." I'll read it in bits or entire, as you prefer.)

> You'll have heard that, as I passionately advised, the Noma Prize is going French this year. Next year it's out [*sic*] turn again, and I guess I'll be hand for it, d.v. Start warming the sake!

> Best B.G.[135]

The Wind-Up Bird and *The New Yorker's* Women

Murakami's primary editor at *The New Yorker* for the first seven or so years of his relationship with the magazine was Linda Asher, who worked in its fiction department for eighteen years, under three different editors: William Shawn until January 1987, Robert Gottlieb until August 1992, and Tina Brown until 1997.

Though she "will make no public claims re writers I brought to the magazine for the first time,"[136] according to Luke, she had already been in the process of soliciting a Murakami story for the magazine when "TV People" was published.[137] This story, "The Windup Bird and Tuesday's Women," was published two months later in November 1990.

Asher also developed a friendship with Murakami. She had lunch with him whenever he was in New York, and in various essays and interviews Murakami refers to Asher as "my editor at *The New Yorker*."[138] Asher does not remember the substance of their conversations, but she does recall once going "with M and Mme Murakami to a soba restaurant in SoHo, a new fashion in NYC." On another occasion, she went with Murakami to hear Grace Paley speak at the City Center on Fifty-fifth Street and "was struck by the degree of Yiddish lilt in her spoken address and wondered how much of that tone/rhythm Haruki had felt and sought to transmit in his translation of her work."[139]

When I ask Murakami about the Grace Paley reading, his eyes light up. "Yes, yes, we went," he confirms. "I can't even really understand Linda very well, but I couldn't understand a word of what Grace Paley was saying!"[140]

In addition to being an editor, Asher has for many years been one of the main translators of Milan Kundera's work. She tells me over breakfast at a café near her Manhattan apartment that she was personally interested in publishing authors in translation— something that the magazine had not been particularly focused on at the time.[141] Her translation work also informed the way she edited translators of Hungarian, Serbo-Croatian, Italian, French of course, and Japanese toward a polished text "with the final English reader in mind." [142]

Under Asher, "The Windup Bird and Tuesday's Women" went through rigorous editing. This, of course, was not unusual for any piece being published by *The New Yorker*. Even now that Murakami is a regular contributor to the magazine (with more than thirty stories published over a period of thirty years), his work continues to be edited significantly—certainly by Japanese standards, where editors (of literary fiction) have been known to be hands-off.

The first two editors of the magazine, Harold Ross and William Shawn, were known for shying away from anything sexual. Robert Gottlieb writes in his memoir that before he arrived at the magazine in 1987, the "fiction department was inhibited in its choices by a number of Mr. Shawn's strictures about language and subject matter. (Sex was a problem. In fact, mentions of all bodily functions except crying were likely to be vetoed.)" Gottlieb also writes that "since I was an editor and publisher of novels, I came with no ground rules about fiction, and so, automatically, the range of subject matter and style was able to expand."[143]

Despite this, when I compare the version of "Windup Bird and Tuesday's Women" published in *The New Yorker* with the one later published in the story collection *The Elephant Vanishes*, I notice that sexual descriptions have been significantly abridged in the magazine's iteration.

For example, the version of the story published in book form by Knopf in 1993 contains the phrase "My pubic hair is still wet." In *The New Yorker* the sentence is "My hair down there is still wet." "Her vagina warm and moistened" is "She's warming up." In the book, there is this passage: "And down below that, it's a whole lot warmer. Just like hot buttercream. Oh so very hot. Honest." This has been deleted from the magazine version. The Japanese original and the version of the story translated for the English book also include this:

> Caress the lips, gently, slowly. Then open them. Slowly, like that. Now caress them gently with the sides of your fingers. Oh, yes, slowly . . . slowly. Now let one hand fondle my left breast, from underneath, lifting gently, tweaking the nipple just so. Again and Again. Until I'm about to come.[144]

In *The New Yorker*, this has been shortened to: "C'mon, now think about stroking me. Slowly. Your hands are so nice . . . oh, yes."[145]

I ask Luke and Asher if they might still have records from editing the story, and they both promise to look through their files. First Asher emails me a page of late-stage edits, and when I see Luke a month later at a Murakami conference in the U.K., he hands me a folder containing two sets of proofs, one from earlier and another from soon before the story went to print.

The proofs seem to have been exchanged primarily between Asher and Luke, but include references to suggestions made by Birnbaum and Murakami. They don't include earlier changes made to the translation, but do reveal how the translation gradually evolved in the final stages of editing. There is the change to a phone-sex scene, from "I didn't towel it dry. So it's still wet. Warm and oh so wet" to, "I didn't towel it dry. So it's still wet.

And warm . . ." in a version of the galleys dated September 19. In the version of the galleys exchanged in early November, immediately before publication, the phrase "C'mon, now think about touching me" has become "C'mon, now think about stroking me."

Murakami has said in an interview that Asher had asked him to "tone down" certain parts of the story.[146] In conversation with me, he recalls, "Back then, there were a number of taboos at *The New Yorker*, and I was told that there wasn't anything to do but accept them, so I relented and a significant amount was cut." He adds, "I liked Linda personally, so I figured I could just trust everything to her; that she would do right by me. I was happy with the set-up of Linda Asher as my editor and Robert Gottlieb above her."[147]

Asher, on the other hand, says that she does not "recall asking for modification of the sexy parts. That discussion may have occurred between Elmer, for instance, and Jay [here Asher clearly means Birnbaum, who was the translator of the piece, not Jay Rubin], upon or after offering the texts to the magazine."[148] Birnbaum, for his part, was still spending most of his time in Europe, and says that he does not recall doing any of the abridging, "so Elmer and Linda must have handled it."[149] When I ask Luke about this again, he responds: "Alfred is right, I think. Alfred was traveling—and in those days communication was not as it is today, so it wasn't easy to keep in touch with him—and once faxes of the ms [manuscript] had their back-and-forth with *The New Yorker*—*The New Yorker* always finalized issues with writers on the phone—I think Alfred agreed that I would act in his behalf as the writer/translator. I remember Linda Asher calling me on the phone in Kamakura and our going through the manuscript. Where there were publishing concerns, as opposed to editorial concerns, like the phone sex scene or names of characters that *The New Yorker* wanted to be sure were not real people, I *think* I discussed with Haruki and then worked out how to resolve and then finalized with Linda."[150] When I share with Luke what the others recall about the editing process, he says that he doesn't recall the details of "who did what when," but that he "wanted them [*The New Yorker*] to want it," and since Birnbaum was on the move he "took over as the writer" and "may have said this is what I'm going to do—to keep as much of it as you could without turning it into white bread."[151]

Gitte Marianne Hansen, a scholar who has written about female characters in Murakami's works, thinks "it is a shame" when some of his more explicit passages are not preserved in translation. She says that even though Murakami has been criticized both in Japan and the West for his depiction of sex—"as journalists are never slow to point out to me when they want a quick comment on the topic, he has in fact been short-listed for the bad sex awards"—in her view, that is precisely the point. "Characteristic of Murakami's sex descriptions are that they often include unsexy language such as 'pubic hair,' 'vagina' and 'penis' ... I often get the impression that sex descriptions in the Murakami world have a lot to do with self-discovery and communication between characters who don't understand each other, rather than sex in the pornographic sense. And that feeling might be lost when these explicit words and images are removed."[152]

There are other interesting exchanges. Take this passage:

"They're not expecting you to write like Allen Ginsberg. Just whatever you can come up with." The September 19 galleys show that an editor at *The New Yorker* (presumably Asher) has suggested replacing Ginsberg with Shakespeare, to which Luke has responded, "How about T. S. Eliot?" Luke has also included a note stating "Author doesn't mind change." The final published version uses T. S. Eliot. In another passage, the name Suzuki has been changed to Kinoshita. The magazine had suggested changing the name, indicating that "a David Suzuki has science show (TV) in Toronto. Maybe find name not identified with any TV/ radio figure?" and Luke had responded by writing "Kinoshita?" Murakami's then editor at Kodansha was Yōko Kinoshita. When I ask Luke if this may have been in the back of his mind when he chose the name, he says, "That I don't know. It may have been a nice gesture to toss her name in if it's true. But I don't remember clearly."[153]

The second line of the story in *The New Yorker* version reads: "Another moment and the spaghetti will be done, and there I am whistling the Overture to Rossini's 'La Gazza Ladra' along with Tokyo's best FM station." "Tokyo" is not in the original Japanese, and was most likely added as part of the magazine's practice—started by its founder, Harold Ross—of "pegging" the circumstantial elements of a story within the first two paragraphs.[154]

In the galleys dated September 19, Asher suggests changing Birnbaum's translation "along with the FM radio" to "along with FM Tokyo Radio," to which Luke responds, "FM Tokyo would be correct except that it doesn't play classical music . . ." In the galleys dated November 8, the line has been changed to "along with a Tokyo classical music station," and Asher has suggested further revising to "along with Tokyo's best FM station" in a November 8 fax, reinserting the "FM station" from the original Japanese, which Luke okays.

Luke believes that the early stories might not have been published if the author and translator were uncompromising. "Of course, that would have hindered further opportunities to publish with the magazine, but the changes asked for here were window dressing."[155]

Murakami included this story—in English—in a 1991 special issue of the literary magazine *Bungakukai* dedicated to his work; it was the only non-Japanese piece in the issue.[156] He had published the original short story in Japanese five years before the translation appeared, and the warm reception the translation had received may have spurred him to start expanding it into a novel soon after he arrived in Princeton early in 1991.

Hard-Boiled Wonderland and the End of the World

We'll freeze to death standing here, so I
guess we might as well do it. Let's tie our
belts together end to end. It won't do us any
good if one of us doesn't make it.

—The Shadow in
*Hard-Boiled Wonderland
and the End of the World*

The Murakamis Go to Princeton

Among Murakami's favorite authors, and among the authors
he had translated, F. Scott Fitzgerald loomed large. Years earlier, Murakami had made a point of visiting Princeton University, where Fitzgerald had been a (far from stellar) student and
which had inspired his first novel, *This Side of Paradise*. Murakami
was impressed not only by the fact that Fitzgerald's papers were
kept there but also by the quiet of the town. He'd thought about

how good it would be to write uninterrupted in such tranquil surroundings.

At the beginning of *Yagate kanashiki gaikokugo* (*A Sad Foreign Language*), a collection of essays serialized in Kodansha's magazine *Hon* (*Books*) in 1991, Murakami writes of having mentioned all this in a conversation with "a certain American." This American, Murakami goes on to say, took the initiative of meeting with "someone from Princeton," and the next thing Murakami knew, Princeton was inviting him for a year's residence as a visiting scholar.[1]

The American of the tale was Elmer Luke, and the "someone from Princeton" was Martin Collcutt, a historian who specializes in Japan. Luke had done "the equivalent of a cold call" and written a letter to Collcutt, who at the time was the director of the East Asian studies department at Princeton. When Collcutt, not long after, was in Tokyo on business, he and Luke met for the first time at a café in Shinjuku to discuss details.[2]

Collcutt, now a professor emeritus, having retired from Princeton several years ago, elaborates in a response to a message from me: "When Luke contacted me, and we later met in Tokyo, I was familiar with some of Haruki's work and felt that he was a very talented, up-and-coming writer, who would be a very attractive visiting fellow for faculty and students, especially graduate students, in Japanese and comparative literature studies at Princeton. Anyway, I spoke to several other faculty members in Japanese literary studies, including Richard Okada (sadly since deceased), and they were all excited at the prospect. Graduate students, too, were enthusiastic."[3]

I later meet Collcutt in person, in Tokyo, where he now lives with his wife. Had there been any objection within the university to inviting a relatively young writer whose reputation was yet to be established within the field of Japanese literary studies? I ask. None that he can recall, he says. Murakami's "growing international recognition" and the East Asian studies department's desire to increase "direct contact with East Asia" and "strengthen the Japanese program" made him an ideal candidate.[4]

Murakami had just returned to Japan at the beginning of the year after spending three years in Europe, but he decided he "didn't want to miss the opportunity to live in Princeton" and "got busy packing again in preparation to leave for America."[5] In early February 1991, the Murakamis arrived at their faculty housing in Princeton.

Hosea Hirata, whom Murakami calls a "drinking buddy"[6]— and who, incidentally, introduced me to Murakami's work when I was a student of his at Tufts University—writes about his first encounter with Murakami in an essay/interview in Princeton's *Gest Library Journal*:

> Early in February 1991, late in the evening, I met Haruki (his first name) for the first time. It wasn't like a planned meeting in a fashionable café (there is no such thing in Princeton); I just landed in front of him, so to speak. The ground was wet and slippery. Someone who had gone to pick him up at the airport knocked on our apartment door. I ran out, slipped, fell, stood up, and found myself in front of him. It was dark and he looked like a bundled up sheep—quiet, compact but somehow dense

and massive. Then I understood completely the raison-d'être of the enigmatic sheep in his novel *A Wild Sheep Chase*. Yōko, his long-time companion (he sometimes refers to his wife in this way in his essays), who looked like his graceful shadow in her black suit, with her long black hair cascading into the darkness around her, was already asking us where the laundry room was.[7]

It took a while for Hirata and Murakami to get comfortable with each other. "First it was a bit awkward because he didn't talk much," says Hirata. But gradually they became friends, helped by living close by and "beer. Definitely, lots of beer ... We lived in a residential area for young Princeton faculty. The Murakamis were given one of the townhouses there. We were always having parties and dinners together. When our son was born, Haruki came to our house after I got back from the hospital. He brought a nice bottle of whiskey. And we really got drunk! There's a similar scene in his story 'Honey Pie.'"[8]

Hirata doesn't quite remember when he first came across Murakami's work, but he does remember buying "a hardcover version (in Japanese) of *Sekai no owari to hādoboirudo wandārando* (*Hard-Boiled Wonderland and the End of the World*) in a second-hand bookstore in Ochanomizu, in the mid-eighties. I also re-member reading *Kaze no uta o kike* (*Hear the Wind Sing*) and feeling excited to discover someone from my generation writing about our experiences in our sort of language."[9]

Starting in 1991, the year Murakami came to Princeton, Hi-rata began teaching Murakami's short stories in his senior seminar. This makes him, with Jay Rubin, one of the first scholars to incorporate Murakami's work into their syllabi at an American university. A year later, Hirata organized a panel on Murakami at the annual conference of the Association of Asian Studies, together with Rubin and Ted Goossen, who had both translated Murakami stories for various magazines. At massive conferences like the AAS, where many panels take place simultaneously, it isn't unusual for individual panels to be sparsely attended. According to the organizers, however, the Murakami panel was packed. Goossen posits that the panel was a turning point in terms of Murakami's position within Japanese literary studies in the U.S.[10] Rubin says, "My greatest regret regarding that panel was that I did not plug my cassette tape of 'The Girl from Ipanema' into the PA system and have the four of us dance to it."[11]

On February 6, soon after arriving in Princeton, Murakami sent Luke a fax informing him of his and his wife's arrival. He writes that Luke had been wrong about their residence, that "This is not an apartment, but a HOUSE," and asks Luke to pass his phone number on to Birnbaum.[12] In another fax sent two weeks later, he also adds that Princeton is the "perfect place for jogging" and that "we are enjoying our new life."[13]

During his first months at Princeton, Murakami spent most of his time cooped up in his "HOUSE" writing the book that would eventually split into two novels: *Nejimakidori kuronikuru* (*The Wind-Up Bird Chronicle*) and the slimmer *Kokkyō no minami, taiyo no nishi* (*South of the Border, West of the Sun*). Murakami tells me that at that stage he was already aware that his work might continue to be read outside of Japan, but he also says that this didn't influence the content of his writing. "Once you start writing a novel you forget those kinds of things and just write."[14]

Luke, on the other hand, suggests that Princeton might have been the "perfect place" not just for jogging but more generally for an author wanting to get a feel for the American reading public. "The American literary scene is basically made up of the publishing industry centered in New York and the universities spread across the country. From Princeton, Haruki was able to engage both."[15]

Murakami does agree that going to live in America was important for his career. He recalls how Japan was "still in the afterglow of the bubble economy" but that "there was hardly any cultural output" from Japan in the U.S. It resulted in "this sense of urgency" once he got to Princeton. "When I was living in Japan I didn't care if my books didn't sell overseas, since I was making a living selling books in Japan, but once I started living abroad I started to feel strongly that I had to find a way to go out into the world. I think that's why I started looking around for agents and publishers."[16]

Which Book Second?

Meanwhile, encouraged by the positive reception of *A Wild Sheep Chase* and his publication in *The New Yorker*, Birnbaum and Luke began to think about Murakami's next book in the U.S.

When Murakami had remarked in his interview with *Asahi Shimbun/Aera* during his first promotional trip to New York that he wanted to publish English translations of his three novels "at the pace of one book a year," he added that this was the ideal pace for publishing in the U.S.[17] KI had apparently agreed, and had started preparing Murakami's second and third books even before the first book was published in the U.S. Machiko Moriyasu, a former editor at KI, says that at the time it was highly unusual for the company to publish translations one after the other by the same writer. With the exception of the Big Three—Kawabata, Tanizaki, and Mishima—there was an implicit understanding within the company that each author would basically be limited to one book. But Moriyasu says that this one-author-one-book policy was scrapped when Pockell and Luke joined the company, and that—thanks partly to the booming economy—they were able to publish multiple volumes by the same author.[18]

One compelling option for Murakami's second U.S. title was *Noruwei no mori* (*Norwegian Wood*). Not only had the book been a massive bestseller in Japan in 1987, but Birnbaum's translation, edited by Jules Young, had already been published in November 1990 as a pair of paperbacks in the Kodansha English Library series. Like *Pinball, 1973* and *Hear the Wind Sing*, these were released only in Japan, but still managed to sell 100,000 copies in the first two months, leading a journalist for *Nihon Keizai Shimbun* to speculate that sales were being driven by bairingyaru ("bilingual gals") who were buying the books as Christmas gifts for their foreign boyfriends.[19]

Initially, it seems there were plans to release the translation outside Japan. In March 1989, *The Christian Science Monitor* reported, "Kodansha International plans a fall release in the US of his book, 'A Wild Sheep Chase,' first published in 1982, followed next year by 'Norwegian Wood,'"[20] and in January 1990 *Nihon Keizai Shimbun* reported that a hardcover edition of *Norwegian Wood* was scheduled to be published by KI in the U.S. that summer.[21]

In the end, however, KI decided against this, based on the judgment, according to Luke, that the book would not go down well with readers in the U.S.—and in particular New York literary circles. Luke says that he, for one, "clearly objected" to publishing it, especially at that stage, when Murakami was still a relative unknown in the U.S. He wasn't thrilled with Birnbaum's translation either, which he recalls as "rather bland, flat, literal, artless, without its own integrity as a translation."[22] Birnbaum says that he scarcely remembers *Norwegian Wood* aside from the fact that "I didn't like its 'soft focus' sentimentality" and that as a result "my translation could only have been less than enthusiastic."[23]

Luke says he also felt that the relationship at the heart of *Norwegian Wood* was "too young." "That is to say, too naive, for Western readers, who were more worldly, more jaded, more 'experienced' at an earlier age. Also, some of the intimate scenes were painful to read, made me cringe a little. I'm trying, as an editor, to channel what readers might think, and I'm thinking, It's a no-go. 'Too' Japanese, won't transport (or translate). Too artless. I actually thought it would squander his readership.

"Yoko, who loved the book, said, OK, you don't have to love it, and you don't have to publish it if you don't love it. But I know she wanted to have it published, and she eventually convinced

Binky [Amanda Urban, Murakami's current agent] and/or Gary [Fisketjon, Murakami's former editor at Knopf] to publish it, and it was a success! There are discriminating younger readers (the very readers who I feared would not like it) who really like it, and the numbers show it. Yoko smelled something that I did not. When I saw Yoko years later, she mentioned *Norwegian Wood* to me, and we laughed about it."[24]

Murakami smiles when I bring this topic up. "Elmer kept insisting that *Norwegian Wood* wouldn't sell in America. But *Norwegian Wood* has sold by far the most [of my books] around the world. So it turns out Elmer was wrong!"[25]

Given the positive reception of *A Wild Sheep Chase*, another option for a second book would have been *Dansu dansu dansu* (*Dance Dance Dance*). Murakami had written the novel after he had finished writing *Norwegian Wood* because he had gotten the urge to revisit the characters from *A Wild Sheep Chase*. It was published in October 1988 in Japan and sold more than a million copies in nine months; it is even mentioned in Murakami's bio for KI's version of *A Wild Sheep Chase*.

Instead, KI chose to go with *Sekai no owari to hādoboirudo wandārando*, which was released in Japan in 1985 and eventually published in the U.S. as *Hard-Boiled Wonderland and the End of the World*.[26] Birnbaum and Luke were happy with the choice. They felt that the novel had even greater potential than *A Wild Sheep Chase* to capture the imagination of American readers. In addition to the humor, another aspect of Murakami's writing that appealed to Birnbaum was the idea of alternate realities: "the concept of coexisting parallel worlds you could drop through." Birnbaum could relate to "doors leading to nowhere," given that in his life he would often find himself "walking through one door and find myself in Japan, walking through another and finding myself in Mexico."[27] Birnbaum tells me that "Murakami's risk-taking still had keen instincts at that time," and that "he wasn't just casting about for 'something else,' hence there was a taut resonance between form and story. For all its deceptively offhand lightness, it has the inevitability of classic tragedy."[28]

Sekai no owari to hādoboirudo wandārando (*Hard-Boiled Wonderland and the End of the World*), Shinchosha, 1985

Luke, too, was drawn to the concept and scale of the book. "*Hard-Boiled* was a clear demonstration of the range that Haruki had, and as it differed so much in theme, narrative, mode from *Sheep* it seemed like showing it off right away, while the iron was still hot (as it were), would lay claim to larger literary territory for him and broaden his readership. Readers who liked *Sheep* wouldn't be going away; we could afford to make them wait for *Dance Dance Dance*."[29]

Side by Side

Birnbaum and Luke immersed themselves in *Hard-Boiled Wonderland and the End of the World*. With *A Wild Sheep Chase*, the two had worked together to edit the translation Birnbaum had completed. This process, according to Birnbaum, was already "far more rigorous" than with the first two books published as part of the Kodansha English Library.[30] But for *Hard-Boiled Wonderland and the End of the World* they took the collaboration one step further. Birnbaum would bring Luke sections of the book as he finished them, and the two would proceed through the manuscript together while the translation was in progress. Sometimes they would translate and edit by hand onto a paper copy, but more often than not they would work straight onto the screen of the computer Birnbaum had carried to Luke's home in Kamakura.[31] At one point, they were working together five to six hours a day, five days a week, sitting side by side, reading passages out loud.[32] Birnbaum suggests half-jokingly that it is possible that the two of them spent more time translating and editing *A Wild Sheep Chase* and *Hard-Boiled Wonderland* than Murakami had spent writing them.[33]

This collaboration between translator and editor reminds me of the collaboration between Jorge Luis Borges and his English translator Norman Thomas di Giovanni. The author and translator sat side by side in the author's office, "aggressively revising" the original text to "increase their accessibility to an American readership"—an effort that seems to have helped get Borges's stories, as well as a long profile of him, published in *The New Yorker*.[34, 35]

It also reminds me of remarks made by Michael Emmerich, the scholar and translator of Japanese literature, during an event for the British Centre for Literary Translation at the University of East Anglia. Emmerich revealed that, for him, getting the first ten percent of a book right seems to take just as long as translating the rest of the book.[36] And in her essay "That Crafty Feeling," Zadie Smith has made a similar observation about the novel-writing process: for her, it is "the first twenty pages" that take longest. The writing of those pages "manifests itself in a compulsive fixation on perspective and voice," she writes. When Smith finally settles on the tone of the book after rewriting the first twenty pages many times, the rest of the book "travels at a crazy speed."[37]

Both Emmerich and Smith emphasize the time it takes to get the "voice" or "tone" right. The task of establishing a narrative voice for a work in translation normally falls upon the translator, which the editor then helps fine-tune. But with *Hard-Boiled Wonderland and the End of the World*, it seems that the translator and editor established the voice and tone of the book together.

Birnbaum says that there were many voices that "needed grappling with" in the novel: "There are, of course, the individual voices of the various characters: the professor, girl in pink, librarian, gatekeeper, colonel, and the duo. But the bigger challenge, and what took the most time, was getting the narrative voices for the two alternating sections—the Hard-Boiled chapters and End of World chapters—right. Elmer was a huge help in that process."[38]

In the Japanese original, the narrative voices in the alternating chapters are distinguished partly through the use of different first-person pronouns: the more formal *watashi* for the Hard-Boiled Wonderland chapters and the more informal *boku* for the End of the World chapters. This difference between *boku* and *watashi* is difficult to capture in English translation, where the only singular personal pronoun available is the neutral *I*. Birnbaum and Luke elected to differentiate between the alternating chapters using different tenses: the Hard-Boiled Wonderland chapters are told in the past tense, while the more dreamlike End of the World chapters are rendered in the present tense. This creates a subtle distance between the two voices and, in Jay Rubin's opinion, gives the End of the World chapters "a timeless quality that may be more appropriate than the normal past-tense narration of the original."[39] Rubin has said that *Hard-Boiled Wonderland and the End of the World* is a book that he has "daydreamed about re-translating for myself simply as a way to get into it more deeply," but that there is no such plan and that he would be "hard pressed not to steal Alfred's brilliant use of past and present narratives for the two halves of the book."[40]

Philip Gabriel, who has been another of Murakami's translators for many years, worked with Luke on the translation of Masahiko Shimada's novel *Dream Messenger* around the same time. "Elmer," he says, "was very hands-on as an editor. How amazed I was when my first pages of *Dream Messenger* came back covered in red and how amazed I was at his thoroughness. Looking back at it now, I can see that . . . I was being way too literal and close to the original, ending up with stiff English. Elmer encouraged me to break out of that and try to produce more fluid English prose. I recall him saying that each character needed to have a distinct voice—I think we may see evidence of that in Alfred's Sheep Man in *A Wild Sheep Chase* and the old professor in *Hard-Boiled Wonderland*."[41]

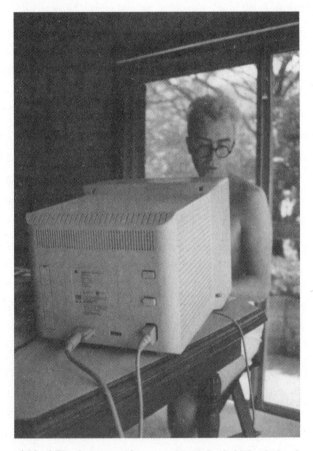

Alfred Birnbaum working on *Hard-Boiled Wonderland and the End of the World* at Elmer Luke's home

Imaginary Beings

The translating and editing of *Hard-Boiled Wonderland and the End of the World* took longer than initially planned. The publication date was pushed back from spring to fall 1991, but Birnbaum and Luke were struggling to meet even this new deadline. On February 20, 1991, Murakami wrote to Luke that while he knew it was "not the end of the world," he was concerned what the delay would mean to publication in the U.K., which had initially been scheduled to coincide with the Japan Fair in London.[42]

On March 18, half a year before the publication date, Luke sent Murakami a fax with an update on his and Birnbaum's progress:

> Work on the manuscript of HARD-BOILED WONDER-LAND proceeds—very satisfactorily though it requires much time. Alfred and I work five or six hours a day on it, every day, going over the [*sic*] each word, tone, voice. HARD-BOILED, because of all the very different characters as well as the timelessness of the End of the World and the timeliness of the Hard-Boiled sections, requires a careful touch. At the same time, I think we are both exceedingly pleased with how the translation is taking shape.

In the same letter Luke asked Murakami several questions.

> Is the Archeology of Animals, by Burtland Cooper, which the main character and the hungry Librarian read from a real book, like the Borges Book of Imaginary Beings? If so, where did you

get it? If it's an invention of yours, (as I suspect it is) it's tremendous! (I just need to be sure for purposes of permission—as with the Borges). Also, are the words "cyntetokerus" (spelling unsure) and "curanokerus" (spelling unsure too) inventions? If so, fine, great actually, but I need to check.[43]

Murakami responded immediately to say that the *Archeology of Animals* was a made-up book but that the "cyntetokerus" and "curanokerus" must have existed. He writes, "[Y]ou can do anything with regard to those miserable creatures. I don't care at all."

Unable to find references to either animal, Birnbaum and Luke proceeded to render them "cyntetokerus" and "curaniokerus." In fact, the proper names of the creatures are Synthetoceras and Cranioceras, but the previous renderings remain in the most recent editions of the translations:

> The cyntetokerus is a smallish horse cum deer with a horn on either temple and a long Y-shaped prong at the end of its nose. The curanokerus is slightly rounder in the face, and sprouts two deer-like antlers from its crown and an additional horn that curves up and out in back. Grotesque creatures on the whole.[44]

When I bring this up to Birnbaum, he says, simply, that "those were the pre-internet days." For the purposes of the story, he adds, "it hardly seems important whether or not the creatures actually existed."[45]

On March 29, just two weeks after the letter above, Luke

wrote to Murakami again to confirm his schedule for the U.S. and U.K. book tours. He added:

> I want you to know that as Alfred and I have worked more and more on the novel, I believe more and more that this novel has the possibility of achieving a good deal. I only wish the edit could go faster, but good things take time.[46]

About six weeks after that, on May 10, now just four months from the scheduled publication date, Luke wrote to Murakami with another update.

> Things have been pure madness around here . . . Some light at the end of the tunnel, though: we've gotten over a major hurdle with HARD-BOILED WONDERLAND, and now we're working on the next, going over every word again obsessively. Want this book to be great.[47]

For That Was His Name

Birnbaum and Luke both believed in the importance of—to borrow the phrase Jay Rubin uses in his book about Murakami—the "music of words." But they didn't always see or hear things the same way. They listened to different music, read different authors, and had lived in different parts of the world. The only time Luke had lived outside of the U.S. prior to moving to Japan in the late eighties was a brief stint in Kyoto. A longtime reader of *The New Yorker*, Luke was drawn to the writing of authors such as Nathanael West, Ann Beattie, and Raymond Carver, and through reading these authors he came to "appreciate a certain economy of language" and the ability of certain writers to "express complex ideas simply."[48] Birnbaum, on the other hand, had grown up moving from one country to another, surrounded by different languages. Although English was the language he used both at home and in school, he had never lived in an English-speaking country for more than three years at a time. Birnbaum also loved to play with words and remembers fondly how Luke, who was keen for Murakami's work to come across as "alive," would occasionally take a phrase that Birnbaum had translated and tell him, "Nobody says that anymore!"[49]

Despite Luke's focus on keeping the prose contemporary, the pair did manage to slip in a phrase that nobody used anymore. In the End of the World chapters, the protagonist is assigned a job at the Library reading old dreams sealed inside unicorn skulls. The following passage describes the endeavors of a professor who comes across a skull belonging to an unidentified creature:

Professor Petrov—for that was his name—summoned several assistants and graduate students, and the team departed for the Ukraine on a one-month dig at the site of the young lieutenant's trenches. Unfortunately, they failed to find any similar skull.[50]

The phrase "for that was his name" is, noticeably, an archaic one, something one might encounter in the opening line of folktales. Douglas Adams, for instance, uses it to comic effect to introduce a new character in *The Restaurant at the End of the Universe*—the second book of the Hitchhiker's Guide to the Galaxy series—published in 1980:

> Trin Tragula—for that was his name—was a dreamer, a thinker, a speculative philosopher or, as his wife would have it, an idiot.[51]

But if the phrase was meant to be funny in *Hard-Boiled Wonderland and the End of the World*, it was only meant to be so to a handful of people—the members of the Birnbaum family—for it was an intertextual reference of sorts to the opening line of Henry Birnbaum's novel, eternally in progress. Although Birnbaum had never been permitted to read his father's novel, he can vividly recall a family friend, who had gotten to read it, teasing his father about the line, exclaiming, "Who says that these days!"[52]

Birnbaum says that he was pleased that he was able to "sneak that phrase into the book."[53] (Luke says that he had actually been the one who snuck the phrase in as a "gift to Alfred.")[54] Birnbaum also suggests that, in hindsight, his literary pursuits may have been motivated to some degree by his desire to have "something to show his father." Henry Birnbaum, upon reading the published book, immediately noted the phrase with pleasure. He also once said to his son, "One thing is for sure, you're definitely more widely read than I am."[55]

The Pink Girl Vanishes

Hard-Boiled Wonderland and the End of the World was a long book; the Japanese original came to around a thousand pages, twice the length of *A Wild Sheep Chase*. Before writing the novel, Murakami had published the novella *Machi to sono futashika na kabe* (*The Town and Its Uncertain Walls*) in the literary journal *Bungakukai*. The world in the novella is similar to that depicted in the End of the World chapters of *Hard-Boiled Wonderland and the End of the World*; the novel can be seen as Murakami's attempt at rewriting this novella, which he considered a "failed work." Murakami felt that he had to "attach something different and go with a twin turbo" for the story and that this something "had to be completely different" from the End of the World chapters. Because he was a fan of Chandler, he decided to try a "hard-boiled plotline." He also decided that he would include "a lot of very strange characters and illogical things," and that this would provide the necessary momentum for the quieter story taking place inside the wall in the End of the World chapters.[56]

Birnbaum and Luke, it seems, felt differently about the effect of the "illogical" components of the Hard-Boiled chapters. They were concerned that readers would stop reading. "American readers aren't as patient with their authors," Birnbaum says.[57] While he has never done a detailed comparison, he tells me that they "must have ended up cutting around a hundred pages."[58]

Though there are subtle cuts to the End of the World chapters—the dialogue between the protagonist and his librarian girlfriend, for instance—perhaps the most obvious omissions are related to the Girl in Pink, a character who appears in the Hard-Boiled chapters. Here, entire scenes have been excised. The English translation is missing four pages of the girl singing about her pink bicycle, as well as the protagonist's long critique of store posters in the supermarket where he is waiting for her.

Birnbaum says that he felt, and still feels, that the portrayal of the Girl in Pink was "far too exaggerated."[59] I ask Luke about this also and he responds, "I think the larger concern for me was that there was (in my humble opinion) chaff that was cluttering the picture—stuff that was repetitious or tangential or less than critical to the narrative or worked against it—the chaff needed to be culled, so that what we had was germane or, if not, appealingly whimsical or amusing or deep. I did not think readers could stick with a story that seemed on the one hand so purposefully constructed (the two worlds) but not tightly held together. Guess I wanted the tight. I thought if we didn't do that, the readers who liked *Sheep* (which was tight) might lose interest and fall by the wayside (thinking one-book wonder, not an uncommon complaint) and that any new readers would be limited to, say, students of Japanese literature. There was also the awareness that Japanese editors did not, do not, edit much. For whatever reason. In translation that lack becomes clear. So—my hubris, perhaps—I felt I had to do what had not been done."[60]

Hosea Hirata, who uses Birnbaum's English translation in one of his classes at Tufts University, points out that what has been excised are "basically the parts when the Pink Girl gets sexually aggressive." He adds, "Perhaps the publisher was worried about her age?"[61] Hirata provides his students with a list of all the deletions, using what he calls his "crude translations" from the original Japanese.

From chapter 21:

"Aren't those huge earrings too heavy to wear all the time?" I asked from behind.

"You get used to them," said she. "They are the same with your penis. Do you ever feel that your penis [is] too heavy?"

"No, not really. I never felt that way."

Why did I have to go and bring up the subject?

*

"Do you always have sex from the front, facing each other?"

"Yeah, most of the time."

"I bet you do from the back too, sometimes."

"Yeah, I guess."

"And there are more ways to do it, right? She on top, or sitting down, or using a chair and stuff . . . ?"

"Well, there are different kinds of people and different kinds of situations."

From chapter 31:

"Hey," the girl called me, putting down the book. "You sure you don't want me to swallow your semen?"

"Not now."

"You're just not in the mood, eh?"

"Right."

"You just don't want to have sex with me."

"Not now."

"That's because I'm too fat?"

"Nothing to do with that," I said. "Your body is really cute."

"Then, why not have sex with me?"

"I don't know," said I. "I'm not sure, but I just feel that this is not the time for me to have sex with you."

*

"I got a hard-on."

"Let me see," said the girl. I hesitated a bit, but decided that I would let her see it. I was too tired to keep arguing about it. And after all I won't be in the world for too long. I didn't think that by showing my healthy erect penis to a seventeen-year girl, it would develop into a grave social problem.

"I see . . ." said the girl looking at my erect penis. "Can I touch it?"

"No," said I.

"But this proves it, right?"

"Oh, well. I guess." I pulled up my pants and stored my penis in them. I could hear a large cargo truck passing by beneath the window.

When I ask Luke if he had considered the Pink Girl's age when he was editing, he says that, while he does not remember the exact details, he couldn't imagine that being the case. "It would have been different if she was twelve or something . . ."[62]

I read him some of Hirata's translations and he responds that while he didn't "shy away from sex," he found the sections "kind of preposterous almost" and that "what I didn't want to happen was for either the author or the book to be dismissed." Luke adds that when "the true Murakami believers" find out about the edits they "will be horrified. But that's okay too. I made the choice. Or we did."[63]

Hirata finds the deletions unnecessary, and says that several are actually problematic. He is particularly disapproving of the "addition (change)" made to the Shadow's speech in the last chapter since it makes "the Shadow more ethically authoritative."[64] Birnbaum also tells me that while he does not recall the details, he remembers that at the very end of the book Luke wanted the Shadow to say "I love you" (where the Japanese original says "I liked you and . . ."). Birnbaum remembers taking exception, that it would not work, but says "Elmer got his way."[65] Luke remembers the conversation well: "In Japanese 'to like someone' can be 'to love someone,' too. Alfred took a couple of nights off and he agreed in the end. We were working closely with the text. That line came out of the moment in the book. I think you got to go for it."[66]

Hirata is not the only one who objects to the abridging. Mette Holm is Murakami's primary translator into Danish and translated *Sekai no owari to hādoboirudo wandārando* in 2014, occasionally using Birnbaum's 1991 translation as reference. She brings up Murakami's translation of Raymond Chandler's *Long Goodbye* into Japanese, and refers to a passage in Murakami's afterword to the Japanese edition:

> I like the description of blondes that appears in this book, that part where Marlowe lists in his head characteristics of various blondes. It is not a truly great description, and, as it rather stands out from the whole, it could well be omitted. Or rather, the novel would hold together better without it. A clever editor would warn: "Mr. Chandler, this part is unnecessary and a bit forced, let's just cut it, shall we?" But after rereading it many times, I realized that I have become strangely attached to this passage, which in the beginning I thought was superfluous. It feels as if we are hearing Chandler's real voice, and this "unnecessariness" (although it is a strange way to put it) penetrates surprisingly deeply into our minds and stays there. For some reason, it sticks in our head.[67]

In Holm's opinion, the long descriptions in *Hard-Boiled Wonderland* have been inspired by Chandler's detours, which "aren't necessarily important to the plot" but "are important for the pacing of the book, as they seem to make the time pass more slowly." She believes that the passages should not be omitted, "since this speeds up the action and alters the reader's experience."[68] She also suggests that the more erotic scenes in Murakami's novels are "fun and nice" and "make the situation more human," and wonders if they were cut because the U.S. is "prudish."[69]

When I ask Murakami about this strong difference of opinion, he says that he is "not the type to suggest that not a single word should be cut." His view is that "it's okay to take out certain parts" as long as the "narrative flow" isn't disrupted. He compares it to a conductor choosing "to skip repetitions in a Beethoven symphony" and says, "I think it can't be helped that publishers in the country of publication maintain a certain level of discretion."

Yet Murakami also seems somewhat conflicted by the question of "faithful" versus "unfaithful" translations: "From the beginning Alfred was more of an introducer than a meticulous translator. So he shapes the translation into the kind of thing he wants to share. Of course, this means he has a lot of fans. But as the author, there are places that make me wonder if he hasn't gone too far . . . [Elmer] is also an American editor, so his mentality was completely different from that of Japanese editors. American editors love editing. They love to cut a lot and move passages around.

"When I saw Hosea the other day, he was telling me that he was using *Hard-Boiled Wonderland and the End of the World* in class but that it's very difficult to teach the book because it's so different from the original. He said that the story changes toward the end and asked if something couldn't be done about it, so I told him you're right, we better do something."[70]

I go back to Birnbaum. "Like I said before, American readers aren't as patient as Japanese readers. There was criticism that the book was baggy even after all the cuts we made. Though the situation has changed now and I'm sure there are plenty of people who would read a Murakami book regardless of how long it is."[71, 72]

In a 2017 interview with novelist Mieko Kawakami, Murakami emphasizes the importance of trust between writer and reader and argues that when trust has been built between the two parties, the reader is willing to "go along" with the writer.[73] The Danish edition of *Hard-Boiled Wonderland and the End of the World* was published in 2014, thirty years after the Japanese original was published, and around a quarter century after Murakami was first published in Denmark. By this time he was already internationally renowned and had gained the "trust" of readers, not only in Denmark but around the world. But back in 1991 this trust between writer and reader (in the English-speaking world) was not as strong. And at least until the turn of the century, even after Murakami changed translators and publishers, his longer works (of both fiction and nonfiction) would continue to be published in English in significantly abridged form.

According to Luke, the (significantly abridged) translation of *Hard-Boiled Wonderland and the End of the World* was sent to Murakami before publication but "no major changes were suggested."[74] When the book was published, the copyright page included the credit, "translated and adapted by Alfred Birnbaum with the participation of the author." On the same page, there is also this line: "The translator wishes to acknowledge the assistance of editor Elmer Luke."[75]

I ask Birnbaum whether or not he would still exclude the material he did if he were translating the book today. "It's hard to say," he responds, "but unless they really serve some concrete function in the plot, I think I'd still be inclined to leave them out."[76]

Jay Rubin and others have expressed interest in retranslating *Hard-Boiled Wonderland and the End of the World*. When I ask Luke how he feels about the possibility of another translator creating an unabridged translation, he replies that he "[doesn't] have a problem with it at all," and that it may even be interesting to have the two translations available for comparison. He adds, "I dare say it would be less good if it were a more 'faithful' translation" and "it would be more successful as an exercise than as a translation."[77]

When I ask Birnbaum the same question, he responds, "The only reason to re-do HBW is to bolster their careers," referring, presumably, to Murakami's other translators and editors. "The book was not originally written for an international readership—unlike the later novels (self-consciously so)—-hence the typical lack of editing glares in an embarrassing amount of unfocused extraneous material (at least from a Western perspective, e.g. the pink girl's dance routine). It hardly matters in the Japanese, but falls apart when translated. I don't believe anything 'they all want' from their camp anymore; it's not about good writing or translating at this late date, it's about marketing a 'director's cut.'"[78]

Alternate Worlds

The working title of *Sekai no owari to hādoboirudo wandārando* in English—handwritten into Birnbaum's translation agreement—had been a direct translation of the original, *End of the World and Hard-Boiled Wonderland*. In an April 1991 interview, Murakami reveals that his Japanese publisher, Shinchosha, had wanted to shorten the original Japanese title to *Sekai no owari* (*End of the World*), but he'd refused because the parallel structure of the narrative was vital to the book. Conversely, he says, KI, his English-language publisher, had asked to shorten the title to *Hard-Boiled Wonderland*. He had refused for the same reason.[79]

When I ask Luke why he wanted to shorten the title, he laughs. "I did that, didn't I? Well, *End of the World* was well-worn as both a concept and title, and I was afraid that the novel would get lost among all the titles in bookstores that start with *The End of the World*. On the other hand, *Hard-Boiled Wonderland* had both a strange and refreshing ring to it." When Murakami rejected the idea, Luke flipped the order of the two parts to make the title *Hard-Boiled Wonderland and the End of the World*. "By bringing *Hard-Boiled Wonderland* to the beginning, we thought we could keep the title feeling new while respecting the author's wish to include both worlds. I still think it's a great title. If you saw *Hard-Boiled Wonderland* on a book it would definitely pique your interest, right?"[80]

Birnbaum, on the other hand, says that he has "always felt embarrassed by the clunky, cutesy-kitsch (dare I say stupid?) title of *Hard-Boiled*, but Elmer voted down my first choice, which was *The End of the World/The Way It Goes*, which I intended as a tribute to Vonnegut's influence."[81]

In interviews and essays, Murakami has often discussed the influence that Vonnegut had on his first two books (*Hear the Wind Sing* and *Pinball, 1973*), and when *A Wild Sheep Chase* (the third book in the "Rat Trilogy") first came out in the U.S., some reviewers detected traces of Vonnegut in the novel. Birnbaum suggests that it's still there in *Hard-Boiled Wonderland and the End of the World*. "I believe the striking similarities (between Murakami and Vonnegut) have to do primarily with his writing style—short

pithy sentences, dry wit, repeating tag lines and overall concept—
parallel realities, hapless everyman protagonists, no villains per
se (everyone's a victim of fate and strange events, to paraphrase
one of Vonnegut's famous dictums). If I had to cite two works
of special resonance I'd say *Slaughterhouse Five* (1969) and *HBW*
(1985): both involve visions of a timeless alternative world trig-
gered by brain damage, to which both Billy Pilgrim and the
nameless 'detective' eventually succumb. Granted, *HBW*'s dream-
world self and severed shadow counterpart are painted in fuzzy
lyrical tones (which Elmer and I highlighted by use of the present
tense) while Pilgrim encounters multiple other players and retains
his real-world cynicism, but both have the same sense of detach-
ment; they are mere observers, not active doers in absurd chains
of circumstance (granted also, this reflects the Japanese 'passive
voice' done-to worldview in general.) I'm one-hundred-percent
sure Murakami would have read *Slaughterhouse* by 1980, even if
he didn't consciously copy any particulars."[82]

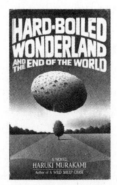

Hard-Boiled Wonderland and the End of the World,
Kodansha International, 1991

A Sophomoric Funk

As with *A Wild Sheep Chase*, *Hard-Boiled Wonderland and the End of the World* was widely reviewed in the U.S. and the U.K. In a *Washington Post* review titled "Down a High-Tech Rabbit Hole," science-fiction writer and critic Bruce Sterling wrote, "The main appeal in the book, and the likely reason why it won Murakami a major Japanese literary prize, is in the extraordinary attitude it manifests, a powerful mélange of disillusioned radicalism, keen intelligence, wicked sarcasm and a general allegiance to the surreal. If Murakami is the 'voice of a generation,' as he is often proclaimed in Japan, then it is the generation of Thomas Pynchon and Don De Lillo [*sic*]." Sterling also pays tribute to Alfred Birnbaum, calling him "a Tokyo-resident 'American by passport' who has made himself a one-man conduit for 'the Japanese New Fiction.'" He touches on Birnbaum's anthology, the "aptly titled *Monkey Brain Sushi*," suggesting that it "demonstrates beyond doubt that there are plenty more where Murakami came from. Slangy, vivid, caustic and political, media-soaked and set on a fast-forward, this 'New Fiction' crowd is fiercely intent on showing the world that Kawabata, Tanizaki and Mishima are history. Given a chance, they may supply the proof."[83]

The reviews that appeared in the U.K. were also largely favorable. *The Observer* published a profile titled "Dreams of high skies and unicorn skulls" by its Northeast Asia correspondent Peter McGill,[84] and *London Review of Books* ran an extended review by Julian Loose, who called Murakami's work "[f]resh, witty and above all eclectic."[85] Loose, who moved to Yale University Press after a couple of decades at Faber and Faber, tells me how he was tapped to write the review: "At that stage I was reviewing a fair number of Japanese titles, I think, simply because I was known to be interested in the area—one thing led to another and a lack of ANY competition made me the 'expert,' for a brief glorious moment . . . Murakami in some ways was a perfect Japanese author for the international market, at least as he emerged (or in the clever choice of books to translate), exotic and ambitious but not too baffling and quite familiar to Paul Auster/magic realist fans in his play with genre and form."[86]

In addition to a two-week tour in the U.S., Hamish Hamilton had planned to have Murakami promote the book in the U.K. Half a year before publication, Luke had written to Murakami about it:

> I know that this makes demands on your time, but September is publication month of HARD-BOILED WONDER-LAND in both U.S. and the U.K., and publicity at that time is critical. In the U.K., as you know, this would coincide with the big Japan Fair to be held at the V&A and other fancy places.[87]

As it turned out, however, the trip was canceled at the last minute. A letter from Andrew Franklin to Murakami dated September 12 stated that while they had received repeated requests for Murakami to appear on television and radio (something Murakami was not willing to do), they had only been able to secure two newspaper interviews and would understand if Murakami chose to cancel his visit.[88] Murakami responded the same day, apologizing for his reluctance about television and radio appearances and agreeing to the postponement. He told Franklin that all he wanted was for the book to be received well in the U.K., and asked if he should just tear up the plane tickets he'd been given.[89]

When I ask Franklin about the cancellation, he responds that he is unable to remember that far back (and has no access to correspondence/files). He agrees with me when I suggest that publishing a second book is harder than a first. "There is the 'shock of the new' with the first book. That is followed by the classic phenomenon of the 'second book syndrome' when it is harder to generate publicity. People like the new. Only the enthusiasts tend to follow an author's second book until they become successful and famous."[90]

Hard-Boiled Wonderland and the End of the World,
Hamish Hamilton, 1991

KI's advertising budget for *Hard-Boiled Wonderland and the End of the World* was not as large as for the first book; according to a memo sent from the New York office to Tokyo, the team had hoped they could rely on "the reputation of A WILD SHEEP CHASE publicity and word-of-mouth."[91] KI did place one ad for the book, a third of a page in *The New York Times Book Review* with the headline "WHAT CAN YOU SAY? FANTASTIC? FOUR STARS? SENSATIONAL."

Just a few pages later was a review of the book by novelist Paul West. Titled "Stealing Dreams from Unicorns," the review begins:

> Enticed by news of Haruki Murakami's Japanese literary prizes and by translations of stories appearing in American magazines, readers might expect his new novel to be as slangy and vivacious as "A Wild Sheep Chase," the 1989 novel that was the first of his many books to appear in English. But they will be disappointed.

West goes on to criticize the language ("inert and commonplace") and redundancies ("which may or may not have come from the Japanese") before concluding, "Alas, the end of the world dwindles fast into a sophomoric funk suffered by a narrator whose prose style cannot be better than it is because—get this—he's not a writer. What an unfortunate bind to get into— one that will not let you write your best."[92]

After he read the review, Luke zipped off a fax to the Murakamis:

> I trust that KIUS has been sending you the HARD-BOILED reviews that have been coming out. With the exception of the

NEW YORK TIMES review, which I'm still angry about (the guy sounds like he didn't read the book), the reviews have been very fine indeed. (Unlike Haruki, you see, I read every review.) Moreover, word of mouth seems to be spreading, which is always good news.

For your information, I attach a couple letters just received. One is from an "ordinary" reader, it seems, in the town where the University of Wisconsin is located; the other is from a bookstore in the town where the University of Michigan is located. Both these universities, by the way, are top-notch, and both these towns have large communities of readers—so I'm very encouraged. Every book I work on doesn't get response like this.[93]

Sales were also relatively quiet. Five thousand copies in hardcover was respectable for a work of literature in translation, but it was still less than half of the sales for *A Wild Sheep Chase*. Luke reflects: "One always wants the book to do well, but I knew it would be less accessible, that the reader would have to work harder. I was sorry it didn't bring in bigger numbers, but I wasn't sorry that we did it the way we did and that it was reviewed well. One has to have a longer view. And in the longer view it was not a problem. I wasn't disappointed in that way."[94]

Both *A Wild Sheep Chase* and *Hard-Boiled Wonderland and the End of the World* have gone on to become long-sellers; these days, the latter is often mentioned in reviews and interviews—together with *The Wind-Up Bird Chronicle*—as among Murakami's major works. But in the early nineties, Murakami was the equivalent of a promising new draft pick on a perennially weak team (as he sometimes describes the Yakult Swallows, his favorite baseball team).[95] He had hit a wall with his second book. "I really felt that I couldn't become global as long as I was publishing with Kodansha [International]," Murakami says. "I thought that sales would gradually increase, so the fact that they had plateaued left me feeling anxious, and I really felt that things couldn't stay the same. Elmer also told me that distribution was going to be a bottleneck as long as I was publishing with Kodansha [International]."[96]

Birnbaum says, "It was true that KI's distribution was less than stellar. So you can understand why he would feel that way. Besides, by then I'm sure he had people around him giving all kinds of advice. He probably had no choice but to look elsewhere."[97]

The Elephant Vanishes
and Dance Dance Dance

The question is really how you keep authors
alive until they break through and garner a
large readership. That's what I stay awake at
night and worry about.

—AMANDA URBAN, interview in
Haaretz, 2009[1]

The Making of a "Meticulous" Translator

I get off the elevator, walk to the end of the narrow hallway, and
press the intercom for Room 806. The door opens almost immediately, and Jay Rubin greets me and lets me into the apartment
he has rented for a few weeks. Rubin has lived in Seattle since
retiring from Harvard in 2006, but he still tries to come to Tokyo
once a year. There is research to do and there are publishing people to meet, but he boasts that the main purpose for his visit is the
jam session he will host for his translator friends in this Roppongi

apartment. Rubin reports that he and his wife, Raku, usually head south to Kyoto and Saga after the jam session, but this year, 2017, they have to come back to Tokyo because their friend Moto (the translator Motoyuki Shibata) is being given an award by Waseda University.

Rubin has not translated anything by Murakami for a while, though he tells me that he's just had dinner with the author and his wife. In the past, Rubin would be asked first, before anyone else, but that is no longer always the case. On the day I visit him in Roppongi, Rubin has just read through the first chapter of *Kishidanchō goroshi* (published in English in 2018 as *Killing Commendatore* in a translation by Philip Gabriel and Ted Goossen) and is hoping to finish it before a symposium on Murakami's work that will be held in the U.K. several months later.

When Rubin was still teaching, he would often get up and start working at half past five in the morning, but these days he wakes up around eight thirty, works for a few hours, and tries to get out as much as possible during the afternoon. He goes on long walks (deliberately choosing hilly paths), accompanies his wife shopping, and spends time with their grandchildren.

Rubin is also working on the introduction to the *Penguin Book of Japanese Short Stories*. He takes out his phone and shows me the cover design his publisher has sent him. The title is in large print, and then under Rubin's name, on the bottom right-hand corner of the cover, is FOREWORD BY HARUKI MURAKAMI. Once Rubin has finished his own introduction, all that will be left for him to do is to translate Murakami's foreword into English. Murakami has contributed forewords to various books Rubin has translated, including his collection of Ryūnosuke Akutagawa stories and his translations of Sōseki's *Sanshirō* and *Kōfu* (*The Miner*). But Rubin was pleasantly surprised when Murakami agreed to contribute one to the Penguin anthology, because it would mean reading works by contemporary Japanese authors in addition to the classics.

Rather than organize the stories chronologically, Rubin has divided them into theme-based sections such as "Japan and the West," "Men and Women," and "Disasters, Natural and Man-Made." Of the foreword that Murakami has written, Rubin tells me, "Murakami says very clearly, 'I don't really know why the stories that are in are and those that aren't aren't. You have to ask Jay Rubin about that.'"[2]

So I ask Jay Rubin about that. "A lot of it," he says, "was sheer accident . . . Things I was asked to translate for *Monkey Business* [the literary magazine] and others that I came across in my research on the censorship system . . . I couldn't have done a review of the entire field and chosen from among thousands of stories. I couldn't have done that in English, let alone Japanese . . . I've suggested to friends that the book should be called *The Penguin Book of Japanese Short Stories that Jay Rubin Happened to Like Over the Past Forty Years*."[3]

Born in 1941 in Washington, D.C., Rubin grew up in the Boston area. His father was a barber and his mother a real estate broker. As a child he wanted to be a postman after reading a book featuring one, but he was never a bookworm. "I got an especially vivid demonstration of how much I was not a bookworm by hanging around with Haruki Murakami, who always had his nose in a book."[4]

The books he remembers from childhood are mostly "biographies of famous men—Thomas Edison (somebody caught him by the ears when he was falling off a train?) and Daniel Boone. I went to the library a lot, would borrow books by Augusta Stevenson. In high school, I read Alan Watts's *The Way of Zen*, which was probably my introduction to anything Japanese."[5]

Rubin attended the University of Chicago, where he "was charmed by the thought that Japanese literature would be a totally useless subject to study . . . I never got resistance from my parents . . . but an uncle of mine made a sour face when I told him I was majoring in Japanese and asked why I wasn't doing Hebrew."[6]

Having studied with Edwin McClellan, the scholar and translator of Japanese literature perhaps best known for his translation of Sōseki's *Kokoro*, Rubin assumed that all professors of Japanese literature translated and began doing so himself. His first translation was included in McClellan's paper "The Impressionistic Tendency in Some Modern Japanese Writers," which is based on lectures McClellan gave at Harvard and Princeton between 1963 and 1964. It quotes a passage from "Unforgettable People," Rubin's translation of a story by Doppo Kunikida.[7] Rubin says that he chose to do his research on Doppo because "he died young, left a small zenshū [complete works]." He adds that McClellan had a lot to do with the choice. "I simply didn't know enough to choose a writer on my own. I think it's fair to say that by the time I finished my dissertation on Doppo, I was finally qualified to begin a dissertation on Doppo. Unfortunately, they don't let you do these things over."[8]

In 1970, around a decade after he first discovered Japanese literature, Rubin completed his dissertation and received a PhD from the University of Chicago. His dissertation included translations of nine Doppo stories.[9] I ask Rubin if it was normal practice at the time to do so much translation as part of a dissertation.

"I don't think there was much 'normal practice' of writing dissertations on Japanese literature back then. I remember thinking it didn't make much sense to write a book about a writer nobody could read, so I decided to make a number of his stories accessible."[10]

The same year, *Monumenta Nipponica*, the journal of Japanese studies issued by Sophia University in Tokyo, published "Bonfire," Rubin's translation of the Doppo story "Takibi."[11] Two years later, the same journal published five more of Rubin's Doppo story translations along with his analysis of them.[12]

After completing his PhD, Rubin moved to Japan to spend a year at the Tokyo Institute of Technology. His plan was to turn his dissertation into a book under the supervision of the literary scholar Jun Etō.

"I've always been fond of a few Doppo stories, will be including 'Unforgettable People' in my Penguin anthology, enjoyed revising that translation for *Monkey Business*. But I was heartily sick of him by the time I finished the dissertation. The Etō influence was too strong and I worked on Sōseki instead."[13]

In 1983, when Kodansha International published a collection of short stories by Doppo, Rubin wrote a review in the *Journal of Japanese Studies* that was critical of the translation. But he did not confine his criticism to the translation:

It is difficult, however, to speak of a need for work on Doppo. Perfectly sound survey courses on Japanese literature can be taught without reference to him. And while his career can tell us much about the literary and intellectual history of the decade between the Sino- and Russo-Japanese wars (indeed, his work as a war correspondent and his experiences in politics, journalism, Christianity, and modern love are no less than fascinating), there is still little doubt that Doppo must be seen as the culmination of his period rather than as a part of the intellectual and artistic revolution that was taking place at the time of his death in 1908. A good book on Doppo would certainly be a welcome addition to Western knowledge of Japan and Japanese literature, but the absence of one could not be called a deprivation.[14]

What seems interesting here are Rubin's criteria for selecting works for translation. In 1983 (several years before he came across Murakami's work), Rubin seems to suggest that the author's importance in literary history—and more specifically whether the author's work is necessary in teaching Japanese literary history in English—is the primary reason for whether a translation is necessary or valuable. Decades later in his own book, *Haruki Murakami and the Music of Words* (first published in 2002 and last updated in 2011), Rubin makes a distinction between academic and commercial translations;[15] still, the review of the Doppo collection leads me to think that, as late as the mid-eighties, Rubin had never entertained the possibility of translating a contemporary author.

Having become an assistant professor of Japanese at Harvard

in 1970, Rubin began translating *Sanshirō* by Sōseki. "I was especially fascinated by *Sore kara* but figured I'd better translate *Sanshirō* first (a) to get my translation skills up to speed, and (b) before I ceased to be young myself and could no longer appreciate its youthfulness. Well, Norma Field got her *Sore kara* (published as *And Then*) out while I was reading *Sanshirō*, and it finally dawned on me that *Sanshirō* was a novel that could never be outgrown."[16]

Rubin completed his translation of *Sanshirō* around the time he became associate professor of Japanese literature at the University of Washington in 1975. Harvard University Press, he says, was "skittish about publishing fiction," so he went with University of Washington Press, which was in his "backyard." The translation was published in 1977 and included a comprehensive introduction and analysis of the novel. "I think I kind of had to include the essay for them to publish it and pretend it was an academic book."[17]

Rubin's translation of *Sanshirō* was reviewed in various journals related to the study of Japan. Alan Turney, known for his translation of Sōseki's *Botchan* and *Kusamakura*, wrote in *Monumenta Nipponica* that "[t]he translation itself is superb. It reads fluently and naturally in English, while remaining faithful to not only the letter but also the spirit of the original. Particularly impressive is the dialogue."[18] J. Thomas Rimer also used the term "spirit of the original" in his review in *The Journal of the Association of Teachers of Japanese*, saying that Rubin's translation was "closer yet to capturing the spirit of the original text than any of the half-dozen other translations of the author's works."[19]

I mention that Alan Turney's review must have felt good to

receive, and Rubin responds, "I remember that 'superb' remark. It appeared in a journal that contained a review of another translation from Japanese that was also supposedly 'superb' but was far from it. I've always viewed that word ironically when it's thrown around by reviewers of translations, especially those without access to the Japanese."[20]

But there were bilingual readers and reviewers too, I suggest.

"Was I aware that bilingual readers would be scrutinizing my work? In those days, it felt as if those were the ONLY kind of readers for translated Japanese literature." As for his Murakami translations, Rubin says, "Most reviewers of Murakami translations don't know a word of Japanese but that doesn't seem to stop them from presuming to comment on the quality of the translation. All they really mean is the translation reads well in English."[21]

Rubin Discovers Murakami

Rubin first came across Murakami's work in 1989, the year after his translation of Sōseki's *Kōfu* (*The Miner*) was published. At the time, Rubin had little interest in contemporary Japanese literature. But one day, several months before Birnbaum's *A Wild Sheep Chase* was published by KI, he received a call from an editor at Vintage.[22] The editor, whose name Rubin cannot recall ("a 'he' and, I think, Japanese"), said he was considering publishing an English translation of *Sekai no owari to hādoboirudo wandārando* (*Hard-Boiled Wonderland and the End of the World*) and asked him if he would read it "to see if it was worth translating."[23] Rubin agreed to the task, thinking "it wouldn't hurt me to discover what kind of junk was being read out there."[24] The call came at a time when Rubin had established himself as an academic and had also completed a novel (which would be published in 2015 by Chin Music Press as *The Sun Gods*). Had Rubin been looking for something new? "That sounds reasonable. I just stumble aimlessly from one thing to the next."[25]

Rubin was amazed by Murakami's imagination. In *Haruki Murakami and the Music of Words*, Rubin recounts strongly encouraging the Vintage editor to publish the book and added that "if, by any chance, they were not satisfied with the translation they were considering, they should let me do it. They ignored my advice on both counts."[26]

Unbeknownst to Rubin, Kodansha International had already signed a contract to publish the translation in September 1988. But what form of publication could Vintage have been considering? With *A Wild Sheep Chase*, paperback rights had been sold before the hardcover edition had been published, and Vintage was a paperback publisher. This seems to suggest that Vintage had been approached to publish the paperback version of what would become *Hard-Boiled Wonderland and the End of the World*. Luke, however, says that was not possible because they did not yet have anything to show publishers at the time.[27]

Rubin says he lost touch with the editor who had gotten him to read the book, and that even after Rubin's translations began to be published by Knopf/Vintage in the nineties, the two never met.[28] The intentions of the Vintage editor, whatever they may have been, are now moot, but thanks to this phone call from a stranger (a device one often encounters in Murakami's work), Murakami gained an ally with whom he would work for more than a quarter of a century.

"Lively" Versus "Faithful"

Having been so impressed by his first encounter, Rubin read all the works of Murakami that he was able to get hold of. Like Birnbaum, Rubin admired Murakami's sense of humor, and took a particular liking to the short fiction.[29] He looked up Murakami's address in the *Bungei Nenkan* (*Literary Almanac*) and wrote him a letter requesting permission to translate some of the stories. He heard from Murakami's agent at the time, the Japan Foreign Rights Centre, and Rubin sent them sample translations of "The Second Bakery Attack" and "The Elephant Vanishes." Rubin soon received a call from Murakami himself, asking if *Playboy* could publish Rubin's translation of "The Second Bakery Attack." Used to publishing academic articles for a limited readership, Rubin "leaped at the chance, whatever scruples I might have had regarding the so-called *Playboy* 'philosophy.'"[30]

"The Second Bakery Attack" was published in the January 1992 issue of *Playboy* together with an ukiyo-e style illustration. (Rubin's translation of "The Elephant Vanishes" ended up being published in *The New Yorker* in its November 18, 1991, issue, so "The Second Bakery Attack" became his second published translation of a Murakami work.) The illustrator, Kinuko

Y. Craft, born and educated in Japan, had been freelancing for *Playboy* for many years. She recalls that the magazine's art directors began commissioning her to create parodies of the works of famous dead artists, and the ukiyo-e style depiction of a scene from "The Second Bakery Attack" was one of them.[31]

When Murakami discusses the translations of his work, he often notes the difference between Birnbaum and Rubin. He mentions Rubin in a September 1991 interview with *Publishers Weekly*, which ran before any of Rubin's translations were even published:

> Murakami is quick to credit the translator of his novels, Alfred Birnbaum: "He's a good man, a good guy. His translation is so lively." Birnbaum, for example, came up with the English title for *A Wild Sheep Chase*; the original was *The Adventure of the Sheep*. "I have another translator, Jay Rubin," Murakami continues. "He's good as well. Alfred is more free, Jay is more faithful to the original." Americans will have a chance to sample Rubin's translation in a September issue of *The New Yorker*, where a story by Murakami will appear.[32]

But a closer look at Rubin's translation of "The Second Bakery Attack" reveals that there are some deviations from the original Japanese. The opening paragraphs, where the narrator muses about free will, have been simplified so that they are around half the length of the original. And throughout the rest of the story, details ("from when they had made the base for a cheesecake";

"with the McDonald logo on it"), descriptions ("The only car in the parking lot was a shiny, red Blue Bird"), and a number of difficult-to-translate metaphors have been left untranslated. In the second half of the story, in which the couple attack the bakery, small actions ("they gave up and moved the car two hundred meters forward") and the narrator's internal monologue are trimmed down so that the English translation seems to move at a slightly faster pace than the original Japanese. I ask Rubin if he made these decisions with the magazine's readership in mind. No, he responds, he has no recollection of any edits being required by *Playboy*.[33]

Fiction Over There

Meanwhile, in the fall of 1991, *New Yorker* fiction editor Linda Asher made her first trip to Japan. In addition to hiking and visiting museums, restaurants, and public baths, she traveled to Kamakura to meet Elmer Luke at his home.[34] After returning to New York, Asher sent Luke a copy of *The New Yorker* that included Rubin's translation of "The Elephant Vanishes." She encouraged Luke to "send me whatever seems interesting in fiction over there—among other things, whatever Alfred Birnbaum may take a notion to translate."[35]

Asher also worked with Rubin to publish another story, "Sleep," in the March 30, 1992, issue of the magazine. Luke wrote to the Murakamis a few weeks later, on April 24, 1992, "I read—and enjoyed—'Sleep.' It's the best work of Jay Rubin's that I've seen. Sometimes I think his work is flat, too flat, but I think he got the voice right in 'Sleep.' A very good piece."[36]

Asher followed "Sleep" with a translation, by Philip Gabriel, of Murakami's 1983 story "Naya wo yaku," published as "Barn Burning" in the November 2, 1992, issue. Luke recalls that there were two translations of the story—the one by Gabriel, and another by Alfred Birnbaum. Asher decided to work with Gabriel's translation. Gabriel had translated several of Murakami's short stories "just for fun" when he was a graduate student at Cornell University; one of them, "Kangaroo Communique," had been published in the San Francisco–based journal *ZYZZYVA* in 1988. Regarding the *New Yorker* story, Gabriel says, "My memory was that soon after I started working at the University of Arizona I got a call from Linda Asher, who said they had read several of the short stories I had translated and wanted to do 'Barn Burning.' Naturally, I was quite happy about that, since I loved Haruki's short stories but wasn't sure I'd have a chance to publish any more. I recall one 2–3 hour phone call from her where we went over the translation almost line by line. She had lots of good questions about word choice, and I had to go back through the original carefully. I recall she felt there was some repetition at the end that should be omitted . . . I recall talking with Haruki about it. He always had the final okay. Having a story published in *The New Yorker* was, of course, a thrill."[37]

In both "Sleep" and "Barn Burning," as in "The Windup Bird and Tuesday's Women," the reference to "Tokyo" has been added to the opening of the story. A paragraph has also been cut from the ending in two of these early *New Yorker* pieces—the final paragraph in "Barn Burning" and the second to last paragraph in "The Elephant Vanishes."

I ask Murakami about having to accept these edits to these early stories. "What can I say—*The New Yorker* has a large number of readers and they also pay really well," he tells me, laughing. He says that if the editor of a Japanese magazine had made similar suggestions, "of course I would change things that I agree with, but in principle I would say no. Not just with *The New Yorker*, but in foreign markets in general, I think you have no choice but to go along with their rules. There are people who criticize me for this, saying, 'I bet you let them do what they want because it's *The New Yorker*.' Yes, that's exactly right! But like I said, I reverse the changes when the story is published in book form."[38]

In Search of a New Publisher

From early on—even as *A Wild Sheep Chase* was just being published by Kodansha International—the possibility of having an American publisher was apparently already on Murakami's mind. Tetsu Shirai, Kodansha's U.S. representative at the time, recalls, "When Mr. Murakami came to New York to promote *A Wild Sheep Chase* he told me something to the effect that 'in Japan I want to continue to work with publishers who have supported me in the past, but in America I want to do what's best in America.' Back then no other Japanese author would say something like that. They were usually all just happy to have their books published [in English]."[39]

When I ask Murakami about this, he says, "I would have, of course, liked to publish with an American publisher, but back then it didn't even occur to me that it was a possibility."

Yet his experience with *Hard-Boiled Wonderland* seems to have strengthened Murakami's determination to move to an American publisher. "I felt like we had established some kind of foundation. But I also felt that I really needed to 'break through.'"[40]

In his essay "Going Overseas—A New Frontier," Murakami writes:

> I was advised by several Americans I had met through work that "it would be difficult to succeed as an author in America unless I signed with an American agent and published with a major American publisher."[41]

At the same time, there were others who advised Murakami against moving publishers, telling him, "Why change the setup when things are going relatively well the way they are?" or "Things won't work out if you try going at it on your own. The American market isn't such an easy place."[42] But Murakami felt strongly that "he wanted to test his ability as a 'rookie writer' in the large American market"[43] and "decided to use [his] own two legs to find an agent and new publisher."[44]

Murakami's essay and interview in *Kangaeru Hito* (*The*

Thinker) magazine gives the impression that Murakami had done everything on his own. But in his 2017 interview with Mieko Kawakami, he also says that "rather than me going around doing things myself, a lot of times it was more a case of people around me helping me out."[45]

When I ask Murakami about this, he says, "I wasn't doing these things strategically from the beginning. Elmer and many others helped me . . . it wasn't like I had this clear ambition, but I found myself in the best position. So I feel very lucky."[46]

Luke agrees. "I don't think Haruki was particularly ambitious or strategic. At least at the time I think he just wanted to be writing. If anything, I was the one who was being ambitious for Haruki. And, of course, Yoko was an important force too."[47]

When I ask Luke what he meant by "important force," he says, "She was someone who was always there," and that the "Murakami empire is based on Murakami's writing, but she's the force that keeps it going. By force I don't necessarily mean a jet force, but she keeps the engines finely tuned and she's very important. When you are an author you need someone to handle everything that's coming so that you can concentrate on writing. Most people don't have that."[48]

Poet Tess Gallagher, who first met Murakami in the home she shared with Raymond Carver, and who has been friends with the Murakamis ever since, says that her "impression of Yoko and Haruki's life together as I have seen it develop allows me to see how Ray and I might have been, had he been able to live longer. Already in the ten marvelous years we shared, we were reciprocal in our support of each other, because we were both writers. Yoko has an uncanny way of knowing exactly what will help Haruki access the worlds of his novels. I remember her announcing one time about the onset of one of the novels. She said simply: 'He's pregnant!' which was both funny, because of course men don't get pregnant with babies—but entirely accurate for the state of being in which a person, a writer, conceives of the material that will be a novel or a short story or a poem! I have felt the strength of Yoko behind and with Haruki at every encounter. She makes many things possible that would not be possible at all."[49]

In any case, Princeton turned out to be a convenient location for an author looking for a new American publisher. Manhattan was less than a two-hour drive away. It also helped that Murakami's responsibilities at the university were relatively light. In the final year of his two and a half years at Princeton, he was a visiting lecturer, teaching a seminar on Japanese literature—notes from which were later published as *Wakai dokusha no tame no tanpen shōsetsu annai* (*An Introduction to Short Stories for Young Readers*)—but even that was just a once-a-week commitment.

Murakami approached a number of publishers. Through a common acquaintance at Princeton, he was eventually able to get a meeting with Sonny Mehta, who headed the Knopf imprint at Random House.

Murakami Meets Mehta

Sonny Mehta was born the son of an Indian diplomat in 1942 and grew up in various cities including Prague, New York, and Geneva.[50] He started out in publishing in the U.K. with the small London firm Rupert Hart-Davis after graduating from Cambridge. He went on to cofound a paperback imprint, Paladin, and serve as publishing director of Pan Books.[51] He then moved to the U.S. in 1987 to take over Knopf from Robert Gottlieb upon Gottlieb's departure to *The New Yorker*.[52] Mehta was at Knopf for thirty years and was the chairman of the Knopf Doubleday Group until his death in 2019.[53]

On November 1, 1991, Murakami took the train from Princeton Junction in New Jersey to Penn Station in New York.[54] According to Murakami, he met Mehta at his home, and the two of them went for a meal at one of Mehta's favorite Indian restaurants.[55] Murakami found Mehta a "very gentle, intellectual, nice person" who "has a mysterious side to him,"[56] and says that he hardly remembers the taste of the food because he was so nervous sitting face-to-face with "a giant of the publishing industry."[57] The two discussed various things over dinner, and by the time dessert was served, Mehta asked him if he wanted to publish with Knopf. Murakami got home that evening at 11:00, which was late for him.[58]

In a letter a few days after their meeting, Mehta told Murakami that he was looking forward to reading the short stories (that presumably Murakami had promised during their meeting to send him) and enclosed books by Cormac McCarthy and Ryszard Kapuściński.[59] A month later, on December 10, Mehta wrote Murakami a short note to say that he had read the short stories Murakami had sent him as well as "The Elephant Vanishes" in *The New Yorker* and that he would be eager to have him on the Knopf list.[60] This was followed by another letter on January 22, 1992, making an offer for world English-language rights for a short story collection.[61]

The timing of their encounter worked very much in Murakami's favor. Mehta was then relatively new to the job at Knopf, especially compared to his predecessors—only two others had been at its head since it was established in 1915, the founder Alfred A. Knopf for more than fifty years until 1968, and Robert Gottlieb for nearly twenty years from 1968 to 1987—but after an initial period of instability and adjustment, he had become, according to a 1990 *New York Times* article, "the power behind the throne at America's largest trade publishing company" and had helped Kazuo Ishiguro's *The Remains of the Day* become a hit in the U.S. Since 1990, Knopf had also published a number of bestsellers—including *Rabbit at Rest* by John Updike, *The General in His Labyrinth* by Gabriel García Márquez, and *Jurassic Park* by Michael Crichton—and was accounting for around 10 percent of Random House's earnings.[62]

Murakami says that the offer from Knopf had made him happy. "I felt like I was finally standing at the start line. The truth of the matter is that today's global publishing culture revolves around New York ... Of course, in my case I first publish my work in Japanese, but New York becomes the hub for distribution to the world market. It was vital that I was able to gain this extremely powerful hub."[63]

Elmer Luke says that he welcomed the news that Knopf had made an offer. "I thought I was handing him off to very capable hands, that Knopf was exactly where he should be," Luke says.[64] Knopf had a long history of publishing Japanese writers, and like many other editors including Robert Gottlieb and Gary Fisketjon, Luke had first encountered Japanese literature through translations published by Knopf under a program started in 1955 by Harold Strauss, when he was editor-in-chief of the imprint.[65] Luke also admired Sonny Mehta, who had been a strong supporter of his friend the Chinese American author Maxine Hong Kingston, and who was "known for crossing borders (in his case, literally as well, coming from UK to take the job)." He adds, "But I was also a bit jealous—wishing I could be along for the ride!"[66]

It is not unusual for authors to "upgrade" publishers the way Murakami did. French scholar Gisèle Sapiro suggests that in the publishing industry, "innovation in the field is mainly supplied by small publishers," giving the example of Elfriede Jelinek, who was initially "discovered" by the relatively small publisher Jacqueline Chambo but moved to the larger and older Editions du Seuil before she was awarded the Nobel Prize. Sapiro writes, "Since they cannot afford to pay high advances on fees to well-known writers, they need to take risks and discover new authors in order to survive. This contribution to the renewal of literary production gives new impetus to the dynamics of the field, yet this very dynamism means small publishers often cannot keep their authors when these achieve recognition."[67]

Murakami further discusses this "upgrade" in his 2010 interview for *Kangaeru Hito* (*The Thinker*) magazine.

> The local staff at KI were mostly American, and they tried very hard, and to this day I'm grateful for that, but the reality was that there were limitations.[68]

Tetsu Shirai says that he understood and was supportive of Murakami's decision, but that at the same time he "didn't see any limitation." He also points out that the house would go on to publish a *New York Times* bestseller—a memoir by two centenarian sisters—a few years later.[69]

When I ask Minato Asakawa—who took charge of the New York office after Shirai—about this, he responds, "We, at least at KA, didn't take the move as a negative thing." He does feel that their ability to market books was limited at the time and that "we should be proud of the fact that the original publisher for the new star novelist in the NY book community was KI."[70]

Stephanie Levi, who was the business manager at KI-USA/KA at the time, recalls that there were "mixed feelings" about Murakami's move, but that "my husband and I were very happy for Murakami-san. Knopf is one of the premier houses for literary fiction, and published Raymond Carver whom Murakami held in high esteem."[71] Kuniaki Ura, marketing manager at KI-USA at the time, also recalls that there were two camps within KI—those who had supported the move and those who had felt betrayed—but that his own position was that it was "the absolutely right choice."[72]

When I press Luke again about why he had encouraged Murakami to move to another publisher when it would most likely mean that Luke would no longer be able to work with him, he responds that his "loyalty towards Haruki was simply stronger than that towards the institution of KI."[73]

When I tell Murakami what Luke had said about his loyalty being with him rather than the company, his expression seems to stiffen momentarily before he says, "I think Elmer wanted to move [publishers] with me. I think it was an opportunity for him as well. But I don't think it was easy to make it in New York as an Asian American editor . . . To do so you've got to be really, really strong."[74]

In Search of an Agent

In contrast to his early interest in finding an American publisher, Murakami initially seems to have had little interest in obtaining an agent. Jonathan Levi, who arranged the evening in the fall of 1989 where Murakami first met Andrew Wylie, observes that "while the notion of an editor translated well between both languages, the role of an agent was unclear to Murakami, since it wasn't a Japanese concept."[75]

But Murakami's thinking seems to have shifted after landing in Princeton in 1991. Luke says that sometime during this period Murakami had asked him to serve as his agent but that he had declined. "I said that I'd do anything for him but I couldn't because I didn't have the contacts necessary to do a good job, but that I would advise him in getting a good agent."[76] Murakami says that he "might have" asked Luke to be his agent,[77] but when I check with the Murakami office, they tell me that it was their understanding that Luke had been the one to suggest that he could serve as Murakami's agent after first being informed of the Knopf offer.[78] When I ask Luke about this, he tells me that he definitely did not suggest becoming Murakami's agent. "What I might have done was offer to serve as a temporary go-between until Murakami found an agent, which is what I did."[79]

On April 24, 1992, and at Murakami's request, Luke faxed a brief note—not from the KI office but from his home in Hirō—to Sonny Mehta's assistant at Knopf with the aim of "keeping the ball rolling" on the Knopf publication:

Dear Jessica:

Spring seems finally to have taken hold here. I can tell by the hayfever.

Just checking in. It's been a bit. I don't mean to prod at all, but want to be sure that all's well. Please get in touch at the above fax number if there's any question.

All best to you,

Sincerely,
Elmer Luke[80]

Hiroo ███
Shibuya-ku, Tokyo ███
Fax ███
24 April 1992

Jessica Green
ALFRED A. KNOPF
Fax ███

Dear Jessica:

Spring seems finally to have taken hold here. I can tell by
the hayfever.

Just checking in. It's been a bit. I don't mean to prod at all,
but want to be sure that all's well. Please get in touch at the
above fax number if there's any question.

All best to you,

Sincerely,

Elmer Luke

copy to 利上

At the time, KI had not officially been made aware of Murakami's plans to change publishers. In a fax to Luke titled "MURAKAMI RUMORS," sent two weeks later on May 7, Leslie Pockell, who was in New York for meetings, wrote in a relatively lighthearted note that he had heard that Sonny Mehta had announced in an internal meeting that Knopf would be publishing a book by Murakami, and also that Murakami was meeting with potential agents.[81]

Another two weeks later, on May 19, Luke seems to still be serving as "temporary go-between":

I have not had a chance to reach Jessica . . . since I talked with you yesterday. As I said, the questions I would like to discuss with her are small issues, technical considerations that are not major but need to be worked out nonetheless. If I am not able to reach Jessica before I leave for the States tomorrow, I will bring the contract with me to New York and talk to her there.

I think that's it for now. I look forward to seeing you both again. I've been thinking more about the matter of an agent for you and would like to discuss further with you. It will be so much nicer (and easier) talking to you face to face![82]

According to Murakami, finding the right agent took some time. "I discussed the matter with Elmer but it wasn't easy finding one. I think we met with three, four different people."[83]

Luke recalls that there were a number of options. There was Andrew Wylie, who had great influence in the publishing world.

There was also an agent who was relatively inexperienced but had the ability to communicate in Japanese. Luke recalls advising Murakami that he should prioritize the agent's connections in the publishing world over ease of communication.[84]

The agent who eventually became the front-runner was Amanda Urban at ICM, one of the world's largest talent and literary agencies. Urban represented Toni Morrison as well as many other authors published by Knopf, including Jay McInerney, Richard Ford, and Raymond Carver. Having joined ICM in 1980, Urban had become executive vice president and co-director of the Literary Department in 1988.[85] In 1991, she was named by *Entertainment Weekly* as among the 101 most powerful people in entertainment.[86]

"I don't know how Binky found out Haruki was looking for an agent," Luke says. "I suspect it was from Gary [Fisketjon], but she knew enough to ring me up (I'm pretty sure we hadn't met before) . . . She went about her courtship gently, unaggressively (certainly in comparison to Andrew Wylie, who came on strong—which was his style, which some people like), and I guess I was her way to him. She invited me to breakfast at the Russian Tea Room, suggested I have blinis (the house specialty) (I did), and at one moment Mike Nichols walked in the door and she excused herself to introduce herself to him . . . After that morning, we'd talk occasionally, and then one day Binky (in a surprising but very smart soft sell) asked me what would it take to get Haruki to meeting and talking to her, were there any writers in particular that she could introduce him to and we could all meet together."[87]

According to Luke, a lunch was set up in the late spring of 1992 to introduce Murakami to Urban and some of the writers she represented. "Binky said she'd invite Tess [Gallagher] (Haruki was very fond of Carver and her, and Binky knew this), but were there any other authors Haruki might be interested in meeting? I suggested Jay McInerney (because his *Bright Lights* had this amazing ear for language I had tried to capture in *Sheep*, and he'd had Japan experience) and Tobias Wolff (who'd recently published *This Boy's Life*, which was wonderful) . . . Binky represented all three authors, all knew Raymond Carver, all had Syracuse University connections."[88]

Luke says that Murakami seemed to be at ease at the meeting. "At the lunch, Haruki was as usual (or as usual as he has become in non-Japan context)—sociable, quietly charming, a little shy but confident, witty, seemingly pleased to be there, and definitely happy to see Tess, whom he had met when Ray was alive and apparently been keeping in touch with. I think that Tobias Wolff did not know Haruki's work then; he does now. On my part, undoubtedly I was glad to be at the table too—and pleased to have had something to do with this guy Murakami, who was in the spotlight and in demand."[89]

Urban says that she does not recall attending the lunch and that she remembers first meeting Murakami at her office.[90] Wolff also has no recollection of the meal. He thinks he did meet Murakami "many years ago, but over coffee. Our brief conversation was conducted through a translator, and we talked mostly about our admiration for the stories of Raymond Carver."[91] Murakami also does not remember whether Wolff was at the lunch. He confirms that Luke introduced him to Wolff "but my memory is that we met at a restaurant in Union Square."[92] On the other hand, Tess Gallagher (who had become close to the Murakamis after they visited Carver's grave with her in July 1991, and who had visited them in Princeton in April 1992)[93] says, "I can't say that I do recall who else was there, although I do recall Ray and I being together with Binky and Mr. Luke."[94] (Raymond Carver had died several years before Murakami began looking for an agent in America.)[95] When I ask Luke why the others seem not to recall the lunch, he responds: "While the lunch was critical to the Haruki story, it was not writ in flashing lights. It would be now, no detail forgotten! Haruki then was fresh and wild and different, but for people whose life is literature, new writers are part of a daily changing landscape. The name Murakami probably did not lodge itself in the literary consciousness until *Wind-Up Bird*—that's five years after the lunch, and it's been another twenty-three years since."[96]

Luke says he was hoping Murakami would choose Urban. "She was capable, her professionalism unquestioned, and her network as wide as could be. So if Haruki went with her, I guess I felt I was doing right by him. I also thought that, no small thing, Yoko could work with Binky, and vice versa."[97]

Even after the meeting, Murakami continued to "agonize" over the choice.[98] Urban—who had not represented any foreign-language authors before—had told him that she could not handle works that she could not read in English.[99] Murakami was also concerned that he would not be a priority at a "big company like

ICM." He had been told that "big firms immediately cut you loose if your sales figures are poor."[100]

Luke says he still pushed for Urban. "There were 'smaller' agents, highly respected, one even suggested by Sonny Mehta, but I presumed to think Haruki needed 'bigger,'" he tells me.[101] "I remember telling Haruki: It's like a marriage—you can always get a divorce. Said marriage has lasted twenty-five years and been good, from all indications, for both sides."[102]

Joining the "Carver Gang"

On June 10, 1992, Luke sent a fax to the Murakamis. He had just visited them in Princeton the previous month.

> Well, as you can see from the fax, I'm back and alive and at work. It's still Japan.

> Seeing you in Princeton was just terrific. You both looked so good and easy. Thanks too for the lovely party—I enjoyed meeting Hosea and Mimi, and seeing Suzuki-san [Murakami's editor at Shinchosha] in such a different part of the world was great fun. Thanks too for letting me impersonate Haruki Murakami at the swimming pool.

> I'm sorry that the time was short and that, once again, we are so far apart. Will that ever change?

I'll be very interested to hear about your meeting with Binky. Of course, if there's anything I can be of help along the way, you know that you can ask at any time.[103]

Five days later, on June 15, Luke received a fax from Yōko Murakami informing him that they had decided to sign with Urban. Luke also received a fax from Urban the following day saying, "Murakami is officially on board. Thank you, thank you, thank you."[104] He wrote to the Murakamis the same day to tell them that he thought they had made the right choice:

> I think that it's a great decision you've made to have Binky Urban be your agent. She's really top of the line, and she has the intelligence and the will and the capacity to represent your interests well—both in the States and internationally . . . For translations of your short stories that people have done, she can read through them, and she can be the one to submit them to various magazines for publication. Because she will be the one person doing this, there will be more coordination and control. And she can deal with all the sticky money matters (for example, the percentage given to translators).[105]

Why did Murakami ultimately decide to go with Urban? Luke mentions "a 'spiritual' connection—due to Binky's having been Ray Carver's agent and to being Gallagher's agent."[106] Murakami himself affirms this. Asked in a 2017 interview with Mieko Kawakami—an author now herself represented by Urban—why he chose Binky after having met with various agents, Murakami responded:

> One thing was that she seemed very efficient, but the fact that she was Raymond Carver's agent may have been a major factor.[107]

And why was Urban interested in Murakami? Urban's policy is not to give interviews related to authors she represents, but in his 2010 interview in *Kangaeru Hito* (*The Thinker*) magazine, Murakami himself suggested why not only Urban but other "super top class" publishing professionals in the New York literary field might have found him worthy of their attention.

> There are probably two reasons. The first is that *Noruwei no mori* [*Norwegian Wood*] had sold more than a million copies in Japan. This fact was known in the American publishing world and it seems that they were interested in me as the author of *Norwegian Wood*.

> The other reason was that I was translating Raymond Carver. Sonny Mehta . . . and Binky both worked with Raymond Carver . . . They were part of the "Carver Gang."[108]

In his essay "Going Overseas—A New Frontier," published five years later, in 2015, Murakami adds a third reason.

I was gradually publishing work in America, and it was relatively well-received, and they saw potential in my future. I
think that the fact that *The New Yorker* valued my work had a
significant impact.[109]

In addition to the two novels published by KI, having short
stories available in English had to have been important. "Back
then the number of works published were still limited, but that
may have even worked in his favor," Birnbaum tells me. "The works
that you could read in America . . . was the best of Murakami."
Birnbaum also emphasizes that "Murakami's passive, introverted
protagonist provided an image that was the complete opposite of
the Japanese corporations that Americans were feeling hostility
towards at the time."[110]

Notably, many of the stories that had appeared in U.S. magazines, such as "TV People," "The Second Bakery Attack," and
"The Windup Bird and Tuesday's Women," have been called rem-
iniscent of Carver's work. The first story published in *The New
Yorker* after Urban became Murakami's agent was "Barn Burning." Gary Fisketjon has said of Carver and Murakami that "their
prose styles are similarly unadorned, their characters often com-
ically anti-heroic" and suggests that "Barn Burning" is the "most
strikingly Carver-like."[111]

When I ask Tess Gallagher, who also serves as Carver's literary executor, whether she perceives the influence of Carver's work
on Murakami's writing, she says that the influence is apparent to
her. She continues: "I would say Haruki takes a step farther than

Ray though—for Haruki has an almost magical element which exceeds Ray's ultra-realistic mode."[112]

"Carver was a major presence for me," Murakami tells me. "I wouldn't go as far as to say that I was guided by Ray, but I would say it was fate or a connection of some kind."[113]

Murakami Meets Fisketjon

Once the matter of the agent was settled, the next step was finding an editor for Murakami at Knopf. The job was given to Gary Fisketjon, who popularized the trade paperback industry by launching the Vintage Contemporaries series at Random House. He saw his fame rise in the eighties through his association with the "literary brat pack," which included authors such as Bret Easton Ellis, Jay McInerney, and Tama Janowitz. After spending a few years as editorial director of the Atlantic Monthly Press, Fisketjon returned to Random House in 1990[114] and worked for Knopf until 2019.[115] For nearly twenty years he spent half his time in New York and the other half in Tennessee, "which in terms of editing is much better since there are fewer distractions, country life in a private office being much less complicated than city life in the offices of an expansive company."[116] Murakami describes Fisketjon as a "warm" person who "unlike most New York publishing professionals . . . speaks in a very leisurely way" and "who, when it comes to publishing fiction, has a sharp eye, just the right amount of stubbornness, and a passion for discovering new work."[117]

Gary Fisketjon and his cat, Carl, in his cabin in Tennessee

Fisketjon tells me that he does not remember whether it was a Japanese friend or his friend Raymond Carver who first introduced him to Haruki Murakami's work. "I somehow got hold of English translations of very early works by Haruki that were prepared for Japanese students studying English. This would've been somewhere in the early eighties, and perhaps Japanese friends had given me one, maybe two slender books . . . It's a distant memory, though I hope I still have these copies somewhere. I doubt the translations themselves were all that impressive, but one can read through even faulty translations and see how impressive the work itself was, and that was certainly the case in this instance."[118]

The two "slender books" that Fisketjon first came across were most likely the Kodansha English Library versions of *Pinball, 1973* (1985) and *Hear the Wind Sing* (1987). *A Wild Sheep Chase* and *Norwegian Wood* were also published as Kodansha English Library paperbacks, but only after 1989 (when the hardcover version of *A Wild Sheep Chase* was published in the U.S.). If Fisketjon had gotten hold of both books together, as he remembers, that would date the discovery not to the early eighties but after 1987.

Fisketjon also discusses his discovery of Murakami's work in an email roundtable with Jay Rubin and Philip Gabriel that was published on the Knopf website:

> My interest in his work derived from an intense though amateurish fascination with Japanese literature and culture for a couple years at Williams College ... I plowed my way through the so-called Big Three (Junichiro Tanizaki, Yasunari Kawabata and Yukio Mishima) and naturally became utterly entranced by Mishima, who became the subject of a very, very long paper I must've spent six months on. So the groundwork was laid in the mid 70s, and when I first encountered Murakami I felt strongly—as I still do—that he properly belongs next in that hugely distinguished line of writers.

> Then, skipping ahead, while by 1986 I was running the Atlantic Monthly Press and certainly would've been keen to publish Haruki, he had his relationship with Kodansha (and I don't poach writers) and so I was a friend in court, as it were, content to spread the word however I could that a great novelist was among us. I moved to Knopf in 1990 and before long so did Haruki, and given my convictions I was the most plausible editor for him.

He also discusses his first in-person encounter with Murakami:

> I think just prior to the publication of A WILD SHEEP CHASE, we had occasion to meet; we talked a lot about Ray's

work, and I confessed my deep admiration of his own novels and my anticipation of the one forthcoming, and Haruki responded that he didn't think it was very good, nor the one to come after, but maybe the next one.[119]

When I try to confirm the timing of his meeting with Murakami, Fisketjon responds, "It must've been after 1986, when I moved to Atlantic Monthly Press. In fact, Ray Carver and I had lunch with Haruki, who was by then a great friend of Ray's and also his Japanese translator. If memory serves, *A Wild Sheep Chase* had already been published by Kodansha and *Hard-Boiled Wonderland* might have been, with *Dance Dance Dance* coming soon."[120]

Carver had to cancel a trip to Japan in the fall of 1987 to undergo cancer treatment; he died in August of the following year. Given that the Kodansha English Library version of *Hear the Wind Sing* was published in February 1987, if Fisketjon's memory about reading the two books together is correct, it would mean that the meeting probably took place sometime in 1987. But Murakami has written that he met Carver only once (and for just a couple of hours), in Port Angeles in 1984. When I ask Murakami if it might be possible that the three of them met and had lunch together, he smiles and says no.[121]

I relay this to Fisketjon, and he responds: "I have a vivid memory of that luck [of having lunch with Carver and Murakami], at some restaurant in the Village on the north side of the street on a very pleasant spring day. Haruki was still with Kodansha then, and *A Wild Sheep Chase* and *Hard-*

Boiled Wonderland were scheduled for publication but hadn't yet appeared, so I suppose it would've been 86 or 87 (I'm bad with years). Haruki was pleasantly surprised that I'd read two earlier books, in not very good English translations done for Japanese students trying to learn the language, and of course eager to read him even in translation. I also recall the fondness between them. So either Haruki simply forgot all about this or else, in a neatly Murakami fashion, it's a story I somehow made up myself."[122]

"Lite" Versus "Literary"

Though the offer that Mehta had made was for a story collection, there seems to have been some discussion about which of Murakami's books Knopf would start with. Murakami says that both he and Knopf had wanted to publish *Norwegian Wood* first, but the contract with Kodansha prevented them from doing so.[123] The English translation of *Norwegian Wood* by Alfred Birnbaum had already been published as part of the Kodansha English Library series and had sold 100,000 copies in two months, with another 40,000 copies selling the following year despite being distributed only in Japan.[124]

Fisketjon, in the meantime, seems not to have known about Murakami's desire to publish *Norwegian Wood* as his first book with Knopf. Asked about the delayed publication of *Norwegian Wood* in the abovementioned email roundtable, Fisketjon responds:

Regarding NORWEGIAN WOOD, I really had to wait for Haruki's interest to be made clear to me, with respect to this book or the order of publication (however out-of-sequence it might be). I can base my decisions only on what's available when it's available, and then start factoring in my thoughts on building a career or controlling its rhythm; that is don't publish two books every five minutes and then disappear for several years, but instead try to maximize the writer's presence in bookstores by pacing publication and thinking about paperback editions as part of that process.[125]

Starting with a collection of stories rather than *Norwegian Wood*, a novel that scholar Margaret Hillenbrand has categorized as "Murakami lite,"[126] may have further helped position Murakami as a "literary author" in the U.S. Jay Rubin, who eventually translated *Norwegian Wood* for publication in the U.S., has also said, "I think I would not have liked Murakami's writing much if I had first read anything else, including NORWEGIAN WOOD (which I would have understood only on the most superficial level). I've been able to enjoy almost everything of Murakami's, knowing that he was the creator of that incredible mind trip, HARDBOILED WONDERLAND, echoes of which are to be found in everything."[127]

Murakami also acknowledges to me that *Norwegian Wood*, which he considers a work of realism, is an anomaly in his body of work. Like Rubin, he thinks that "in a way, people got *Norwegian Wood* because I had published *The Wind-Up Bird Chronicle* . . . If I had published *Norwegian Wood* first people may have assumed that was the kind of writer I was."[128]

A Selection of Selections

Murakami had a month-long trip to Mexico (a research trip for the Japanese magazine *Mother Nature's*) scheduled for July 1992.[129] Birnbaum was to join him in Mexico partway through, so it was important that they get as much done as possible on the collection of stories, *The Elephant Vanishes*, before they made the trip. The selection of titles to be proposed to Knopf was "done in a flurry," says Luke. "Due date was soon, and there was a furious back and forth between Haruki and Yoko and me and with Alfred and Jay. I read everything, worked on a bunch, and by July 2, 1992, I made my initial recommendations to Haruki."[130]

Before the publication of the collection, Murakami made changes to some of the stories, including "A Slow Boat to China." "This was the first short story I had ever written. I didn't really know how to write a short story and when I reread it later there were several places I wasn't satisfied with. I rewrote it a couple of times so there are three versions [in Japanese] of this work. My memory is not clear on this, but I think the translation for the American book was based on the second version."[131]

On September 18, 1992, Luke wrote to Murakami:

On Monday, I faxed Gary the revised translation of "Slow Boat to China" that I worked on a bit with Alfred (Alfred had promised it to Gary when they talked together in New York). You know, Haruki, I have come to like this story a lot. It is also a much stronger story, I think, than as it was in its earlier version.[132]

Given that Luke did not have the ability to read literary works in Japanese, this probably was not the first version of the story in English translation. Birnbaum says he does not remember the details, but one possibility is that he had translated the earlier version of the story (he does recall translating most of the stories in the Japanese collection *Chūgoku yuki no surō bōto* [*A Slow Boat to China*] soon after discovering Murakami) and updated it for the Knopf collection.

Luke received a reply from Murakami the following day saying that he and his wife had gone to New York the previous day "to talk with Binky and Gary." He wrote that "Gary is a nice person" and that at their meeting at the Knopf office he was given the final list of stories to be published. He added, "You have your taste, of course. Alfred has his taste. Gary has his taste," but that he thought the contents were "quite reasonable." He also mentioned that they decided on the order of stories. [133]

Seventeen stories were included in the collection compiled by Fisketjon. Murakami had published six short story collections in Japanese between 1980 and 1991. All but two of the stories included were from these collections: three stories from *Chūgoku yuki no surō bōto* (*A Slow Boat to China*), two stories from *Hotaru, naya o yaku, sono ta no tanpen* (*Firefly, Barn Burning and Other Stories*), five stories from *Panya saishūgeki* (*The Second Bakery Attack*), two stories each from *TV piipuru* (*TV People*) and *Kangarū biyori* (*A Perfect Day for Kangaroos*) and one story from *Kaiten mokuba no deddo hīto* (*Dead Heat on a Merry-Go-Round*). These last two collections comprised work initially written for small magazines—the stories in the former for a magazine delivered to members of the department store Isetan and the latter for Kodansha's publicity magazine IN★POCKET—and these "lighter" pieces may not have matched the poetic priorities of the time (though Birnbaum liked them, particularly those in the latter collection, and did sample translations of many of them). A number of the stories in *Kaiten mokuba no deddo hīto* were later published in translation in various magazines (including *The New Yorker*) and were also included in the 2005 short story collection *Blind Willow, Sleeping Woman*, but many in *Kangarū biyori* remain unpublished in English translation.

When *The Elephant Vanishes* was released in Japan in 2005, Murakami emphasized in his introduction that Fisketjon had been responsible for the selection of stories, and that the book as a result reflected one editor's "taste" or "bias." He also suggested that if a Japanese editor had put together a collection of stories in 1992, the lineup probably would have looked very different.[134]

It is true that the final selection of seventeen stories was made by Knopf, but as Fisketjon himself acknowledges, he chose based on what was available to him in English translation. In that sense, the selection was influenced by the selections made by Birnbaum and Rubin and other translators. Of the final seventeen stories, nine were translated by Birnbaum and eight by Rubin. Birnbaum and Rubin's translations were used even in cases where certain stories had already been published (in magazines and anthologies) in translations by others (such as "Naya o yaku" translated as "Barn Burning" by Philip Gabriel and "Shi-

gatsu no aru hareta asa ni hyakupāsento no onnanoko ni deau
koto ni tsuite" translated as "On Meeting My 100% Woman
One Fine April Morning" by Kevin Flanagan/Tamotsu Omi).
When Murakami's second book of collected stories, *Blind Willow, Sleeping Woman*, was published in 2005, it would also include
the work of just two translators, Philip Gabriel and Jay Rubin. I
ask Fisketjon if consistency of voice was a consideration in his
choice of translators. "Jay and Phil were always instrumental to
my thinking, and Alfred's a worthy compatriot. And it did seem
to me very important indeed to rely on existing strengths in the
translations rather than push things out willy-nilly."[135]

Birnbaum remembers discussing the anthology with Jay Rubin during a party at Murakami's Aoyama apartment (the only
time, as far as he recalls, that the two of them met). He says that
their "tastes were completely different" and there was "no overlap
between the stories we had translated or wanted to translate."[136]
Rubin has said similarly that "the ones that he [Birnbaum] liked I
usually didn't like. We almost never asked for the same stories. It
was downright strange."[137]

Twelve of the seventeen stories selected by Fisketjon over-
lapped with the recommendations made by Luke. The five stories
included in the anthology that Luke did not recommend were
"The Kangaroo Communiqué," "On Seeing the 100% Perfect
Girl One Beautiful April Morning," "The Fall of the Roman Empire, the 1881 Indian Uprising, Hitler's Invasion of Poland, and
the Realm of Raging Winds," "Family Affair," and "A Window."
Luke says that he was of the opinion that the last two (both translated by Rubin) should not be included.[138]

There were four stories on Luke's list that did not make the cut. He says he pushed for inclusion of "Tony Takitani" and "New York Mining Disaster" (both translated by Birnbaum). These two stories were later published by *The New Yorker*, in translations by Jay Rubin and Philip Gabriel, respectively, and included in the 2005 Knopf anthology *Blind Willow, Sleeping Woman* (also edited by Fisketjon). The other two that Luke had recommended (with the caveat "perhaps too slight though?") were "The Rise and Fall of Sharpie Cakes," translated by Birnbaum, and "Losing Blue," translated by Rubin.[139] The former was eventually published in English in *Blind Willow, Sleeping Woman* (in a new translation by Jay Rubin), and the latter was first published in English in a supplement for the *Independent* and other papers to commemorate the Exposición Universal de Sevilla in 1992.

More than half of the stories included had first been published in magazines, including *Granta*, *Playboy*, and the *Threepenny Review*. Five stories—the most of any magazine—were first published in *The New Yorker*. When I ask Murakami if there were stories that he wanted to include that were left out, he "can't think of any," but says there was one, "The Last Lawn of the Afternoon," that he wasn't all that thrilled about that did make the cut. "I don't like that story, so I said I didn't want to include it, but Gary said 'I like this.'"[140]

At the final meeting between the Murakamis and Fisketjon regarding *The Elephant Vanishes* on September 14, 1992, it was also decided that they would include "On Seeing the 100% Perfect Girl One Beautiful Morning" and drop "New York Mining Disaster."[141]

Fisketjon chose to open the collection with "The Wind-Up Bird and Tuesday's Women," the story that had been published in *The New Yorker* in November 1990 and which Murakami, with the encouragement of his agent, was in the process of expanding into *Nejimakidori kuronikuru* (*The Wind-Up Bird Chronicle*) and serializing in the literary magazine *Shinchō*.[142] "There might've been some vague inkling," Fisketjon says, that the story would turn into the next book Knopf would be publishing, but placing the story first in the book had more to do with setting the "tone and feeling" for the collection.[143]

The title, *The Elephant Vanishes*, was the title of the final story in the book. He recalls that "it stood out quite clearly" as something that "might appeal to readers who at the time would've had no idea who this writer was" but also was an "honest reflection of Haruki's work."[144]

The translations continued to be edited until close to the publication date. On December 7, 1992, just three months before publication, Rubin sent Fisketjon a fax:

Happy Pearl Harbor Day. Thanks for the 1st-pass galleys of Elephant. Sorry I haven't had a chance to look at them until now—and only at my own translations with a few exceptions (marked with *). This is going to be a wonderful book. I assume there will be indications of who translated what.

He attached two pages listing around sixty corrections.[145] A month later, on January 3, 1993, Rubin sent Fisketjon another fax:

Happy New Year. I hope you got my message on Pearl Harbor Day (I only write on holidays). It consisted of a long list of revisions. I've had a chance to read a bit more in the proofs, came across a few more questionable points, some of which I suspect you've caught already.

He suggested eight new corrections, including several to Birnbaum's translations.[146]

Three weeks after Rubin's second fax, Luke (who had also received a copy of the latest galleys) wrote Murakami:

Dear Haruki:

Gee, terrific seeing you. And thanks for the good meal. Times like that I feel annoyed we're not nearer. Be good to have a drink and share a meal with you more than twice a year (which, I got to admit, isn't so bad, given where we live).

I'm so glad things have worked out so well for you in the U.S.—not only with Princeton but also Binky and Knopf. Naturally I had hopes that they would, but I didn't dare hope that all this would happen, and that, among other major achievements, you'd be teaching a graduate seminar! Taihen [da] kedo, I think it's really marvelous.

I haven't had time to read through all the stories in THE ELEPHANT VANISHES carefully yet. I did go over a few, like LEDERHOSEN (which made me laugh out loud again) (congratulations, by the way, on its getting published in HARPER'S—another excellent magazine) and SLOW BOAT and THE SILENCE and THE DANCING DWARF. And really, Haruki, I think that what you have here is very, very fine. The other stories, in particular those I haven't read before (like Jay's new translation of 100 PERCENT WOMAN), I will read more carefully and tell you what I think—right now, I'm trying to meet a preliminary deadline for DANCE 3 so time is a little tight. Gomen nasai.

I did want to say, though, that I think it's very important that the book include the translators' names—also, which stories were translated by whom. As you said, this is only a galley proof and Knopf might be rectifying the problem; but I would recommend that you still might mention this to Gary Fisketjon just in case he has overlooked the matter. And since they are going to press soon, this probably should be done soon. Sorry for pushiness, but giving translators credit for their contribution is critical, as you know from your own translation work.

. . .

Anyway, hope it feels good to be back in Princeton and that the old jet lag isn't too bad on your system. Lots of things happening this 1993 for you—gambatte ne, may the cock crow loudly, good health, and all best. Needless to say, call if there's anything I can do. Yoroshiku to you and Yoko.[147]

25 January 1993

Dear Haruki:

Gee, terrific seeing you. And thanks for the good meal. Times like that I feel annoyed we're not nearer. Be good to have a drink and share a meal with you more than twice a year (which, I got to admit, isn't so bad, given where we live).

I'm so glad things have worked out so well for you in the U.S.--not only with Princeton but also Binky and Knopf. Naturally I had hopes that they would, but I didn't dare hope that all this would happen, and that, among other major achievements, you'd be teaching a graduate seminar! Taihen kedo, I think it's really marvelous.

I haven't had time to read through all the stories in THE ELEPHANT VANISHES carefully yet. I did go over a few, like LEDERHOSEN (which made me laugh out loud again) (congratulations, by the way, on its getting published in HARPER'S--another excellent magazine) and SLOW BOAT and THE SILENCE and THE DANCING DWARF. And really, Haruki, I think that what you have here is very, very fine. The other stories, in particular those that I haven't read before (like Jay's new translation of 100 PERCENT WOMAN), I will read more carefully and tell you what I think--right now, I'm trying to meet a preliminary deadline for DANCE 3 so time is a little tight. Gomen nasai.

I did want to say, though, that I think it's very important that the book include the translators' names--also, which stories were translated by whom. As you said, this is only a galley proof and Knopf might be rectifying the problem; but I would recommend that you still might mention this to Gary Fistekjon just in case he has overlooked the matter. And since they are going to press soon, this probably should be done soon. Sorry for pushiness, but giving translators credit for their contribution is critical, as you know from your own translation work.

Also, as far as book design design is concerned, there are three places which seem, to me, a little strange and misleading. The problem occurs in THE FALL OF THE ROMAN EMPIRE and SLOW BOAT, the two stories that have numbered parts. On pages 115-116 and 222-223 and 227-

Chip Kidd, Optic Translator

The task of designing the cover for *The Elephant Vanishes* was assigned to Chip Kidd. Now one of the best-known book designers in the world, Kidd has been responsible for Murakami's hardcovers at Knopf for over a quarter of a century. His Upper East Side apartment displays many of the books he has designed over the years, and many of Murakami's books are displayed together with the object that inspired the cover. Kidd once even held a publication party for Murakami out on his balcony with an expansive view of Manhattan.[148] He says he had never read Murakami before being assigned *The Elephant Vanishes*, though he remembers somebody recommending *A Wild Sheep Chase* to him. "To this day, I rarely get much time to read books that I'm not working on—I'm actually a very slow reader, but I think also a careful one, which helps in my profession."[149]

Kidd was immediately drawn to Murakami's work. "I loved the casual surrealism of it. What's going on in the stories is usually very strange, but it's told in such a calm, direct, matter-of-fact way that it provides a wonderful contrast of Form and Content."[150]

How did Kidd approach the design of *The Elephant Vanishes*? "I always say that I'm inspired by the text, because it's actually true. A designer then works as a kind of visual filter for that text, an optic translator, if you will . . . In regards to designing a cover for a short story collection, if the title of the book refers to one of the stories, then I concentrate on that particular piece. My apologies if that's just stating the obvious, but in this case I started thinking about elephants; it would have been foolish not to . . . I guess the problem I set up for myself was, 'How do you show an elephant without actually showing an elephant?' It was similar, actually, to the problem two years earlier for 'Jurassic Park'—how do you suggest a dinosaur without literally showing one? The answer in this case is what you see, it's a collage I created out of images from old catalogue pages for German industrial water heaters. I had found them at a flea market years before and bought them for some kind of future use. This of course was years before the internet. But how does someone think to do such a thing? I have no idea, it was pure intuition. The design process often is."[151]

Murakami has written about how important it was that Kidd has designed all of his American hardcover editions, and that when he first saw Kidd's cover of *The Elephant Vanishes* he was stunned by the innovation of the design—it reminded him of the gloomy machine featured in David Lynch's *The Elephant Man.*[152]

The Elephant Vanishes, Knopf, 1993

Looking back on that first book, Kidd muses, "It suddenly occurs to me that this cover doesn't look Japanese at all. Which is really weird, when you think about it, and arguably misleading. But I would also say that most of my designs for Haruki ever since also don't look overtly Japanese. Or similar to each other, for that matter. Which so far has seemed to work out okay for everyone involved."[153]

Chip Kidd in his office at Knopf

The "Winter Years"

The Elephant Vanishes—wrapped in its wonderfully strange Chip Kidd cover and duly crediting the translator of each story—was published in March 1993, a year and a half after the publication of *Hard-Boiled Wonderland and the End of the World*. Murakami now had one of the best literary publishing teams behind him.

He was working with top-class editors, designers, and marketing teams. But once again sales were—at least according to Murakami—poor.

"Both Gary and [Sonny] Mehta told me before the book was published not to get my hopes up because 'short story collections don't sell in the American market unless you are a very well-known author' but as they predicted, hardcover sales were discouraging. I remember when I did a book signing at the Princeton University Coop we only sold fifteen copies. These were my 'winter years' in the American market."[154]

Fisketjon, on the other hand, was less disappointed. He wrote in his email roundtable with Rubin and Gabriel that the book "enjoyed sales and reviews beyond most collections even by not-well-known American writers,"[155] and in a 2014 interview with Japan's national broadcaster NHK, he recalled that sales were around ten to twelve thousand copies.[156] (The Haruki Murakami office has a record of the hardcover edition selling 5,448 copies.)[157]

Fisketjon and Murakami obviously had different expectations. Fisketjon was likely comparing the numbers to other translated short story collections by writers who had yet to establish themselves in the U.S. Murakami was accustomed to seeing bigger numbers. "Whenever I published a book in Japan I was selling at least 100,000 copies, so I thought 10,000 copies was low. But I had been told that short story collections don't sell in America, and decided that it couldn't be helped, that I had to bank on the novel."[158]

The New York Times bestseller list had a small section beneath it titled "And Bear in Mind," where books picked up by the editorial team were listed. *The Elephant Vanishes* was included with a brief blurb: "Stories that render Japan as a country sunk in a spiritual torpor; bizarre events are frequent but little noted." This may not have been the ideal way to find one's way onto the bestseller page, but Murakami writes that being picked up by the mainstream press during these "winter years" served as moral support.[159]

The New York Times, which had published a harsh review of *Hard-Boiled Wonderland and the End of the World*, was much kinder to *The Elephant Vanishes*. Herbert Mitgang writes: "No question that Mr. Murakami is the most international voice among the current generation of Japanese novelists. He demonstrated that in 'A Wild Sheep Chase,' an imaginative novel in which modern and traditional forces clashed symbolically, as well as in the novel 'Hard-Boiled Wonderland and the End of the World.'" After touching on a few stories, Mitgang concludes: "Nearly all the short stories in 'The Elephant Vanishes' are fun to read, but Mr. Murakami seems better as a long-distance runner in fiction."[160] While a number of people, including his translators Rubin and Birnbaum, would disagree with Mitgang on this point, this is consistent with Murakami's self-evaluation that he is first and foremost a novelist.[161]

The review in *The Washington Post* was also relatively positive. It was by writer D. T. Max, who would several years later write a long piece in *The New York Times* about the complicated relationship between Raymond Carver and his editor Gordon Lish, titled "The Carver Chronicles" (which Murakami would later translate into Japanese).[162] Max acknowledged Murakami's talent, writing that "the cumulative effect is to remind us that, of Japan's finest post-war novelists, Murakami is certainly the one who, were he better known, would give American readers the most pleasure," but also predicted that "it is unlikely" that the book would "help Murakami's American cult grow into a crowd."[163]

Birnbaum and Luke's Last Dance

The publication of *The Elephant Vanishes* essentially marked Murakami's move from Kodansha International to Knopf. But before this decision was made, Kodansha International was already in the process of having *Dance Dance Dance* translated. Back on March 20, 1991, Luke had sent a fax to Murakami:

> Alfred Birnbaum wanted me to tell you that he would be very pleased to translate DANCE DANCE DANCE. He plans to go to China(!) after our work on HARD-BOILED WONDERLAND is done. And sometime after he is back, he should be getting started on DANCE DANCE DANCE. Good news, ne![164]

Murakami wrote back the same day agreeing that it was good news and saying, "I am so glad . . . that Alfred will do the translation of DANSU3" because "he is the best translator I could get."[165] Six months later, on September 13, 1991, a translation agreement was finalized between KI and Birnbaum with a deadline of April 20, 1992.[166]

Hard-Boiled Wonderland and the End of the World had been translated and edited in unusually close collaboration. (Birnbaum says that he has since tried to set up similar situations with other editors but that they have all refused.) With *Dance Dance Dance*, however, Luke and Birnbaum corresponded mostly by post and fax, because Birnbaum had moved abroad, first to London (from September 1992 to May 1993) and then to Myanmar (from June 1993 onward). Birnbaum recalls at one point reading through the proofs in a room in Myanmar with no electricity, which limited his working hours to daytime.[167]

By this time, Luke and Seward had also moved, from Kamakura to an upscale neighborhood in the center of Tokyo. "It was in Hirō, which was a little embarrassing, the address. (We used to tell people we lived in Ebisu, which then was unhip and we were on the border of.) An English friend was moving back to London, and we took over his lease on the first floor of a house. Semai [small], but very pleasant with a tiny yard and a hori kotatsu [sunken heater-table], a tiled shower and ofuro [bath] that had a pilot light, and the wc was wood-cased and suspended over the sit-down toilet. Alfred used to visit often. I'd forgotten all these details . . . A sudden old memory emerges (like in *Hard-Boiled*): Alfred biking over soon after we'd moved, maybe even the first night, with newly made pot of black beans."[168]

At this point Luke was working on a freelance basis. Despite the relative success of the first two Murakami books, Kodansha International had chosen not to renew Luke's contract. And although *Dance Dance Dance* bears the notation of being "translated and adapted," Birnbaum and Luke did not adapt it as heavily as they had *Hard-Boiled Wonderland and the End of the World*. It may have been that the physical distance between translator and editor did not afford them ease of collaboration, or it may have been a difference in the material itself.

The fact that they had worked together on two novels and at least a dozen short stories (a few remain unpublished) did ease the distance. *Dance Dance Dance* was a sequel to *A Wild Sheep Chase*, and narrative and character voice had been established with the first book. They also knew each other well by then and were able to discuss the work candidly.

Still, the fact that the new book was a sequel presented its own challenges. For one thing, it meant that voice and diction of the two books had to be kept consistent. Sounds and images were particularly important to Birnbaum, no less so than the novel's overall direction. The reader had to be able to hear and see even as they were reading words.

This focus on sounds and images is something Birnbaum shares with Murakami, who talks about having composed his first novel by first shooting scenes as if for a movie. As a translator himself, he appreciates that "it is not enough to find words that match: if images in the translated text are unclear, then the thoughts and feelings of the author are lost."[169] In the afterword to his translation of *The Great Gatsby*, he also suggests that translation is "fundamentally an act of kindness."

Reading the passages out loud during the translation process, which Murakami says he also did many years later when translating *Gatsby*, helped Birnbaum "hear" the book—for example, the voice of the memorable Sheep Man from *A Wild Sheep Chase* and *Dance Dance Dance*. The Sheep Man is a short, slouching, bowlegged man, dressed from head to toe in a sheep costume made of sheep fleece, genuine sheep horns, a hood with wire-enforced sheep ears, black leather mask, gloves, and socks. In *A Wild Sheep Chase*, the Sheep Man appears toward the end of the book to deliver bad news to the protagonist about his girlfriend with "the most perfect ears" who has suddenly—like many a woman in a Murakami novel—disappeared. "You'llneverseethatwomanagain," he says, his speech rendered without spaces.

In *Dance Dance Dance*, the Sheep Man reappears, greeting the protagonist by saying, "Beenalongtime." Speaking in the royal "we," the Sheep Man once again gives the protagonist some valuable insight:

It'stheonlyway.Wishwecouldexplainthingsbetter.Butwe-toldyouallwecould. Dance. Don'tthink. Dance. Danceyour-best, likeyourlifedependedonit. Yougottadance.[170]

Birnbaum says that he had struggled to translate the Sheep Man's distinct speech and that this was the voice he had "heard" when rereading earlier drafts of his translations.[171] "I couldn't imagine a crazy guy in a sheep costume talking normal. I saw him as a genuinely original quirky character, hence a chance to inject a bit of zany cartoonish humor (Murakami included a funny drawing of him, after all). I wanted something close to baaaaa yet still intelligible."[172]

On January 25, 1993, a year before the publication of *Dance Dance Dance*, Luke wrote in a fax to Murakami, "Right now, I'm trying to meet a preliminary deadline for DANCE 3."[173] Five months later, on June 25, he wrote to Murakami again:

Oh yes, got your manuscript of DANCE DANCE DANCE back today. Sorry that the timing was lousy and this stage of the process was so rushed for you. I'd like to think you can trust that all the effort that has gone into the translation will have created something you'd be pleased for. So far, the signs are good. Next week we go into k[i]yozuri [proofs].[174]

The editing process had taken at least half a year. In Luke's recollection, Murakami took part by suggesting minor changes[175] (and the letter referring to the manuscript seems to suggest this), but Murakami tells me he never checks the manuscripts of his English books.

"Reading galleys is a lot of work! I do read the book [the English translation] when it's published, but I don't really read the translations at the galley stage . . . But over the years I've always had assistants who are fluent in English, so I've had them read the translations and let me know if they come across anything very different [from the original]. In that sense I'm checking them, but I can't do it myself. I don't have the time. It's still true now . . . And the thing is, once I publish something [in Japanese] I don't reread it, so the more time goes by the more I forget. This means that when the translation comes out about three years later, and I start reading the book, I enjoy it. I really do! I read the book wondering what's going to happen next, and when I reach the end, my reaction is that it was a very good read. So even if things are changed in the translation, I probably wouldn't even notice it most of the time. My take is that it's all fine as long as the book is interesting."[176]

Murakami also says that he cannot really judge the quality of translations himself. "There are quite a few people who compare Philip's and Jay's translations and say they prefer one over the other. They say things like, 'Philip's is easier to read' or 'Jay's has a unique sense of humor,' but when I compare them I don't feel like there is any significant difference. It's my own work after all."[177]

Dance Dance Dance was published in January 1994 by Kodansha International in the U.S. and Hamish Hamilton in the U.K. One might have expected KI to have less investment in their Murakami books by this point, but in a memo to executives in 1993, Gillian Jolis, the marketing director, wrote that *Dance Dance Dance* could be Murakami's "break-out book" and requested that they increase the promotional budget.[178]

For the U.S. editions of *A Wild Sheep Chase* and *Hard-Boiled Wonderland and the End of the World*, Shigeo Okamoto had been commissioned to design new covers, but with *Dance Dance Dance* the Kodansha team decided to use the cover from the Japanese edition of the book, designed by Maki Sasaki.[179] The bio on the back of the book places emphasis on Murakami's relationship with *The New Yorker* and is otherwise simple and straightforward, which Luke says was done to reflect the fact that Murakami's reputation was on the rise.[180]

Dance Dance Dance, Kodansha International, 1994

Soon after the book was published, a reviewer for *Publishers Weekly* wrote, "All the hallmarks of Murakami's greatness are here: restless and sensitive characters, disturbing shifts into altered reality, silky smooth turns of phrase and a narrative with all the momentum of a roller coaster. If Mishima had ever learned the value of gentleness, this is the sort of page-turner he might have written."[181] *Los Angeles Times* staff writer Michael Harris also offered a positive review: "*Dance Dance Dance* successfully mixes genres—the philosophical quest, the topical satire, the whodunit. Murakami's characters, from kids to cops, are vividly drawn, no matter how unlikely the situations they encounter. The narrative voice—increasingly sure of itself as the speaker's mental health improves and he begins to take ethical stands and becomes capable of love—pulls like a diesel."[182]

The New York Times reviewed the book two days in a row. The review by Donna Rifkind that appeared on January 2 in the Sunday *Book Review* was on the critical side. While praising the humor and Birnbaum's translation, Rifkind wrote, "The book never quite decides what it wants to be. At times it reaches for the urbane whimsicality of Mr. Murakami's earlier novel, while elsewhere it attempts to be a more serious investigation into the depths of human identity. Knocked off balance by such vacillation, 'Dance Dance Dance' stumbles where it ought to glide."[183] The review that appeared in the Arts section the following day was by Herbert Mitgang—who, having at that point written relatively positive reviews of all but one of Murakami's books available in English translation outside Japan, was arguably one of the most influential reviewers (and supporters) of Murakami's early work. In "Looking for America, or Is It Japan?" Mitgang emphasized Murakami's originality: "Haruki Murakami, Japan's most popular novelist, writes metaphysical Far Easterns with a Western beat ... True, in his fiction there are echoes of Raymond Chandler, John Irving and Raymond Carver, but Mr. Murakami's mysterious plots and original characters are very much his own creation." Mitgang closes his review by referring to the translation: "Mr. Murakami's keen translator, Alfred Birnbaum, who keeps 'Dance Dance Dance' hopping, valiantly interprets the author's numerous references to American music, books and movies. In fact, he may even exceed the challenge now and then by dropping in a New Yorkism, as when the freelancer says: 'Before noon I drove to Aoyama to do shopping at the fancy-schmancy Kinokuniya supermarket.' Wonder how you say fancy-schmancy in Japanese?"[184]

The original Japanese for "fancy-schmancy Kinokuniya supermarket" is simply "Kinokuniya." When I ask Birnbaum about this, he shrugs. "Well, Kinokuniya was a fancy-schmancy super-market, wasn't it? I certainly never shopped there."[185]

The Beginnings of a Backlist

The reviews of *Dance Dance Dance* may have been positive, but according to Minato Asakawa, who was heading the Kodansha America office at the time, it, too, did not become the "break-out book" that Jolis had hoped it would be.[186]

Luke's recollections are similar to those of Asakawa. "If sales are any indication, yeah, it might have been a disappointment. It doesn't have the form or construction or tightness of his previous work . . . I liked it the least of the three I worked on, but it does seem to me that this 'other' dimension that Haruki has gone on to explore and is known for is established here . . . and it's what readers continue, on some level, to respond to."[187]

Yet hardcover sales don't tell the whole story. Prior to publica-tion of *Dance Dance Dance* in hardcover, Vintage had obtained pa-perback rights to *A Wild Sheep Chase* and *Hard-Boiled Wonderland and the End of the World*, printing 20,000 copies of each title.[188] And when Vintage published the paperback edition of *Dance Dance Dance* a year later, *The New York Times* picked it up as one of its "New and Noteworthy Paperbacks" and described it as "a Japanese 'Twin Peaks.'"[189]

In any analysis of print runs and sales, there is a tendency to focus on hardcover figures, but true bestsellers are made in pa-perback (and more recently in e-book form). And as Murakami's editors in the U.S. and U.K. have acknowledged, backlist sales of Murakami's books increase significantly when a new book is published—a trend, it seems, that was already being established in the mid-nineties.

Murakami is aware of this. "Books become longsellers in paperback ... So I'm really pleased when my books come out in trade paperback. And in my case they are published by Vintage, and they are strong."[190]

5

The Wind-Up Bird
Chronicle

When you read Haruki Murakami, you're reading me, at least ninety-five per cent of the time.

—JAY RUBIN, interview in
The New Yorker, 2013[1]

Becoming a *"New Yorker* Author" 2

Robert Gottlieb stepped down as editor of *The New Yorker* in June 1992. He went back to Knopf, and rather than taking on a leadership role, he chose to take a position that would allow him to edit only the books that he wanted to work on.[2]

Fortunately for Murakami, the departure of Gottlieb first and Linda Asher several years later did not prove detrimental to his relationship with the magazine. After publishing Philip Gabriel's translation of "Barn Burning" just months after Gottlieb's departure, *The New Yorker* did not publish another story by Murakami for nearly three years. Nevertheless, in 1993 the magazine asked him to sign a contract that gave the magazine first right of refusal for the English translations of his stories. Murakami signed without hesitation.[3]

Murakami's position as a "*New Yorker* author" was further cemented by his inclusion in a photo feature on writers associated with the magazine, with portraits by the celebrated photographer Richard Avedon. Fourteen fiction writers were brought together in Manhattan (and three others in London), and the resulting images were published in the June 27, 1994, issue alongside a short article by senior editor Daniel Menaker.

Murakami has written about the photo shoot in an essay published soon after he moved from Princeton to serve as writer-in-residence at Tufts University in Massachusetts.

> The authors who gathered for the shoot included (around ten) names familiar to the magazine including John Updike, Ann Beattie, Bobbie Ann Mason, Jamaica Kincaid, Michael Chabon, Nicholson Baker, William Maxwell.[4]

When the Japanese edition of *The Elephant Vanishes* was published in 2005, Murakami once again mentioned the photo shoot in his foreword, emphasizing the fact that he was the only one in the group (in New York) that was not from North America, and added an anecdote about how John Updike had come up to him after the shoot and said, "I always read your work. They are all terrific."[5]

Avedon's subjects included people from all walks of life:

celebrities, models, political leaders, murderers. Geoff Dyer—whose collection of vignettes about jazz Murakami has translated into Japanese—writes in an essay about the photographer that because all the people who entered Avedon's studio were stars, "even if you weren't famous when you went in, you sort of were when you came out." Dyer adds that "[to] be photographed by Avedon thus afforded a double means of *recognition*. Consequently, people turned up for their session as if for a once-in-a-lifetime opportunity, almost, as the saying goes, for a rendezvous with destiny."[6]

At the time of the photo shoot, John Updike had been writing for *The New Yorker* for nearly forty years—he would ultimately have almost one hundred and fifty stories as well as five-hundred-odd reviews and poems and critical essays published in the magazine (including, later in 2005, a review of Murakami's novel *Kafka on the Shore*).[7] Ann Beattie had been contributing stories to the magazine for nearly thirty years (forty-eight of them would later be collected and published in 2010 as *The New Yorker Stories*). Alice Munro had almost thirty stories published in the fifteen years she had been contributing. William Maxwell had not only contributed his own short stories but also edited many of them during his forty-year career as a fiction editor there.[8] Michael Chabon, who was one of the two youngest writers in the group at just thirty years old and had been writing professionally for only five years, already had a dozen stories in the magazine. By contrast, Murakami had had just a handful of stories published and was clearly the least "*New Yorker*" of the seventeen "*New Yorker* authors."

As with the "first-look" deal, the Avedon photo shoot had been arranged under the editorship of Tina Brown, who before coming to *The New Yorker* had made her mark by helping to increase *Vanity Fair*'s circulation during her nearly ten-year tenure as editor, in part by featuring photographs of celebrities on the front covers, including, famously, a nude photograph of a pregnant Demi Moore by Annie Leibowitz in 1991.[9] At *The New Yorker*, Brown hired Avedon and began to publish photographs for the first time in the magazine's history.[10] Brown has also been credited with attempting to bring ethnic diversity to a magazine that was once described by John Updike as being "race blind."[11] It is not clear if the desire to portray diversity played some part in the decision to incorporate Murakami into what was otherwise an exclusively Anglophone portrait of *New Yorker* authors, but scholar and translator Stephen Snyder suggests that "Murakami, strategically positioned between Minimalists Bobbie Ann Mason and Ann Beattie . . . serves as a safe and familiar marker of the foreign."[12]

What is clear is that such visual portrayals can have a significant impact on the public image of an author. Murakami makes appearances only rarely, and almost never in Japan. Most of the available images of the author are by photographers whose names also carry and impart high levels of prestige—like Avedon, Marion Ettlinger, and Nobuyoshi Araki. This, along with *The New Yorker*'s reputation and influence—its reported circulation was around 600,000 in 1991 and would surpass one million in 2004—meant that Murakami's fame now extended far beyond the normal reaches of literary culture.[13]

Murakami's work began to be published in *The New Yorker* fairly regularly again after Bill Buford was appointed fiction and literary editor in April 1995. Buford had been editor of the British literary magazine *Granta* for sixteen years before being hired by Tina Brown to revitalize the publication of fiction in the magazine, which Brown herself admitted had suffered after she had taken over.[14]

Murakami was already on Buford's radar. Buford—who had coined the term "dirty realism" in an issue of *Granta* in 1983 and helped increase the readership of American writers like Raymond Carver in the U.K.—published Alfred Birnbaum's translation of the Murakami short story "Lederhosen" (in significantly abridged form) several years before he moved to *The New Yorker*.[15] And on July 31, 1995, a few months after Buford became head of the fiction department, *The New Yorker* published another story, "The Zoo Attack." During Buford's seven-and-a-half-year tenure, the magazine published seven works of fiction by Murakami, an average of about one piece a year, including two excerpts from the novel *The Wind-Up Bird Chronicle*, two stories later published in the collection *after the quake*, and three stories eventually collected in the anthology *Blind Willow, Sleeping Woman*. Under Brown and Buford, *The New Yorker* also published a long profile of Murakami by Ian Buruma titled "Becoming Japanese" (December 23, 1996), which included information about the upcoming publication of *The Wind-Up Bird Chronicle*. Murakami has suggested that these features encouraged Knopf to invest more heavily in the book's promotion and helped set the stage for publication in October 1997.[16]

Murakami also mentions that, for his part, he created a setup by which he gives translators half his contributor's fee when one of his stories is published. "According to my system, translators [of my books] don't receive royalties from publishers. Instead I buy the translation from them. And I keep all of the rights. But when a translation is sold to a magazine I make sure to compensate them—give them a kind of bonus. That's why I've always had a good relationship with my translators. Philip, Jay, Ted, I've been working with them all for a long time. *The New Yorker* pays really well ... So I think the translators did pretty well for themselves."[17]

A Changing of the Guard

By the fall of 1992, all of the novellas and novels Murakami had written in Japan had seen publication in English or were forthcoming. He had written two novels while in Princeton that he could now proceed with: *Kokkyō no minami, taiyo no nishi* (*South of the Border, West of the Sun*) and *Nejimakidori kuronikuru* (*The Wind-Up Bird Chronicle*). Murakami was convinced that the latter was stronger.[18] The first volume of the novel was also starting to be serialized in the literary magazine *Shinchō* and set to continue through the summer of 1993, after which it would be published as a book. But Murakami felt he could not afford to wait until the novel was published in book form in Japan. He began arranging for an English translation of *Nejimakidori kuronikuru* even before the original began to be serialized in *Shinchō*.[19]

The two obvious choices for translators were Alfred Birnbaum and Jay Rubin, as they had both worked on *The Elephant Vanishes*. But when I first speak to Birnbaum about this time, he tells me that he was "never asked to translate *The Wind-Up Bird Chroni-*

cle." Once management shifted from KI to ICM and Knopf, he says, he had basically "been dropped" from Murakami's English translation team.[20]

A letter from Murakami to Luke in mid-September 1992 gives a different picture of that transitional moment. Murakami writes to Luke that he had discussed the matter with Alfred while in Mexico: "He [Birnbaum] told me he was not going to do translation anymore at least for a couple of years or so because he's got a lot of things to do, his own things." Murakami adds that this was "sad news" because Birnbaum was a "fabulous translator" and that the three of them had been getting along very well. He also adds that Birnbaum "is not merely a translator" and has his own way of "express[ing] something."[21] Murakami concludes by saying that he will ask Rubin to translate *The Wind-Up Bird Chronicle*, and that he hopes too to identify younger translators for his work, asking Luke to help him evaluate the translations in that event. About the potential new translators, Murakami writes that while they might not be as good as Alfred, he had to consider all possibilities. Murakami, it seems, was not looking "to drop" Birnbaum, and was only eager to keep publishing in English in a timely manner.

In July 1992, when Murakami and Birnbaum were in Mexico, Birnbaum was completing drafts of the translations for stories in *The Elephant Vanishes* as well as the novel *Dance Dance Dance*. Birnbaum had also just decided to pursue an MA in Burmese studies at SOAS at the University of London. It would have been during this hectic time that he was asked—if he was asked—about the possibility of translating a work that was yet to be published even in Japanese.

Rubin shares his recollection of this time in *Haruki Murakami and the Music of Words*:

> Having translated all the long works up to *Dance Dance Dance*, Alfred was feeling justifiably burnt out by the time Murakami started writing *The Wind-Up Bird Chronicle*. In the meantime, I had translated some of the short stories and was eager to do more when Haruki said he needed a translator for his next novel. The timing of Alfred's fatigue couldn't have been better for me. Alfred not only stopped translating Murakami for a while, he left Japan to live and work in Myanmar, marrying a Burmese woman.[22]

Regarding his decision to "start translating it [*The Wind-Up Bird Chronicle*] into English while the first volume of it was still being serialized," Rubin writes:

> Of course, as a scholar, it would have made sense for me to have waited to see how the book turned out, to judge whether it was an important part of Murakami's oeuvre, to decide whether Murakami was superior to his contemporaries, or if he was genuinely a spokesman for his time or his generation and the work was sure to enter the canon, but by then I'd be dead, and so would Murakami ... I suppose I might be accused of having betrayed my responsibilities as a scholar by involving myself in "the industry," but it has been an adventure I'm glad I didn't miss.[23]

Murakami, in retrospect, tells a similar story: "Around the time, Alfred was getting busy with his own work and couldn't find the time to translate longer works, so I was grateful that Jay entered the picture."[24]

When I bring this up when I next speak to Birnbaum, he acknowledges that his memory is fuzzy and it is possible that it had happened that way. The next day he writes me an email:

> Your asking about the Mexico trip with Murakami really brought those years into focus and let me see in hindsight how volatile a transition period it was for me. I guess I shut it out of my memory, consciously or not, because it was such a troubled, lost, disruptive passage. Hope your late-30s are more stable.[25]

Birnbaum's hesitation about making a long-term commitment to Murakami in turn had an effect on Luke's prospects. Responding to Murakami's mid-September letter, Luke wrote:

> About who should be the next translator of your novel, if there is no need to decide right away, can I suggest that you wait as long as possible. I agree, by the way—you and Alfred and I were a terrific team.[26]

By this time, however, the decision seems to have already been made.

In a September 18 letter Rubin wrote to Murakami:

Thanks for rushing me the copy of Shinchō. I'm very interested in the novel and almost surely want to translate it, but let me share my reactions with you about what I've read so far.

I was initially disappointed to find that so little of the first chapter had changed from the story, which was not one of my favorites. Since Alfred translated it so well, I wonder whether there will be difficulties in re-translating . . . By the time I reached the end of Chapter 1, I realized I liked the original Nejimaki-dori story better than I had remembered, and knowing now that it is the introduction to a novel, there seemed to be more emphasis on the potential for expanding on the husband and wife's relationship.

Chapter 2 then immediately proceeded to do this—and very effectively. My favorite part so far is the argument about toilet paper and paper towels: in some ways, it seems to be examining Boku's attitude toward his wife more deeply than earlier works have done—which was a theme I enjoyed the hints of in "Pan'ya saishūgeki." . . .

It was strangely disconcerting to meet Kanō Malta in Chapter 3 since I last saw her sister as some kind of ghost in that story . . . I guess I'm uncomfortable with these psychic elements and am worried how the book is going to develop. If the Malta parts begin to take over, I may find myself not enjoying the book as much, and that could affect my translating . . .

So, yes, I am very interested, and am flattered that you would ask me to take on a full-length novel.[27]

Murakami wrote back a week later to say that the first six installments were already available as galleys, and while he was still making changes, he should be able to send them within a few days. At the same time, he told Rubin that he expected the supernatural elements of the story to take on greater prominence as the novel progressed, so Rubin should not hesitate to let him know if he was not interested in taking on the translation of such a project.[28] Rubin replied the same day:

Thanks for today's fax. I'm looking forward to reading as much of Nejimakidori chronicle as you can send me. I'm also expecting to translate it. Especially since you have left my choice of [which] stories [to translate] entirely to me (and seemed to prefer it that way), I guess I feel uncomfortable committing to such a big project without reading it first, but I fully expect to want to do it. In general, I'd say I'm much more comfortable with hints of the unexplainable impinging on everyday life (as in "The Elephant Vanishes") than with out-and-out ghost stories (the way Nezumi enters late in Hitsuji as a ghost that doesn't reflect in the mirror). I was absolutely mesmerized by the "Sekai no owari" chapters of Sekai no owari and "Odoru Kobito" remains a favorite.[29]

A few weeks later, Rubin wrote to Murakami to thank him for having had Kodansha send him a copy of *Kokkyō no minami, taiyō no nishi* (*South of the Border, West of the Sun*), which had just been published in Japan. He wrote, "The 17-year old protagonist interests me much less than the cast of characters in Nejimaki-dori kuronikuru" and that he was "looking forward to reading the Kuronikuru pages when you get the chance to send them. The idea of translating an entire novel of yours is exciting."[30] Two days later, Rubin writes Murakami again to inform him that he has read up to part 8 of *Nejimakidori kuronikuru* (in proofs sent to him by Shinchōsha) and to confirm that he wants to translate the novel.[31]

The "changing of the guard" also coincided with a shift in Murakami's own writing. Murakami thinks Birnbaum preferred "pop stuff," a sensibility that Murakami seemed to be leaving behind. "My style has changed from around 1990. My prose has become more meticulous, which means Alfred's tendency to translate freely can be a problem. I want my work to be translated properly. But back when I was writing *A Wild Sheep Chase* and *Hard-Boiled Wonderland* my style wasn't as established so I felt that it couldn't be helped if things were changed a bit. At least back then."[32]

Reflecting upon this switch, Murakami is matter-of-fact. In the forty years he has been writing, he says, "there are many people who were able to come along with me for a certain period but gradually were unable to keep up. There's nothing you can do about that . . . Sometimes you just have to part ways. But I've seen and talked to Alfred many times since. I went to his wedding in Myanmar [in 1998] too."[33]

Books 1 and 2 of *Nejimakidori kuronikuru* (*The Wind-Up Bird*

Chronicle) were published simultaneously in separate volumes in Japan in April 1994, followed by Book 3 in August 1995. Rubin's translation combined these three volumes into a single book, which was published in the U.S. in October 1997 and in the U.K. the following year. This was three and a half years after the publication of the English translation of *Dance Dance Dance*, despite the early start Rubin had had. Given that Murakami had been hoping to publish a book a year in the U.S., a pace that would be extraordinary for even a prolific writer in English, those years must have felt long to him. If he had waited until Book 3 had been published in Japanese to start the translation process, the gap between novels would have become even longer, and the momentum generated from his initial success in the late eighties and early nineties could have been lost. That Murakami secured this translation seems to me an indication of his ambition and his sense of the moment.

The Long Goodbye

In the years after Murakami moved from KI to Knopf, Birnbaum co-translated, with Philip Gabriel, one of Murakami's nonfiction books (*Underground: The Tokyo Gas Attack and the Japanese Psyche*, published in 2000) and a story for *The New Yorker* ("Folklore of Our Times" in 2003), but he never got the opportunity to translate any of his novels again. Birnbaum tells me that the "short break" he wanted to take turned out to be a "long goodbye."[34]

"The question about Murakami & co distancing themselves from me is complicated and my feelings obviously have changed over the years—it's been a long time—but to try to reconstruct what I thought at the time: the real issue at first was whether or not it was a simple misunderstanding/miscommunication, some dissatisfaction with me or more insidious motives (but on the part of whom?). Of course I felt bitter and betrayed and generally let down, as you say, but more than anything it was just confusing. What they call 'ghosting' these days. All communication just stopped and no one answered my letters (before the age of emails, and I didn't have a current phone number—anyway I'm no good over the phone). Of course I did send occasional queries to the Murakami Office saying I'd be happy to do some translations if/when, but all I ever got back was an officious 'we'll let you know'—never anything personal. Contact with Binky was a one-way street, from her side. But now, in retrospect, I guess I'm glad I don't have to do his catalogue any more. The later stuff keeps getting worse and worse, at least to me. Sour grapes perhaps, but I don't even read him anymore."[35]

When I ask Luke about Birnbaum's falling out of favor as Murakami's translator, he says, "Alfred does not remember, and I do not know full details myself. But two things: Alfred wanted to do other creative things (as Haruki mentions Alfred saying to him), and also Alfred was not a slave to schedule, which in publishing one MUST be . . . Maybe part of the reason they went looking for somebody else . . . I was hoping Alfred would stick with Haruki, thought he could do well by him, and Haruki by Alfred, but Alfred had his mind elsewhere and he had not the required discipline to keep at it."[36]

Dance Dance Dance was the last Murakami book Birnbaum and Luke worked on together. Their Murakami collaboration lasted just five years, though they have continued to be involved in promoting Japanese literature in translation. While in Myanmar, Birnbaum translated Miyuki Miyabe's mystery novel *Kasha* (translated as *All She Was Worth*), which was published by Kodansha International in 1996. He has also gone on to translate a number of works by Natsuki Ikezawa. From 2004 to 2005 he also served as an advisor to the Japanese Literature Publication and Promotion (JLPP) program sponsored by the Japanese Cultural Affairs Agency.

As he sits feeding the fire in his living room, I ask him whether he planned to continue translating Japanese literature (he had recently also done some translations from the Burmese), and he said that he might if he came across a work he liked, then added, "I've done Haruki and Natsuki, so perhaps I'll try my hand at something by an Akiki."[37] (It's typical Birnbaum humor: Haruki means "spring trees," Natsuki "summer trees," and Akiki would mean "autumn trees"—except that there is no such name). He has since gone on to translate a novel by the Japanese writer Toshihiko Yahagi, which was acquired by MacLehose Press.

Once Luke completed *Dance Dance Dance*, few projects from KI came his way. "Working in Tokyo in the late 80s/early 90s was a true adventure, new, different, often thrilling ... But working for corporate KI was not the easiest fit. I brayed against the old-world rules and conventions of the place, and I'm sure I was an asshole about it. In any case, my departure from KI was by mutual agreement. I was wanting to return to New York, and they were ready for that to happen. At the time, they were more ready than I was."[38]

"After KI, I returned to New York (with cat). I'd been out

of the country for six years. Any cred I'd had was gone, had no currency. I had many interviews, people were intrigued about life in Japan, but I just couldn't land a full-time editorial job. Several contributing things; very bad economic times; no real interest in Japanese or Asian fiction or nonfiction, not like now. (Also, Gary was handling Haruki, and while Haruki was now represented by Binky, he hadn't broken through on a significant level so the interest wasn't there—and that'd been my so-called calling card.) . . . Bob Gottlieb even recommended me to Sonny Mehta . . . Yes, how come he didn't hire me?! Well, even as he was a great early supporter of my dear old friend Maxine Kingston, fiction translated from East Asia was barely beginning to make inroads. And translation was still a dirty secret. Anyway, I wish I had got to work with him, but no matter now . . . Robert and I then bought that apartment you visited us in—those were bad economic times, remember, so it was affordable with yen; place was a shambles, had to be totally renovated, so my time was completely taken up by that. When the place was done, I got offered a position at Morrow. The editor-in-chief had an Asian line of books (but no Japanese), but mostly what I did was general fiction and nonfiction, including Colleen McCullough (of *Thorn Birds* fame), Tom Wicker (on race in the US), a book on staying married(!) that I inherited . . . Morrow was in flux, so when a new publisher was hired and the editor-in-chief left the company, I too was out. That was my woeful period of why-did-I-ever-choose-this-ridiculous-profession."[39]

Since being let go by Morrow, Luke has primarily worked as a freelance editor and publishing consultant. For almost a decade he did not work on any Japanese fiction, but when the Japanese government launched the aforementioned JLPP program in 2002, he began editing Japanese works in English translation again. Luke has also been involved in compiling anthologies (including an anthology for which I was co-editor and a *Granta* issue devoted to Japan) and advising various programs involving the exchange of writers and translators. He says that these are all opportunities that "came my way thanks to my work with Haruki and Alfred."[40]

When Birnbaum brought Murakami to the attention of KI in the mid-eighties, Murakami was not the national celebrity that he would become in Japan a few years later, nor the international celebrity he is now. Given the massive success of *Norwegian Wood* in Japan, however, it seems quite likely that Murakami's work would have eventually been translated into English. But Birnbaum and Luke's achievement was in getting Murakami published when he was (if this was ten years later Murakami might have missed the chance to become a "front-runner"), prioritizing translations that they believed would increase the chances of his books winning acceptance by Western readers, and positioning his work as "literature" to be taken seriously.

This strategy in itself is not unusual; neither is it unusual to see such translator-author partnerships come to an end. The American translator Norman Thomas di Giovanni and Jorge Luis Borges provide another example. After a period of close collaboration between 1967 and 1972—and despite the fact that these translations they produced together helped Borges achieve international fame—the author ended their collaboration.[41] When Borges's wife sold the English translation rights to a different publisher after the author's death, the Giovanni translations went out of print.[42]

Unlike Giovanni's Borges translations, most of Birnbaum's translations of Murakami's fiction remain in print today, comprising an important part of Murakami's body of work in English, although a number of translations, including *Hear the Wind Sing*, *Pinball, 1973*, *Norwegian Wood*, and several short stories, have been replaced by newer translations by Jay Rubin, Philip Gabriel, and Ted Goossen. It is entirely conceivable that the earlier translations that established Murakami's voice in English will gradually fade from Murakami's oeuvre, especially given the relatively unusual nature of his agreements with translators. While authors generally retain copyright of the translated editions of their work, the translation copyright, at least in the U.S. and U.K., usually remains with the translator. With Murakami's work in English, however, the author retains the translation copyright. In other words, the translation is essentially a "work-for-hire," and the translator has no say in how it may or may not be used. And while some of the earlier English translations of Murakami's works published by Kodansha International gave the English translation copyright to Alfred Birnbaum, these rights are also now retained by the author; Birnbaum sold the rights to Murakami at the author's request.

In *The Scandals of Translation*, Lawrence Venuti discusses Milan Kundera, who famously rewrote the English translations of his own works. Venuti gives the example of Kundera's English (re)translation of his novel *The Joke*, which the author "cobbled together not just from his own English and French renderings, but also from the 'many fine solutions' and the 'great many faithful renderings and good formulations' in the previous translations." It is not clear, according to Venuti, if the translators gave Kundera permission to reuse parts of their translations to patch together a new version; in any case, the title page does not give recognition to the translators.[43]

Though Murakami himself has to date made no attempts to rewrite his English translations the way Kundera has, the fact that he retains translation rights does leave open the possibility. Murakami also tells me that he is particularly keen on seeing new versions of the works originally translated by Birnbaum for the American market.

"The publisher isn't really hot on the idea of changing ships part way through, since many people have read the books in the current translations. But for example, I've done translations of *The Catcher in the Rye* and *The Great Gatsby*. I think that there is a need to publish new translations after a certain period of time has passed. I think you need to adjust to the times. I feel that Alfred's translations were highly effective when they came out, but at this point I think it would be better if the translations are a little more faithful to the original."[44]

When I ask Lexy Bloom, who replaced Fisketjon as the editor responsible for Murakami's translations at Knopf starting with *1Q84* in 2011, if there was any chance they would change their minds and publish new translations, she responds, "Basically, we did not feel that the demand was great enough to warrant the publication of the unabridged editions, since they were already such classics, and so beloved by readers here in their current forms. I wasn't aware that Haruki felt strongly about it, however, and obviously if he continues to feel this way, we'd be open to reconsidering."[45]

Birnbaum suggests that he has no desire to see his "literary fame" survive him and that he has "never had the illusion that [he] was creating anything that wasn't disposable."[46] When I mention this to Luke and ask him how he feels, he responds: "I don't know if I thought about 'creating something that would last' as much as I was hoping to create something that would make an impact. But then, to varying degrees, I feel similarly about every book that I work on that I care about. Murakami was special, I really cared about his books that I worked on, and I really cared about him, so I was personally gratified that the impact we (Alfred, KI publishing staff in US and Japan, KI resources, and me) managed to make helped start the Murakami engine. But you know—and I don't mean to sound like 'poor ignored me'—editors are largely unseen and unacknowledged, we stand behind the writer and the translator, behind the publisher and the agent, so the gratification is quiet and private. Which is all right—it's the job description— and maybe why I do it too. 'Lasting' probably falls in the same category. But re Murakami's lasting, it's indisputable he's touched a chord with a significant international readership. As with any writer with any readership at all, it is in the context of time that such success is achieved. And for the moment, at least, and surely for a bit longer, given the ripple effect of readership, his writing will be around and he will be read. It is, I think, by now a matter of fact."[47]

Elmer Luke and Alfred Birnbaum at the Albany airport in 2012

The Windup to the Publication of
The Wind-Up Bird Chronicle

The editing of the English edition of *The Wind-Up Bird Chronicle* had started, arguably, in November 1990, seven years before the publication of its hardcover edition, when Linda Asher and others had prepared the story "The Windup Bird and Tuesday's Women" for publication in *The New Yorker*. When Asher found out that the novel based on the first Murakami short story she had published was being translated into English, she asked Murakami to select a section for excerpting in the magazine.[48]

In a 2010 interview, Murakami said that, in response to Asher's request, he discussed the matter with Rubin and chose the excerpt.[49] But when I ask him about this, he tells me that he "had almost no interest in excerpts" and had left the process to Rubin. "If they tell me they want to excerpt a certain section I have no choice than to say that sounds fine. As you know, in Japan there isn't the practice of publishing novel excerpts."[50]

Rubin isn't clear on whether he discussed the selection with Murakami in person or over the phone. But he is clear that the choices they ended up making were from his favorite parts of the book and could also be read as stand-alone stories.[51]

Asher similarly says that she has very little memory of her work on the excerpts. "I don't recall any of the doings or my work on the Murakami excerpts—except for the great pleasure and interest I felt in the process and his writing and the interchanges with the translators."[52]

The first excerpt of *The Wind-Up Bird Chronicle* was published in *The New Yorker* in the summer of 1995. Titled "The Zoo Attack," it was an abridgement of the tenth chapter of Book 3 of the Japanese edition of the novel.

In book form—in both the Japanese original and the English translation—the chapter is called "The Zoo Attack (or, A Clumsy Massacre)." When I compare the books to the story, I see that around 120 lines have been left out of the story. For the most part, the cuts are to passages that do not immediately make sense within the parameters of the excerpt—the interaction between Nutmeg Akasaka and Tōru Okada, for instance, the calls of the Wind-Up Bird, etc. In other words, a new story—one that does not exist in the Japanese—was crafted from a chapter in the book especially for *The New Yorker*. This practice is not unusual at the magazine and was repeated with *1Q84* in 2011 (by combining three chapters) and *Killing Commendatore* in 2019 (by combining two chapters).

The later Murakami excerpts for *The New Yorker* were created by Deborah Treisman, the magazine's fiction editor since 2002 (and Murakami's editor since late 1997). However, in the case of *The Wind-Up Bird Chronicle* excerpts, Rubin suggests that he must have been the one who undertook the larger piecing together of the story and that Asher's editorial suggestions were primarily at the word and sentence level.[53]

Asher recalls "finding that the two segments we published were almost incontestably suited in form to the then quite strict standard of 'short fiction' the magazine demanded; novel sections were rarely manipulable to that standard at that time. And I felt strongly that the political and historical episodes represented material rarely seen from that part of the world and would have significant impact."[54]

"The Zoo Attack" was published in an issue marking the fiftieth anniversary of the end of World War II. Other pieces included "Did the Bomb End the War?" by Murray Sayle and an excerpt from *Hiroshima* by John Hersey, which *The New Yorker* first published in 1964, devoting a whole issue to the piece after other publications had turned it down. The cover featured an illustration by Lorenzo Mattotti, in which a woman carrying a child is escaping from a mushroom cloud.

A year and a half later, *The New Yorker* published the profile of Murakami titled "Becoming Japanese" by Ian Buruma, in which he wrote that *The Wind-Up Bird Chronicle* "is different from anything else he [Murakami] has written: it reeks not of butter but of blood." He introduces scenes from the book: those in which soldiers shoot dozens of bullets into bears left in an abandoned zoo and reflect afterwards that "it was so much easier to kill humans on the battlefield than animals in cages"; a later scene in which the soldiers kill Chinese prisoners by thrusting "their bayonets into the Chinese men with tremendous force . . . they twisted the blades so as to rip the men's internal organs, then thrust the tips upward." Buruma also emphasizes Murakami's "rediscovery of Japan's history" and quotes Murakami as saying, "I take war very seriously" and "the most important thing is to face our history, and that means the history of the war."[55]

In January 1997, a month after Buruma's profile, the magazine published a second excerpt. This was an edited version of chapter 28, "The Wind-Up Bird Chronicle #8 (or, A Second Clumsy Massacre)" from Book 3 of the Japanese original (chapter 26 in the English translation). Examining drafts and proofs,

I notice that the excerpt seems to leave out details that humanize the veterinarian, the main protagonist of the section, and that most of these changes have been suggested by the magazine. One example is a passage about the vivid blue mark on the veterinarian's cheek:

> While still a child, he hated this mark, this imprint that only he, and no one else, had to bear upon his flesh. He wanted to die whenever the other children taunted him or strangers stared at him. If only he could have cut away that part of his body with a knife! But as he matured, he gradually came to a quiet acceptance of the mark on his face that would never go away. And this may have been a factor that helped form his attitude of resignation in all matters having to do with fate.

These sentences have been cut in the draft sent to Rubin on December 16, 1996.[56] In a new draft created two days later on December 18 and sent to him as proofs on December 31, passages in which the veterinarian is thinking longingly of his family have also been cut:[57]

> A hollow quiet ruled the house. This was no longer the home he loved, the place where he belonged.

> For them, he would gladly have given up his life. Indeed, he had often imagined doing so, and the death he had endured for them in his mind seemed the sweetest deaths imaginable.

The title for the magazine excerpt also evolved over multiple passes. In Rubin's first draft, it is "The Wind-Up Bird Chronicle #8 (or, A Second Clumsy Massacre)," a relatively straightforward translation of the original Japanese, which would eventually be used as the chapter title of the book in English. On December 16, *The New Yorker* has suggested the alternative title "Clean Up Hitting."[58] Two days later, presumably following discussions with Rubin, the title has become "Another Way to Die," a phrase that has been lifted from the piece.[59] Sometime after January 2, the subtitle has been added: "Last orders of a Japanese officer in Manchuria during the final moments of the Second World War."[60]

The two excerpts and the profile frame *The Wind-Up Bird Chronicle* as a serious work of literature that engages with Japan's responsibility in World War II. This emphasis would be reproduced in publishing copy, reviews, and other materials related to the book.

A "Salable" Book

Murakami had initially planned on ending *The Wind-Up Bird Chronicle* after two volumes. But he says that after some time had passed he had gotten the urge to write a third volume.[61] Rubin ended up spending nearly five years translating and editing the book.

For him it didn't feel like a long time. "It's new every day and it's fun to plunge into a text and go through this process that finally you can't entirely explain. It isn't just thinking through a series of ideas. A lot of it is coming up with images and phraseology that you couldn't have imagined coming up with until you do it. So that little bit of mystery keeps it fun."[62]

But there was one problem with the translation Rubin produced. At approximately 290,000 words, it was far longer than the 125,000 words initially proposed in a draft contract with the publisher.[63] "Knopf had a maximum figure in their brains about how long the book could be to be salable at that stage of his career," Rubin writes in *Haruki Murakami and the Music of Words*. "Concerned at what an editor might do to the text," Rubin submitted two versions.[64] The first was a complete translation; the second a version that, in Rubin's estimation, was abridged by 25,000 words. The publisher went with the abridged version.[65]

Murakami, unsurprisingly, says he would have preferred not to have the novel abridged. But he says that he did not feel that he could express his opinion firmly. "Back then I had just become a Knopf author so couldn't say much. When they said it was too long I told myself it couldn't be helped."[66]

Rubin made the majority of cuts and changes at the end of Book Two and beginning of Book Three. He chose sections that he believed were "rendered almost irrelevant by Book Three" and rearranged material that he thought was not "meant to be as chaotic" as he had found it, and created a translation that he says was "tighter and cleaner" than the original.[67] His abridged version left out chapters 15, 18, and parts of chapter 17 of Book 2; combined the first chapter of Book 2 with other chapters and moved the second chapter to later in the book; and removed chapter 26 (although, as Rubin himself has suggested, the editing is "much more complex" than that).[68] Interestingly, the final paragraph of his Book 2 combines the final paragraph of chapter 17 with several sentences from (the deleted) chapter 18, creating an ending to Book 2 that has quite a different feel from the original Japanese.

Rubin has donated his papers related to the translation of *The Wind-Up Bird Chronicle* to the Lilly Library at Indiana University. When I look at the book proofs and correspondence available for viewing in 2018, I don't notice any major edits to Rubin's abridged translation. His letters to Fisketjon, Robert Glover (Fisketjon's assistant at the time), and Debra Helfand (the production editor and later copy chief) do show that smaller editorial changes continued to be made over half a year, until quite close to the publication date of October 1997:

March 31, 1997

Dear Rob (if I may)

Here are all the pages of Book One, including front matter. I've put some information on p. iv. There are a few questions still unresolved, mostly small, but some more substantial.

1. I am still not satisfied with the opening paragraph. Too many "was"es. One question I discussed with Gary was the appropriateness of giving the opera title in English to bring out the bird image, and we tend to prefer English.

*

There are several passages I have marked "OMIT(HM)" to indicate that Haruki specifically designated these as deletable. I tend to agree with him, but Gary may feel differently.

*

April 17, 1997

Dear Rob and Gary:

I assume you got the pages of Book One I sent on March 31. Here are Books Two and Three. I don't have any major quarrels with the editor, am grateful for the many things she caught (especially dangling modifiers, about which I'm always screaming at my students!). There are a few matters I should call to your attention, though: I enclose a new Page 1 with a rewritten opening paragraph. The rest of the page incorporates revisions suggested by the copy editor, though the proper editorial/typesetting markings need to be put in next to the title and elsewhere.

I consulted a couple of opera reference books, found Rossini's opera only as La Gazza Ladra, though I would still like it to appear as The Thieving Magpie, which not only foregrounds the bird image but also simplifies matters in later chapters when the text discusses the meaning of the title. Let me know if you are getting protests about not using the Italian.[69]

*

May 9, 1997

Dear Gary:

Thanks for sending me the copy of Book 1 of the Wind-Up Bird. What arrived today, though, was a printout of the text before copy editing. I need the copy-edited version with my responses. I hope that's what you are using there for putting together the sampler, including the new version of page 1. Meanwhile, in case you can use them now, here are a few revisions I made after sending in the complete ms:

. . .

Hope all is well with you. We'll probably be in touch soon.[70]

*

August 18, 1997

Dear Rob:

Here are the corrections. I didn't even come close to getting them in before you left on Friday. It would have taken us hours to do this over the phone and finally would have been impossible. I find it incredible that nobody bothered to send me a copy of the galleys when there was still a chance for me to go through them with the new editor's markings on them—the whole thing, not just the relatively few pages you managed to cull.[71]

*

Aug. 25, 1997

Dear Rob:

While waiting for Gary's return call, I decided to search the chapters that might need "Residence" to replace "house," and this is what I came up with. If I understood you correctly, Deborah [*sic*] Helfand has replaced the expression "the house" with the expression the Residence without quotation marks. I like that much better than what I had.

. . .

I hope Deborah [*sic*] caught all these—and more, if I missed any. There are a lot of other "house"es in the text, but these are the only ones my computer caught that seemed to me to need changing.[72]

Rubin seems to have approached his abridging of *The Wind-Up Bird Chronicle* quite differently from the way Luke and Birnbaum approached the abridging of *Hard-Boiled Wonderland and the End of the World*. In the latter case, Luke and Birnbaum retained the overall structure of the book, cutting sentences and passages throughout the book to create a "tighter" text.[73] With *The Wind-Up Bird Chronicle*, which Rubin suggests is "a compilation of self-contained short stories, its great power deriving from cumulative effect and variety than structural wholeness,"[74] the translator seems to have been less constrained by concerns about the structural integrity of the work.

Another significant difference between the two approaches is the level of collaboration between translator and editor. Rubin basically worked alone in creating a shortened version of *The Wind-Up Bird Chronicle*, and the publisher accepted it, he says, "without a whimper."[75]

Fisketjon remembers the criticism he faced for the final version of the book. "The main and perhaps only bone of contention was my refusal to publish THE WIND-UP BIRD CHRON-ICLE except in one volume, given that the peculiar Japanese release—two hardcovers at one time, followed by a surprise third—suggested there were obvious cuts waiting to be made. This was agreed all around at the time, by Haruki and Jay Rubin and Binky as well; but once it became an item of interest and outrage on the Internet, suddenly it loomed as some great problem. On my behalf I'd offer that this book was the crucial steppingstone for Haruki, who previously had neither secured or maintained publishers throughout Europe nor approached in this country the sales he then achieved and since has increased considerably. So if that was my fault, I'll gladly take the blame."[76]

Would Fisketjon have attempted a similar edit if Rubin hadn't created an abridged version and had sent him just the complete translation?

"I should hope so, starting with the fact that the Japanese publication of WIND-UP BIRD would've been completely impossible in the U.S., where nothing of the sort had ever been attempted ... Jay kindly and wisely saw there was a different route, and that's the one we at Knopf chose to take."[77]

Rubin has maintained a degree of separation between his two roles as translator and editor by dividing the process into two distinct stages, and was able to protect himself from accusations of overstepping his role by creating, keeping, and making public the existence of an unabridged translation. The unabridged translation donated by Rubin to the Lilly Library will be made accessible in 2026.[78]

Birnbaum, on the other hand, worked closely with Luke in abridging the manuscript, often bringing to editing sessions drafts marked with sections that he felt could be left out. As far as today's English readers are concerned, the different processes create similar results, in that in both cases only significantly abridged versions of the books are available to them. In the case of *Hard-Boiled Wonderland and the End of the World*, however, no unabridged translation remains—neither Birnbaum nor Luke have copies of earlier drafts or proofs. As a matter of fact, due to the collaborative nature of the translation/editing process, a "complete" unabridged translation simply never existed.

Murakami says that he did not check the abridged translation of *The Wind-Up Bird Chronicle* before publication. But—as with *Hard-Boiled Wonderland and the End of the World*—he is hoping that a "complete" English version will eventually be published.

"The biggest problem with *Wind-Up Bird* is the gap between

Book 2 and Book 3," Murakami tells me. "Jay has remade that part a bit, and the fact that it's different from the original became a problem, and there are still quite a lot of people who are unhappy about it. These dissatisfied voices are so strong that Jay tells me that he is also feeling down about it, that he wants to publish an accurate translation, but that Knopf isn't thrilled about the idea."[79, 80]

A Most Elegant Object

Chip Kidd, tasked with the cover design for the book that was being billed as Murakami's major new novel, eventually came up with a design based on a wind-up toy bird. Kidd explains his process in his book *Chip Kidd: Book One*:

> *The Wind-Up Bird Chronicle* was the most ambitious and intricate design for a work of fiction I'd ever attempted and is probably only matched in complexity by *The Cheese Monkeys* [Kidd's own novel]. In this sweeping novel of both contemporary and wartime Japan, the narrator is constantly haunted by the sound of what he imagines to be a wind-up bird, which he never sees. While I'm usually loathe to go so literal with title and imagery, the idea was to make the device on the jacket so relatively large that it can't be perceived on a whole when wrapped around the book and so becomes completely abstracted . . . Chris Ware's astonishingly imagined rendering of the interior workings of the wind-up bird were surprinted over Geoff [Spear]'s photo-

graph with a hi-gloss spot-laminate that contained tiny bits of flaked metal to help give it that extra glint . . . It should also be said that all of these bells and whistles added a tremendous amount to the per-book costs, which Sonny very generously approved—a testament to Knopf's commitment to the book, and to the author.[81]

Kidd's efforts did not go unnoticed. The arresting design—which, in yellow and orange and blue, included a large bird's eye on the front cover and a wind-up key on the back—captured the attention of several reviewers. In *The New York Observer*, Philip Weiss wrote that "designer Chip Kidd helped make *The Wind-Up Bird Chronicle* the most elegant object a novel could ever be."[82]

The Wind-Up Bird Chronicle, Knopf, 1997

The writer Pico Iyer, who tells me that he first began reading Murakami seriously after coming across *The Wind-Up Bird Chronicle*, has this to say about the cover: "He (Murakami) seemed a very big deal in New York even then—one of the maybe four or five international writers who was getting a lot of press and attention—and none of that has changed much since. And I did and do feel that the Chip Kidd covers that accompany his Knopf editions, and all the time and energy that go into them, play a part in making him seem one of the most cool, unexpected, cutting-edge writers around."[83]

Rubin, on the other hand, remembers objecting to the design when he was shown it before publication. Personally, he actually liked the design, he says, but in the book itself the wind-up bird is not a mechanical toy. He informed Knopf of this inconsistency, but as far as he recalls he did not receive a response.[84]

Great Expectations

Murakami was satisfied with how *Nejimakidori kuronikuru* (*The Wind-Up Bird Chronicle*) had turned out in the original Japanese. He says, "*A Wild Sheep Chase*, *Hard-Boiled Wonderland and the End of the World*, and *The Wind-Up Bird Chronicle* were each important stepping stones, but with the first two I was still unable to write as well as I thought I was capable of. With *The Wind-Up Bird Chronicle* I felt that I did everything I could, so it's central to my body of work. If I may say so myself, I think that it's a well-written book."[85]

Reviews recognized that the novel was a turning point for Murakami. Michiko Kakutani, *The New York Times*'s chief book critic, wrote, "'The Wind-Up Bird Chronicle' is a wildly ambitious book that not only recapitulates the themes, motifs and preoccupations of his earlier work, but also aspires to invest that material with weighty mythic and historical significance."[86] Jamie James, art critic for *The New Yorker*, wrote two days later in *The New York Times Book Review* that while Murakami "has yet to find a wide following abroad" and had been treated as a "lightweight" by Japanese critics, *The Wind-Up Bird Chronicle* was "a big, ambitious book clearly intended to establish Murakami as a major figure in world literature," and that "the new book almost self-consciously deals with a wide spectrum of heavy subjects: the transitory nature of romantic love, the evil vacuity of contemporary politics and, most provocative of all, the legacy of Japan's violent aggression in World War II." Yet while James goes on to suggest that "Murakami has written a bold and generous book, and one that would have lost a great deal by being tidied up,"[87] Kakutani reaches the opposite conclusion: "[W]hile Murakami seems to have tried to write a book with the esthetic heft and vision of, say, Don DeLillo's 'Underworld' or Salman Rushdie's 'The Moor's Last Sigh,' he is only intermittently successful. 'Wind-Up Bird' often seems so messy that its refusal of closure feels less like an artistic choice than simple laziness, a reluctance on the part of the author to run his manuscript through the typewriter (or computer) one last time."[88]

Notably, unlike negative reviews of Murakami's earlier work, Kakutani's opinion was met with ardent disagreement. In a review in *The New York Observer*, Philip Weiss even criticizes Kakutani in defending Murakami's novel: "What have we come to that a reader as hateful of daring and spirit as Michiko Kakutani has become the certifier of the Literary? She's been too long at the job, and a lot of the candles have flickered out. She likes her books crafted, stoop-shouldered, tidy, and the giant, howling *Wind-Up*

Bird Chronicle scared her. She called it confused and messy and filled with 'portentous red herrings.' The only thing I can say about Ms. Kakutani's criticisms is that they're all true—and they don't matter a whit. There are many big things wrong with *Great Expectations*, too. I read this book as what J. D. Salinger called an 'amateur reader,' thankful to wander around in a powerful story-teller's hold. And unlike the stuffy juggernauts that Don DeLillo and Thomas Pynchon wheeled out this year, *The Wind-Up Bird Chronicle* lacks mannerism. It is written in plain speech and contains passages that are simply transcendent."[89]

The reported sales figures of the hardcover of *The Wind-Up Bird Chronicle* range from 14,000 copies (in a 2002 book by Matthew Strecher)[90] to "around 20,000 copies" (in a 1998 interview with Murakami).[91] The book, however, was picked up as an Editors' Choice and introduced under the bestseller list: "This big book by Japan's most popular novelist wrangles with big subjects: the evanescence of love, the vacuity of politics, the legacy of aggression in World War II"—a crib of James's review. At the end of the year, the book was also picked up as one of the Notable Books of the Year, and a year later, it was mentioned one more time, as a New and Noteworthy Paperback.

Knopf, according to Fisketjon, published *The Wind-Up Bird* "very aggressively" and was more than satisfied by the novel's reception. "I do believe it was a giant step forward from [Murakami's] excellent, and pretty successful, earlier work in terms of scale and scope and ambition, and so extraordinary overall . . . This is one of those rare instances where my expectations—which I'd set as high as I possibly could—were actually fulfilled, in both acclaim and sales. Haruki was, as I mentioned, fully established already at a level that few translated writers were, and his readership rivaled that of some highly admired American writers."[92]

Fisketjon also emphasizes the impact the book had on sales of Murakami's earlier books. "It was around this time, I think, that I noticed a remarkable fact: that each and every one of his books in Vintage paperback sold more copies year after year—the first example of that I'd ever experienced; and this demonstrated that if a reader enjoyed his or her first Murakami, he or she would then read another and another, and introduce friends to his work, and they would then do the same. I can't overestimate how important this is, and how rare: even Cormac McCarthy, who became a best seller with *All the Pretty Horses*, subsequently enjoyed better sales of his prior novels, some more than others, but those sales didn't increase for all of them year after year, as Haruki's did. I hope to see this happen again sometime before I retire, but I'm not holding my breath."[93]

The Wind-Up Bird Chronicle seems to have also been the book that captured the attention of a critical mass of an important and influential group of readers: other writers. For Roland Kelts, reviewing for *The Philadelphia Inquirer*, the book was nothing short of a revelation. As he recounted to me: "I was living in New York in the late 90s, and it felt like the era of the big sprawling inventive 'postmodern' novel, massive and very male. David Foster Wallace, Don DeLillo and Thomas Pynchon all dropped heavy tomes, and suddenly Haruki Murakami was in the mix . . . The story was immediately addictive and mesmerizing . . . this Japanese novelist had a unique gift for reinventing mundane but closely observed realities—the rotary telephone that looks like a deep sea creature; the alleyway with the absent cat and the always blurry clairvoyant young girl. In the same story, he takes us to Manchuria and the horrors of the Japanese occupation there, the ghosts embedded in the land, and an excruciating, deftly paced scene in which a soldier is skinned alive.

"For anyone who'd read Murakami before, the book felt like its author had marshalled his talents and concentrated them into one dazzling performance. For readers new to Murakami, he was a portal to another universe, another way of looking at and experiencing both the isolation of urban anomie in Tokyo and the repressed, unprocessed memories of the war in Asia ... A lot of New York friends told me that they loved the book but were befuddled by the ending, and I realized at the time that an elliptical ending to a riveting story was not such a bad thing."[94]

David Mitchell, for whom Murakami has been an influence from relatively early in his own career, was another author who had been pleasantly surprised by the publication of *Wind-Up*:

"In 1996 I was teaching English in a small town north of Hiroshima. It was pretty much the last pre-Internet year, and I read a lot, often exchanging books with other English teachers and foreigners. One dog-eared old paperback that came my way was the English translation of *A Wild Sheep Chase* by one Haruki Murakami. I'd never heard of him, though back then, few people outside Japan had. I loved its tone, its urbanity, its drive and its Japan ... It looked a lot like the Japan of the nineties—nondescript, grey, suburban, alienated—but it hid spaces where strangeness, transgression or the occult could happen. The book went to unfashionable, unliterary places like Sapporo, off the beaten track of Japanese culture. Its characters were existentially untethered. They lived in bars, coffee shops and tiny rooms with no view to speak of. They worked, had odd conversations, drank beer, slept, and worked. Family rarely entered the picture. They made no plans for their futures. Not unlike English teachers in Japan, now that I think of it."

Mitchell proves Fisketjon's observation that readers who enjoy one Murakami work go on to read the rest of his oeuvre. "In 1998, my then girlfriend (these days Mrs Mitchell) gave me a slim, two-volume bilingual edition of *Norwegian Wood*—then the only version in English. There was a Doutor coffee shop in Hiroshima near the city office where I used to stop on my way home from work, just so I had a third place to go to that wasn't a classroom or my apartment. One evening I started to read *Norwegian Wood* there and read both volumes in a single sitting ... I finished the final page as the staff at Doutor were shutting up shop for the night. Twenty years later, I still remember the afterglow of the story; yet I've never really worked out why it affected me so much. It's a quiet novel, lacking the genre tropes of *A Wild Sheep Chase*. It's just about a young man at university in Tokyo with a dead best friend; a love interest with a fragile grasp on sanity; an older woman. Perhaps Murakami presents an alternative version of our younger selves; complex, sexual, musical, cool, faintly tragic, Japanese (if you're not) yet culturally cosmopolitan and contentedly-doomed to outsider status. It's a seductive prospect. Certainly it seduced me. At the time I was scrabbling around for ideas for my difficult second novel, and an indecent number came from *Norwegian Wood*. The homage (shall we call it) is there in the title; *Number9dream*, like *Norwegian Wood*, is a John Lennon song.

"[B]ut for me, the masterpiece is *The Wind-Up Bird Chronicle*. It's a Murakami cocktail of quirkiness, emotional nuance, longing and a kind of metaphysical magic, mixed to perfection. The novel is grounded by historical elements relating to the thirties and forties Japanese puppet state of Manchukuo in north-east China, a period not widely discussed in popular culture, to say the least. (Endlessly re-hashed samurai TV dramas; yes, annually. Films about photogenic airmen and sailors sacrificing themselves for the fatherland and, of course, eventual peace; all you can eat. Fact-based narratives about the scorched earth subjugation of Korea and China? Good luck.) *The Wind-Up Bird Chronicle* impressed me from the first page. It was like no other novel I'd ever read, Japanese or otherwise . . . When you're a young writer still searching for your voice, or voices, a novel like *The Wind-Up Bird Chronicle* is exhilarating, liberating, and a challenge. It tells you, 'Fiction can be this innovative and still work as a piece of art'; it tells you, 'If this writer can follow the wilder promptings of his or her imagination, you should, too'; and it tells you, 'Remember, this is how high the bar is: try to write something this good; chances are you'll fail, but try.' The novel has a killer last line, which I shamelessly nicked, though I no longer recall where I used it. Nobody's ever noticed, anyway."[95]

Junot Díaz, who had made his debut with the short story collection *Drown* in 1996, was living in New York when he first read *The Wind-Up Bird Chronicle*: "I remember it both ways—to a certain segment of the literary population *WBC* struck like lightning and it certainly put Murakami on the English map in ways that nothing he'd written before had. He vaulted into the stratosphere of 'serious' writers. I read the book with great interest and talked about it obsessively but I didn't have a lot of conversants. For a lot of folks the arrival of *WBC* was something that they didn't much pay attention to. To be fair, it's rare for books in translation to have the kind of reception that the country reserves for its linguistic confreres. Took a little while for Murakami's popular reputation to catch up to the excitement that he provoked among the cognoscenti."[96]

Pico Iyer is one of the rare Anglophone writers who first came across Murakami through the Kodansha English Library series. But it was only with *The Wind-Up Bird Chronicle* that he "took him on in earnest."

"I was asked to review it by the Books Editor at *TIME* then, Janice Simpson, because I spent time in Japan and often reviewed for *TIME*; and I think everyone felt that this was his magnum opus, which would seize the attention of the world.

"I was in Nara, in our silent, two-room, rented flat in the middle of a Murakami-worthy suburb dating from the late seventies, with McDonald's, KFC and Mister Donut ringing the nearest train-station.

"I was stirred by the intensity and seriousness of the sequences set during the war in that book—the mix of unrealism and hyper-realism, I suppose—and now, twenty-one years on, I suppose that book does look like his one great attempt at a huge masterpiece, taking in not just the easy glide of life now, but what contrasts with it in the generation immediately before his own.

"And I remember being struck at how he almost seemed to suggest (as I read it) that the suffering and reality of war was a solace, or gave direction and groundedness to life, in comparison with the dream-like drift and painless ease of the post-war suburban life he otherwise chronicles.

"All of which is a way of saying that I understand just why and how Murakami is so popular everywhere in the world; wherever I go, from Delhi to London to Singapore to Dubai, people seem to be gobbling down Murakami, as the rare contemporary master who catches the frictionless challenge of middle-class suburbia, the sense of missing meaning and lost identity that haunts us here and there amidst the pleasure of hearing Coltrane and the convenience of heating up pasta. Every traditional society that feels it's lost its moorings, even as it's moved into a new modern comfort, must be tugged by that fleeting sense of having missed the boat that he evokes so plangently.

"And I can see how he's as easy to consume as bottled water, and as easy to translate. He's struck a global chord by speaking from and for a global apartment in a condo that people in most developed countries can relate to.

"But for me this is precisely the Japan that is least compelling and deep, even if it's not illusory. He writes for everything other than what made me want to move to Japan, which has to do with its stubborn ancientness, its rites and values, all the things that in fact make it sometimes painfully distant and different from everywhere else, and grounded to a fault."[97]

As *The Wind-Up Bird Chronicle* was the first Murakami novel to be published following the disbanding of the Birnbaum/Luke duo, I can't help wondering how they had been observing the developments with the new book. Birnbaum says that he was "so preoccupied with getting married in 1997/8" that he "didn't pay attention to *Wind-Up* when it came out."

"I don't think I saw a copy until I went to Tokyo later that spring. I was surprised they didn't try to reshape or reduce the rambles/excesses further in the English translation. Had I been the editor I would have pressed for cuts or a serious reworking of the material. I'm not sure if the novel really even needed a Book 3."[98]

Luke, for his part, says that he recalls reading the book when it was first published. "Knopf under Sonny Mehta being the finest, best publisher in the US, knew how to publish it. The Chip Kidd jacket art was eye-catching, dazzling. But I was disappointed editorially. The prose—of the translation, that is—had no tightness, it was flabby, and the novel went on and on and on far too long, didn't keep my interest, and didn't resolve organically. And this after something like 25,000 words had to be cut almost arbitrarily. It should have been cut more. I don't think my response was proprietary in any way—I really tried to keep myself out of it—it was an honest, fair response and one, when I reread the book last year, I had all over again. But the book made its mark, made a huge splash, and some critics loved it. Not all did, but those who did were utterly crazy about it. I was not vocal about my criticism because I also thought that as I was no longer working with Haruki I should back off, let others do their job without any noise from me. I think I wrote to Haruki to say what a great job Knopf had done and how beautiful the book was. And now, twenty years later, what the *Wind-Up Bird* achieved is history. No one can argue with that."[99]

Regardless of their personal opinions, Luke and Iyer have been proven correct in seeing *The Wind-Up Bird* as the book that cemented Murakami as a writer of international stature and historical importance. It was a development, Fisketjon reiterates, that was helped by strategic decisions made by Murakami's publishers and other collaborators: "To boost his standing with foreign publishers, who at the time weren't plentiful, I sent a box of our edition to the Frankfurt Book Fair to hand out to my friends abroad; we didn't control translation rights, but I wanted to do what I could to help his agents correct what was then a sort of failing. As you know, his roster of publishers around the world soon filled up beautifully."[100]

To the U.K. and Beyond

Initially, Murakami's supporters and publishers in the U.K. had found little success. Clare Alexander, who had bought the rights to *A Wild Sheep Chase* for Hamish Hamilton, was not involved in the publication of *Hard-Boiled Wonderland and the End of the World*, and Andrew Franklin also left the publisher in the mid-nineties. Sales were also modest.[101] But this began to change in the late nineties when the then independent Harvill Press began acquiring U.K. rights to Murakami's books. Harvill Press was headed by Christopher MacLehose, who over his career has introduced British readers to international writers like W. G. Sebald, Javier Marías, and Peter Høeg, as well as American authors such as

Raymond Carver and Richard Ford. When he was at Harvill, MacLehose published primarily translations, at one point from thirty-two languages. More recently he published Stieg Larsson's novels in English translation at MacLehose Press—which he started after leaving Harvill—and helped turn the Millennium Series into a global hit.[102]

MacLehose does most of his editing at home, working in the greenhouse in his garden on nice days and sitting at the kitchen table when the weather is cold. When I ask what he does when he's not working, he responds, "Hah! I wonder if editors anywhere in the world ever relax or even sleep. The work that one is privileged to do with the translations we publish is all-absorbing, and if it goes on deep into the night that is hardly a surprise. There are so many administrative chores to accomplish during the working days. I have the great blessing of a wife who is also working in the same world and so is understanding of the hours I keep."

Christopher MacLehose in his greenhouse with his dog, Miska

MacLehose remembers that it was Gary Fisketjon who introduced Harvill Press to *The Wind-Up Bird Chronicle*. "We made our offer to the American agent, ICM, who had, I think, taken over the handling of the rights from the Japanese publisher at that time."[103]

When I ask Fisketjon about this he replies, "It's very sweet of Christopher to remember. Christopher was not only an old friend indeed but also, in my view, the best UK publisher for Haruki— this based in part on the general excellence I'd witnessed for many years by then, and perhaps most intensely on the happy collaborations he and I had shared with other authors. Most particularly with Ray Carver, who I'm sure would've told Haruki how happy he was to work with Christopher."[104]

MacLehose says that it was true that he was the first to publish Carver in the U.K. when he was at Collins. "I offered the agent $1000 for WHAT WE TALK ABOUT . . . He refused point blank. I asked him what he might accept. He said he would accept a maximum of $500! It wasn't worth a cent more, he said. They don't make agents like that nowadays."[105]

Harvill Press printed 60,000 copies of *The Wind-Up Bird Chronicle*.[106] MacLehose says that the critical reception was "immediately favourable and the commercial success of the whole oeuvre was assured from that time onwards."

"There were individual critics and admirers of the work whose enthusiasm led Murakami to come to London, to take part in a public discussion—in a theatre in central London, which was sold out weeks before the event—and to meet chosen critics and booksellers. I believe the author must have recognised how very welcome he was and how numerous were his admirers in this country."[107]

Harvill followed the publication of *The Wind-Up Bird Chronicle* in 1998 with *South of the Border, West of the Sun* in 1999 and both *Underground* and *Norwegian Wood* in 2000. They continued to be relatively ambitious with their print runs: 20,000 copies of *South of the Border, West of the Sun* and *Norwegian Wood*, and 5,000 copies for the nonfiction book *Underground*.[108] The press also purchased the rights to *A Wild Sheep Chase, Hard-Boiled Wonderland and the End of the World*, and *The Elephant Vanishes*, and published them as part of a series of paperbacks linked by design, which were displayed prominently in Borders, Waterstones, and other major bookstores.[109]

Harvill's Haruki Murakami paperback series

MacLehose says that it had always been Harvill's intention to acquire all of the earlier works. "There were working at Harvill at that time fans of his work, chiefly John Mitchinson, who had been a senior bookseller in the Waterstones chain, who knew and loved all of the earlier novels. I still like the uniform series of the reissues. And they were all of them commercial successes. Perhaps none more so than *Norwegian Wood*, which we also published in a special limited edition in two volumes, one green and one red, in a metal box. Those editions now are treasures for collectors. They were modelled, of course, on the original Japanese editions."[110]

The Harvill marketing director at that time was Paul Baggaley, another former manager at Waterstones (who went on to be publisher at Picador and recently moved to Bloomsbury, where he is editor-in-chief). Baggaley became a Murakami fan when he ran a bookstore in Charing Cross, where he would import Murakami titles from the U.S. that were out of print in the U.K. He had joined Harvill Press in June 1998, soon after *The Wind-Up Bird* was published in hardcover. Baggaley says his personal involvement was with the paperback and "with all subsequent books before the sales to Random House" and that his experience and the networks he built as a bookseller helped expand Murakami's readership at Harvill.

"As a bookseller in the late 80s Murakami was always regarded as a cult writer with a certain number of committed fans—but there was never a critical mass (hence his books went in and out of print). As I ran shops in central London and Hampstead amongst others, I had a very literate clientele and in Charing Cross Road, a cool young customer base and in Hampstead a US/international centric base—both included keen Murakami fans and I felt strongly that if we could appeal to these readers the rest would follow. Getting Waterstones onboard at the start was key as they had the right bookselling profile, the critical mass of shops to support it and the promotions to make the books visible. The groundwork was done with the Waterstones team and my relationship with them certainly helped—and then when the WH Smith influence on Waterstones took over (through Our Price book buyer Scott Pack being brought in to head the buying team), there was another obsessive Murakami fan in a key position. Books Etc too were early adopters."

The paperback reissues were also important in increasing Murakami's visibility. "I was very involved in commissioning the series look along with the editor Vicky Miller—we asked Jamie Keenan to create a brand that we could roll out across all the books—the type style was particularly effective we felt, and we would try to reissue a book every six months to keep the momentum going."

Baggaley agrees that the publication of *The Wind-Up Bird Chronicle* (his favorite Murakami book) marked a turning point in Murakami's U.K. trajectory. "I think it was the right book at the right time in the UK—and with a publisher for whom it was so important that it couldn't be allowed to fail. It was a big book that allowed for a reassessment of his career—it took him from out-of-print cult writer to a writer on the international stage."[111]

Rubin's translation of *The Wind-Up Bird Chronicle* was further edited in the U.K. version. In a February 9, 1998, fax addressed to "Victoria Miller, Assistant to Christopher MacLehose," Rubin writes: "Thank you for the proofs of THE WIND-UP BIRD CHRONICLE. I'm sorry to say that I like most of the revisions that your editor has suggested, which improve upon my version. I have nothing to say about British usage, however," and then attaches two pages of comments, in which he resists quite a few of the changes.

Is "boom box" totally unusable in Britain? "Ghettoblaster" has ugly racial and class overtones that I dislike and that are absent from the original. I see that page 379 has "music machine." How would that be?

A "shrine fortune" is a paper slip one receives at a Japanese shrine with predictions as to which areas of one's life are going well or badly. Not that hard to grasp from context.

Changing this to cricket would be entirely inappropriate for Japan, where baseball is virtually the national pastime. You might add the word "inning" after "third" for clarity.[112]

It isn't clear how much impact the Harvill editors' text-level changes had on the reception of the book in the U.K. But there is no question that having strong and well-connected allies in the market helped. I ask MacLehose—just as I had asked most of the people I have interviewed—if he ever imagined that Murakami would become the international phenomenon he is today.

"I don't think a wise publisher will ever suppose that his writers will become celebrated throughout the world as Murakami has become. I do remember sharing our belief in him with European publishers, one of whom at least, the German publisher, did take on his work as a direct result of our evident success."

When I ask how he would position *The Wind-Up Bird Chronicle* within Murakami's larger body of work, MacLehose responds, "I think I will wait to see what marvelous works are still to come from Murakami before deciding on a preference overall."[113]

Christopher MacLehose with his cat, Mitsuko

Back in Tokyo, when I squeeze in one last question about his upcoming work, Murakami looks amused. "I wonder. At my age all my friends are retired." He adds, "I find it strange that I'm the only one continuing to sweat," and lets out a laugh. "I'm the type that only begins to write when I get the urge to write, so I'm always waiting for that feeling to well up inside me. And when it doesn't, I spend my time translating . . . The interesting thing is that when I was in America, back when my novels weren't selling [outside Japan], I remember being envious of Ryūichi Sakamoto and others who were being well received because with music there is no need for translation. But while writing takes time, it lasts. Translations are a big part of that equation. And you need a certain level of breadth. So you don't want to find yourself in a situation where you've published just one or two books. You need to keep adding to the pile, and that pile as a whole leaves behind a certain 'world.' That's very important. That's why it's important to write a lot."

When I ask him if he ever feels like his books sell too well around the world—that he's gotten "too big"—Murakami shakes his head. "I'm just glad that they sell," he says.[114]

Acknowledgments

This book, which ends in 1998 (the year, it so happens, that I first read Murakami in English translation as a sophomore in college in the U.S.), is very much a work in progress. That is to say, the story has continued to evolve, even as I was preparing this book for publication. Murakami has continued to publish new work; on the request of the author, Jay Rubin has begun work on a new translation of *Sekai no owari to hādoboirudo wandārando* (*Hard-Boiled Wonderland and the End of the World*), and some of the other key figures in this narrative have left publishing, retired, or passed away. Waseda University, which is Murakami's alma mater and where I currently teach, has announced that it will be opening the Haruki Murakami Library in spring 2021. A more comprehensive picture of the author's thoughts and adventures will no doubt emerge as his personal papers are gradually made accessible.

When I was first writing the book in Japanese that this English edition is based on, I spent nine months scribbling additions in the margins of an early galley and, to my editor's consternation, continued to make emendations and amendments until a few weeks before publication. Half a year before the scheduled publication date for the English edition, and three months after the initial deadline, I find myself doing the same. I have no doubt that I will continue to make changes until the final hour. Once the book goes to print, I will have to let it go for a moment, but I imagine it won't be long before the next chapter of the story begins to take form in my mind.

I write both fiction and nonfiction in Japanese, but all of my book-length publications in English to date have been translations and edited volumes of translations. This means (though norms on this are changing) that I rarely see my name on the cover of a book. It is a strange feeling to see my name featured so prominently here (in Michael Salu's elegant design) when this book is—like any book but probably more so than most others—a work of collaboration. I am grateful to the many people who took the time to share their thoughts and recollections with me—in Japanese and in English, in one-to-one conversation or email correspondence or that outdated thing, the phone call. I am grateful to the editors of both the Japanese and English versions of the book—particularly Yuka Igarashi at Soft Skull Press and Junko Ogawa at Misuzu Shobō, who each brought her own unique perspective and editing style to the shaping of the book. I am grateful to friends who commented on the manuscript at various stages with such care, patience, and good humor: Polly Barton, David Boyd, Junot Díaz, Michael Emmerich, Ted Goossen, Roland Kelts, Marjorie Lieu, Gitte Marianne Hansen, Yuko Matsukawa, Masatsugu Ono, Allison Markin Powell, William Roff, Kayoko Takeda,

Acknowledgments

Ginny Tapley Takemori, Anna Zielinska-Elliot. I would also like to thank the staff of the Haruki Murakami office for responding to my many queries and requests with such grace and candor. I am of course very grateful to the author, Haruki Murakami himself, who was generous with his time and his consideration and whose work continues to amaze and entertain and provoke. All have been invaluable to the writing of this book—and to me. Just as when you are reading Haruki Murakami—presumably in translation—you are reading the work of the many people who have engaged with the text published in his name, when you are reading David Karashima, you are reading the wide array of individuals whose efforts have been a part of the narrative.

Notes

1. *Pinball, 1973* and *Hear the Wind Sing*

1. Lesser, Wendy. *Why I Read: The Serious Pleasure of Books*. New York: Farrar, Straus and Giroux, 2014. 152.
2. Birnbaum, Alfred. Interview with author. November 20, 2015.
3. Birnbaum, Alfred. Interview with author. November 20, 2015.
4. "Letter from the Chancellor." *East West Center News*, University of Hawaii. Vol. 2, No. 2, April 1962.
5. Birnbaum, Alfred. Interview with author. January 4, 2018.
6. Birnbaum, Alfred. Email interview with author. January 20, 2018.
7. Strecher, Matthew C. "Magic Realism and the Search for Identity in the Fiction of Murakami Haruki." *The Journal of Japanese Studies*, vol. 25, no. 2 (Summer 1999).
8. Birnbaum, Alfred. Interview with author. July 12, 2012/May 5, 2014.
9. Palaima, Carolyn. "From a Shared Border to Western Hemisphere Concerns: The History of Latin American Studies at the University of Texas at Austin." Title VI 50th Anniversary Conference, March 19–21, 2009, Washington, D.C.
10. Murakami, Haruki. *Uzumaki neko no mitsukekata. Murakami asahidō jyānaru*. Illustrated by Mizumaru Anzai. Tokyo: Shinchosha, 1996. 26–27, 30. My translation.

11. Birnbaum, Alfred. Interview with author. January 11, 2016.
12. Birnbaum, Alfred. Interview with author. January 11, 2016.
13. Birnbaum, Alfred. Interview with author. July 12, 2012.
14. Murakami, Haruki. "Shōsetsuka ni natta koro," in *Shokugyō toshite no shōsetsuka*. Tokyo: Switch Publishing, 2015. 42.
15. Birnbaum, Alfred. Interview with author. November 20, 2015.
16. Birnbaum, Alfred. Interview with author. January 11, 2016.
17. Birnbaum, Alfred. Interview with author. January 11, 2016.
18. Birnbaum, Alfred. Interview with author. January 11, 2016.
19. Birnbaum, Alfred. Interview with author. July 12, 2012.
20. Murakami, Ryū, and Haruki Murakami. *Wōku donto ran. Murakami Ryū vs Murakami Haruki*. Tokyo: Kodansha. 1981.
21. Birnbaum, Alfred. Interview with author. November 20, 2015.
22. Murakami, Haruki. *Hashiru koto ni tsuite kataru toki ni boku no kataru koto*. Tokyo: Bungeishunju, 2007.
23. Murakami, Haruki. "Kikigaki: Murakami Haruki kono jūnen 1979–1988." *Murakami Haruki bukku, Bungakukai shigatsu rinji zōkangō*. Edited by Yutaka Yukawa. Tokyo: Bungeishunju, 1991. 44. My translation.
24. Murakami, Haruki. "Kikigaki: Murakami Haruki kono jūnen 1979–1988." *Murakami Haruki bukku, Bungakukai shigatsu rinji zōkangō*. Edited by Yutaka Yukawa. Tokyo: Bungeishunju, 1991. 44.
25. Birnbaum, Alfred. Email interview with author. January 4, 2018.
26. Birnbaum, Alfred. Interview with author. March 21, 2017.
27. Birnbaum, Alfred. Interview with author. July 12, 2012.
28. Birnbaum, Alfred. Interview with author. March 21, 2017.
29. Young, Jules. Email interview with author. June 22, 2017.
30. Young, Jules. Email interview with author. September 30, 2017.
31. Birnbaum, Alfred. Interview with author. March 21, 2017.
32. Murakami, Haruki. Interview with author. January 24, 2018.
33. Wray, John, and Haruki Murakami. "The Art of Fiction No. 182." *The Paris Review*, issue 170, Summer 2004.

34. Murakami, Haruki. Interview with author. January 24, 2018.

35. Birnbaum, Alfred. Interview with author. November 20, 2015.

36. Wray, John, and Haruki Murakami. "The Art of Fiction No. 182." *The Paris Review*, issue 170, Summer 2004.

37. Birnbaum, Alfred. Interview with author. January 11, 2016.

38. Memorandum of an agreement between Kodansha Ltd. and Alfred Birnbaum for a translation of Haruki Murakami's *Hitsuji o meguru bōken.* August 19, 1987.

39. "Besuto serā uochingu: Sarada kinenbi tanka no kaze ni notte nihyakumanbu." *Yomiuri Shimbun.* January 7, 1988.

40. Murakami, Haruki. Author page. Shinchosha homepage. www.shinchosha.co.jp/harukimurakami/author.html. Last accessed February 20, 2020.

41. Birnbaum, Alfred. Interview with author. November 20, 2015.

42. Murakami, Haruki, and Motoyuki Shibata. *Honyaku yawa.* Tokyo: Bungeishunju, 2000. 18. My translation.

43. Birnbaum, Alfred. Interview with author. January 3, 2018.

44. Birnbaum, Alfred. Interview with author. March 21, 2017.

45. *03 Tokyo Calling Sōkangō Nyū Yōku ni mirai wa aru ka.* Shinchosha, 1989.

46. Birnbaum, Alfred. Email interview with author. March 25, 2019.

47. Birnbaum, Alfred. Interview with author. March 21, 2017.

2. A Wild Sheep Chase

1. Murakami, Haruki. "Amerika de Zō no shōmetsu ga shuppan sareta koro" in *Zō no shōmetsu tanpensenshū 1980–1991.* Tokyo: Shinchosha, 2015. 26. My translation.

2. Luke, Elmer. Interview with author. September 1, 2014.

3. Luke, Elmer. Interview with author. September 1, 2014.

4. Luke, Elmer. Interview with author. February 12, 2018.

5. Luke, Elmer. Interview with author. September 1, 2014.

6. Luke, Elmer. Email interview with author. July 30, 2017.

7. Luke, Elmer. Email interview with author. July 30, 2017.

8. Luke, Elmer. Email interview with author. July 30, 2017.

9. Luke, Elmer. Phone interview with author. February 13, 2019.

10. Luke, Elmer. Email interview with author. July 20, 2017.

11. Luke, Elmer. Email interview with author. January 22, 2018.

12. Luke, Elmer. Email interview with author. January 23, 2018.

13. Luke, Elmer. Email interview with author. January 22, 2018.

14. Luke, Elmer. Email interview with author. June 18, 2018.

15. Luke, Elmer. Phone interview with author. November 22, 2015/ Email interview with author. December 12, 2015.

16. Parks, Tim. Email interview with author. March 22, 2019.

17. Luke, Elmer. Email interview with author. September 19, 2017.

18. Luke, Elmer. Phone interview with author. May 2, 2019.

19. Luke, Elmer. Phone interview with author. February 28, 2019.

20. Luke, Elmer. Email interview with author. September 19, 2017.

21. Luke, Elmer. Email interview with author. July 18, 2017.

22. Luke, Elmer. Email interview with author. July 18, 2017.

23. Murakami, Haruki. "Kaigai e dete iku. Atarashii furontia," in *Shokugyō toshite no shōsetsuka*. Tokyo: Switch Publishing, 2015. 269. My translation.

24. Shirai, Tetsu. Interview with author. April 3, 2017.

25. Shirai, Tetsu. Interview with author. March 1, 2017.

26. Luke, Elmer. Email interview with author. July 18, 2017.

27. Luke, Elmer. Email interview with author. May 3, 2018.

28. Luke, Elmer. Interview with author. September 1, 2014.

29. Luke, Elmer. Email interview with author. July 19, 2017.

30. Luke, Elmer. Email interview with author. October 19, 2019.

31. Asakawa, Minato. Email interview with author. May 1, 2018.

32. Shaw, Stephen. Email interview with author. April 13/14, 2018.

33. Luke, Elmer. Email interview with author. April 23, 2018.

34. Shaw, Stephen. Email interview with author. April 22, 2018.

35. Katō, Norihiro. Email interview with author. May 1, 2017.

36. Luke, Elmer. Email interview with author. January 22, 2018.
37. Luke, Elmer. Phone interview with author. November 22, 2015.
38. Birnbaum, Alfred. Interview with author. January 11, 2016.
39. Murakami, Haruki. *A Wild Sheep Chase*. Translated by Alfred Birnbaum. Tokyo: Kodansha International, 1989. 1, 4, 7, 8, 9, 10, 75, 80.
40. Murakami, Haruki. *A Wild Sheep Chase*. Translated by Alfred Birnbaum. Tokyo: Kodansha International, 1989. 150, 152.
41. Rubin, Jay. *Haruki Murakami and the Music of Words*. London: Vintage, 2005. 189.
42. Reagan, Ronald. "President Ronald Reagan Remarks to 1988 Republican National Convention," Heritage Foundation website, accessed March 2013, www.reagansheritage.org/html/reagan_rnc_88.shtml.
43. Luke, Elmer. Interview with author. July 25, 2012.
44. "Murakami Haruki sekai wo mezasu." *Asahi Shimbunsha*, *AERA*, November 21, 1989. My translation.
45. Murakami, Haruki. *A Wild Sheep Chase: A Novel (Trilogy of the Rat Book 3)*. New York: Vintage, 2010. Kindle.
46. Bloom, Lexy. Email correspondence with author. March 15, 2019.
47. Luke, Elmer. Phone interview with author. November 22, 2015.
48. Murakami, Haruki. Interview with author. January 24, 2018.
49. Shirai, Tetsui. Interview with author. March 1, 2017.
50. Murakami, Haruki. "Īsuto Hanputon: Sakkatachi no seichi" in *Henkyō, kinkyō*. Tokyo: Shinchosha, 2000.
51. Cheng, Anne. Email interview with author. April 20, 2017.
52. Shirai, Tetsu, and Gillian Jolis. "A Wild Sheep Chase Marketing Strategy Summary." December 5, 1989.
53. Birnbaum, Alfred. Email interview with author. September 29, 2017.
54. Molasky, Michael. Conversation with author. April 2017.
55. Jolis, Gillian. "Proposed Promotion Budget Dance Dance Dance." January 21, 1993.

56. Murakami, Haruki. Interview with author. January 24, 2018.

57. Shaw, Stephen. Email interview with author. April 15, 2018.

58. Luke, Elmer. Email interview with author. September 19, 2017.

59. "Murakami Haruki 'Hitsuji o meguru bōken' beikoku de shuppan, kokusaisei ni takai hyōka." *Asahi Shimbun*, Evening Issue. November 13, 1989.

60. Fuerbringer, Jonathan. "World Markets; A Long Ride on Tokyo's Turmoil." *New York Times*, January 26, 1992.

61. Luke, Elmer. Interview with author. September 1, 2014.

62. Cheng, Anne. Email interview with author. April 20, 2017.

63. Luke, Elmer. Interview with author. July 25, 2012.

64. Fuhrman, Janice. "Japan's Literary Brat Pack Is Finding a Place in Sun." Associated Press article in the *Los Angeles Times*, September 15, 1989. www.latimes.com/archives/la-xpm-1989-09-15-vw -273-story.html. Last accessed February 20, 2020.

65. Chapman, Tom. "Making of 'You Gotta Have Wa': Tom Chapman conducts in-depth interview with Bob Whiting on best sell." September 29, 1989. Digitized by Jessica Suchman and Catherine Nissley for Robert Whiting's homepage at JapaneseBaseball.com. www.japanesebaseball.com/writers/display.gsp?id=44491. Last accessed February 21, 2020.

66. Whiting, Robert. Email interview with author. December 23, 2017.

67. Shirai, Tetsu, and Gillian Jolis. "A Wild Sheep Chase Marketing Strategy Summary." December 5, 1989.

68. Notes from Haruki Murakami office. March 5, 2019.

69. Mitgang, Herbert. "Books of the Times: Young and Slangy Mix of the U.S. and Japan." *New York Times*, October 21, 1989.

70. Shirai, Tetsu. Interview with author. March 2, 2017.

71. Murakami, Haruki. "Sentoraru pāku no hayabusa" in *Murakami rajio*. Tokyo: Magazine House, 2001. 166–169. My translation.

72. Luke, Elmer. Email interview with author. May 25, 2017.

73. Cheng, Anne. Email interview with author. April 20, 2017.

74. "Murakami Haruki 'Hitsuji o meguru bōken' beikoku de shuppan, kokusaisei ni takai hyōka." *Asahi Shimbun*, Evening Issue. November 13, 1989. My translation.

75. Cheng, Anne. Email interview with author. April 20, 2017.

76. Shirai, Tetsu. Interview with author. June 3, 2017.

77. Levi, Stephanie. Email interview with author. June 15, 2017.

78. Luke, Elmer. Phone interview with author. March 25, 2018.

79. Levi, Jonathan. Email interview with author. April 24, 2018.

80. Notes from Haruki Murakami office. April 12, 2019.

81. Luke, Elmer. Phone interview with author. November 20, 2015.

82. McInerney, Jay, and Haruki Murakami. "PEN Conversations with Distinguished Foreign Writers: Haruki Murakami." December 3, 1991. archive.pen.org/asset?id=291. Last accessed February 21, 2020.

83. Luke, Elmer. Email interview with author. November 13, 2018.

84. Murakami, Haruki. *Tōi Taiko*. Tokyo: Kodansha. 1990. Kindle. My translation.

85. Murakami, Haruki. Interview with author. January 24, 2018.

86. Martin, Douglas. "Herbert Mitgang, Wide-Ranging Author and Journalist Dies at 93." *New York Times*, November 21, 1993.

87. Mitgang, Herbert. "Books of the Times: Japanese Put a Spin on Baseball." *New York Times*, July 15, 1989.

88. Mitgang, Herbert. "Books of the Times: Young and Slangy Mix of the U.S. and Japan." *New York Times*, October 21, 1989.

89. Murakami, Haruki. *A Wild Sheep Chase*. Tokyo: Kodansha International, 1989.

90. "Bei Nyūyōku Taimuzu, Murakami Haruki-shi o zessan." *Yomiuri Shimbun*, Tokyo evening edition, October 24, 1989. My translation.

91. Ryan, Alan. "Wild and Wooly." *Washington Post*, November 12, 1989.
92. Kometani, Foumiko. "Help! His Best Friend is Turning into a Sheep!" *Los Angeles Times*, October 15, 1989.
93. Mitgang, Herbert. "Books of the Times: Young and Slangy Mix of the U.S. and Japan." *New York Times*, October 21, 1989.
94. Arensberg, Ann. "Just the Myths, Ma'am." *New York Times*, December 3, 1989.
95. Birnbaum, Alfred. Email interview with author. September 29, 2017.
96. Ryan, Alan. "Wild and Wooly." *Washington Post*, November 12, 1989.
97. Leithauser, Brad. "A Hook Somewhere." *New Yorker*, December 4, 1989.
98. Leithauser, Brad. Email interview with author. October 24, 2017.
99. Jolis, Gillian. "Proposed Promotion Budget Dance Dance Dance." January 21, 1993.
100. Moriyasu, Machiko. Interview with author. July 6, 2017. Email interview with author. July 12, 2017.
101. "Murakami Haruki 'Hitsuji o meguru bōken' beikoku de shuppan, kokusaisei ni takai hyōka." *Asahi Shimbun*, evening issue. November 13, 1989.
102. Luke, Elmer. Interview with author. September 1, 2014.
103. Kuniaki, Ura. Interview with author. April 23, 2019.
104. Luke, Elmer. Phone interview with author. February 28, 2018.
105. Murakami, Haruki. Interview with author. January 24, 2018.
106. Updike, John. "Subconscious Tunnels." *New Yorker*. January 24, 2005. www.newyorker.com/magazine/2005/01/24/subconscious -tunnels. Last accessed February 21, 2020.
107. Shirai, Tetsu, and Gillian Jolis. "A Wild Sheep Chase Marketing Strategy Summary." December 5, 1989.
108. Alexander, Clare. Email interview with author. June 9, 2017.

109. Hiatt, Fred. "Haruki Murakami's Homecoming." *Washington Post*, December 25, 1989.
110. Alexander, Clare. Email interview with author. June 9, 2017.
111. Franklin, Andrew. Email interview with author. July 11, 2017.
112. Murakami, Haruki. Interview with author. January 24, 2018.
113. Alexander, Clare. Email interview with author. June 9, 2017.
114. Franklin, Andrew. Email interview with author. July 11, 2017.
115. Luke, Elmer. Email interview with author. May 25, 2017/Phone interview with author. March 25, 2018.
116. Murakami, Haruki. "Amerika de Zō no shōmetsu ga shuppan sareta koro" in *Zō no shōmetsu tanpensenshū 1980–1991*. Tokyo: Shinchosha, 2015. 13. My translation.
117. Murakami, Haruki. "Shōsetsuka ni natta koro" in *Shokugyō toshite no shōsetsuka*. Tokyo: Switch Publishing, 2015. 272–273. My translation.
118. Pace, Eric. "William Shawn, 85, Is Dead; New Yorker's Gentle Despot." *New York Times*. December 9, 1992.
119. Murakami, Haruki. "Ryokō no otomo, jinsei no hanryo" in *Murakami Asahidō wa ikanishite kitaeraretaka*. Tokyo: Shinchosha, 1987. 248–249. My translation.
120. Gottlieb, Robert. Phone interview with author. March 22, 2017.
121. Weiss, Phillip. "Forget DeLillo and Pynchon—Murakami's the Guy for Me." *New York Observer*. December 22, 1997. observer.com/1997/12/forget-delillo-and-pynchonmurakamis-the-guy-for-me. Last accessed February 21, 2020.
122. Gottlieb, Robert. Phone interview with author. March 22, 2017.
123. MacFarquhar, Larissa. "Robert Gottlieb, The Art of Editing No. 1." *Paris Review*, issue 132, Fall 1994.
124. Gottlieb, Robert. *Avid Reader: A Life*. New York: Farrar, Straus and Giroux, 2016. 214.
125. McPhee, John. "Editors & Publisher." June 25, 2012. *New Yorker*.

July 2, 2012. www.newyorker.com/magazine/2012/07/02/editors -publisher. Last accessed February 21, 2020.

126. "The New Yorker Names a New Fiction Editor." *New York Times*. December 14, 1994.

127. Birnbaum, Alfred, ed. *Monkey Brain Sushi: New Tastes in Japanese Fiction*. Tokyo: Kodansha International, 1991.

128. Gottlieb, Robert. Phone interview with author. March 22, 2017.

129. "1990 The Noma Award for the Translation of Japanese Literature." Pamphlet for ceremony on October 4, 1990 at Hotel Frankfurt Intercontinental/Gottlieb, Robert. *Avid Reader: A Life*. New York: Farrar, Straus and Giroux, 2016. 229.

130. Gottlieb, Robert. *Avid Reader: A Life*. New York: Farrar, Straus and Giroux, 2016. 229.

131. Luke, Elmer. Interview with author. July 25, 2012/Gottlieb, Robert. Phone interview with author. March 22, 2017.

132. Luke, Elmer. Email interview with author. January 22, 2018.

133. Birnbaum, Alfred. Email interview with author. February 20, 2020.

134. Murakami, Haruki. Interview with author. January 24, 2018.

135. Gottlieb, Robert. Letter to Elmer Luke. April 10, 1991.

136. Asher, Linda. Email interview with author. December 10, 2017.

137. Luke, Elmer. Interview with author. July 25, 2012.

138. Murakami, Haruki and Masashi Matsuye. "Murakami Haruki kuronikuru" in *Kitaru beki sakkatachi*. Tokyo: Shinchosha, 1998.

139. Asher, Linda. Email interview with author. December 9, 2017.

140. Murakami, Haruki. Interview with author. January 24, 2018.

141. Asher, Linda. Interview with author. May 7, 2013.

142. Bil'ak, Peter, and Linda Asher. "Translation Is a Human Interchange." Netherlands: *Works That Work*, issue 1, Winter 2013.

143. Gottlieb, Robert. *Avid Reader: A Life*. New York: Farrar, Straus and Giroux, 2016. 213–214.

144. Murakami, Haruki. *The Elephant Vanishes.* Translated by Alfred Birnbaum and Jay Rubin. New York: Knopf, 1993. 15.

145. Murakami, Haruki. "The Windup Bird and Tuesday's Women." Translated by Alfred Birnbaum. *New Yorker.* November 26, 1990.

146. Murakami, Haruki and Masashi Matsuye. "Murakami Haruki kuronikuru" in *Kitaru beki sakkatachi.* Tokyo: Shinchosha, 1998. 185.

147. Murakami, Haruki. Interview with author. January 24, 2018.

148. Asher, Linda. Email interview with author. December 9, 2017.

149. Birnbaum, Alfred. Interview with author. August 13, 2017. Email interview with author. September 29, 2017.

150. Luke, Elmer. Email interview with author. September 23, 2017.

151. Luke, Elmer. Phone interview with author. May 2, 2019.

152. Hansen, Gitte Marianne. Email interview with author. March 13, 2020.

153. Luke, Elmer. Phone interview with author. April 18, 2019.

154. Bell, Susan. *The Artful Edit: On the Practice of Editing Yourself.* New York: W. W. Norton & Company, 2007.

155. Luke, Elmer. Phone interview with author. August 10, 2017.

156. Murakami, Haruki. "Kikigaki: Murakami Haruki kono jūnen 1979–1988." *Murakami Haruki bukku, Bungakukai shigatsu rinji zōkangō.* Edited by Yutaka Yukawa. Tokyo: Bungeishunju, 1991. 44.

3. Hard-Boiled Wonderland and the End of the World

1. Murakami, Haruki. "Purinsuton—hajime ni" in *Yagate kanashiki gaikokugo.* Tokyo: Kodansha, 1994. 10. My translation.

2. Luke, Elmer. Email interview with author. March 15, 2017.

3. Collcutt, Martin. Email interview with author. March 20, 2017.

4. Collcutt, Martin. Interview with author. April 5, 2019.

5. Murakami, Haruki. "Purinsuton—hajime ni." in *Yagate kanashiki gaikokugo.* Tokyo: Kodansha, 1994. 10. My translation.

Notes

6. Murakami, Haruki. "Saraba Purinsuton" in *Yagate kanashiki gaikokugo*. Tokyo: Kodansha, 1994. 257. My translation.
7. Hirata, Hosea. "Haruki Murakami in Princeton." *The Gest Library Journal* 5, no. 1 (1992): 10–25, library.princeton.edu/eastasian /EALJ/hirata_hosea.EALJ.v05.n01.p010.pdf. Last accessed Feb. 20, 2020.
8. Hirata, Hosea. Email interview with author. March 30, 2017.
9. Hirata, Hosea. Email interview with author. March 30, 2017.
10. Goossen, Ted. Interview with author. May 2, 2013.
11. Rubin, Jay. Email interview with author. June 27, 2013.
12. Murakami, Haruki. Letter (fax) to Elmer Luke. February 6, 1991.
13. Murakami, Haruki. Letter (fax) to Elmer Luke. February 20, 1991.
14. Murakami, Haruki. Interview with author. January 24, 2018.
15. Luke, Elmer. Interview with author. March 25, 2017.
16. Murakami, Haruki. Interview with author. January 24, 2018.
17. "Murakami Haruki 'Hitsuji o meguru bōken' beikoku de shuppan, kokusaisei ni takai hyōka." *Asahi Shimbun*, Evening Issue. November 13, 1989.
18. Moriyasu, Machiko. Interview with author. July 6, 2017.
19. "Murakami sakuhin no eiyaku (bukku endo)." *Nihon Keizai Shimbun*. January 14, 1990.
20. Kambara, Keiko. "A '60s Refugee Speaks to '80s Youth. Interview: Best-selling Japanese Author Haruki Murakami's Searching Message Is Snapped Up by Millions in Japan." *Christian Science Monitor*. March 30, 1989.
21. "Murakami sakuhin no eiyaku (bukku endo)." *Nihon Keizai Shimbun*. January 14, 1990.
22. Luke, Elmer. Email interview with author. April 27, 2019.
23. Birnbaum, Alfred. Email interview with author. April 27, 2019.
24. Luke, Elmer. Email interview with author. January 22, 2018.
25. Murakami, Haruki. Interview with author. January 24, 2018.

Notes

26. Birnbaum had already signed a contract with KI to translate the book on September 27, 1988.
27. Birnbaum, Alfred. Interview with author. July 12, 2012.
28. Birnbaum, Alfred. Interview with author. April 27, 2019.
29. Luke, Elmer. Interview with author. September 21, 2017.
30. Birnbaum, Alfred. Interview with author. July 12, 2012.
31. Luke, Elmer. Interview with author. March 25, 2018.
32. Luke, Elmer. Email interview with author. March 16, 2017.
33. Birnbaum, Alfred. Interview with author. July 12, 2012.
34. Venuti, Lawrence. *Scandals of Translation: Towards an Ethics of Difference*. London: Routledge, 2002. 4–5.
35. Borges, Jorges Luis. "Autobiographical Notes." *New Yorker*. September 19, 1970.
36. Emmerich, Michael. "Panel: Life as a Translator." British Centre for Literary Translation Summer School 2012. July 24, 2012.
37. Smith, Zadie. *Changing My Mind: Occasional Essays*. New York: Penguin Books, 2010.
38. Birnbaum, Alfred. Interview with author. March 21, 2017.
39. Rubin, Jay. *Haruki Murakami and the Music of Words*. London: Vintage, 2005. 117.
40. Rubin, Jay. Email interview with author. June 26, 2013.
41. Gabriel, Philip. Email interview with author. May 6, 2018
42. Murakami, Haruki. Letter (fax) to Elmer Luke. February 20, 1991.
43. Luke, Elmer. Letter (fax) to Haruki Murakami. March 18, 1991.
44. Murakami, Haruki. *Hard-Boiled Wonderland and the End of the World*. Translated by Alfred Birnbaum. Tokyo: Kodansha International, 1991. 97–98.
45. Birnbaum, Alfred. Interview with author. March 21, 2017.
46. Luke, Elmer. Letter (fax) to Haruki Murakami. March 29, 1991.
47. Luke, Elmer. Letter (fax) to Haruki Murakami. May 10, 1991.
48. Luke, Elmer. Interview with author. July 25, 2012.

49. Birnbaum, Alfred. Interview with author. July 12, 2012.

50. Murakami, Haruki. *Hard-Boiled Wonderland and the End of the World*. Translated by Alfred Birnbaum. Tokyo: Kodansha International, 1991. 102–103.

51. Adams, Douglas. *The Restaurant at the End of the Universe*. New York: Del Rey, 2008. 76.

52. Birnbaum, Alfred. Interview with author. April 30, 2013.

53. Birnbaum, Alfred. Interview with author. August 13, 2017.

54. Luke, Elmer. Email exchange with author. November 30, 2019.

55. Birnbaum, Alfred. Interview with author. August 13, 2017.

56. Murakami, Haruki. "Kikigaki: Murakami Haruki kono jūnen 1979–1988." *Murakami Haruki bukku, Bungakukai shigatsu rinji zōkangō*. Edited by Yutaka Yukawa. Tokyo: Bungeishunju, 1991. 44. My translation.

57. Birnbaum, Alfred. Interview with author. August 13, 2017.

58. Birnbaum, Alfred. Interview with author. July 12, 2012.

59. Birnbaum, Alfred. Interview with author. August 13, 2017.

60. Luke, Elmer. Email interview with author. April 29, 2019.

61. Hirata, Hosea. Email interview with author. January 31, 2018

62. Luke, Elmer. Phone interview with author. March 25, 2018.

63. Luke, Elmer. Phone interview with author. June 6, 2019.

64. Hirata, Hosea. Email interview. January 31, 2018.

65. Birnbaum, Alfred. Interview with author. February 5, 2019.

66. Luke, Elmer. Phone interview with author. February 28, 2019.

67. Holm, Mette. "Translating Murakami Haruki as a Multilingual Experience." *Japanese Language and Literature*, vol. 49, no. 1, Special Section: Beyond English: Translators Talk about Murakami Haruki (April 2015): 125–126.

68. Holm, Mette. "Translating Murakami Haruki as a Multilingual Experience." *Japanese Language and Literature*, Vol. 49, No. 1, Special Section: Beyond English Translators Talk about Murakami Haruki (April 2015): 125–126.

69. Holm, Mette. Email interview with author. March 12, 2020.

70. Murakami, Haruki. Interview with author. January 24, 2018.

71. Birnbaum, Alfred. Interview with author. August 13, 2017.

72. Birnbaum's comment reminds me of a *Los Angeles Times* review that stated, "The least successful parts of the book are the science-fiction trappings. The Professor and his mind-scrambling projects are expounded at tedious length; they are both abstract and murky. There is a long section in which the narrator, accompanied by the Professor's virginal but eager granddaughter, trek through perilous underground tunnels and swamps, threatened by leeches, monsters and floods. We get no sense of adventure, much less of tension; it is like one of the duller journeys in the Land of Oz." Eder, Richard. "Tokyo the Day After Tomorrow: Hard-Boiled Wonderland and the End of the World." *Los Angeles Times.* September 15, 1991.

73. Kawakami, Mieko, and Haruki Murakami. *Mimizuku wa tasogare ni tobitatsu.* Tokyo: Shinchosha, 2017. My translation.

74. Luke, Elmer. Interview with author. July 25, 2012/Phone interview with author. November 22, 2015.

75. Murakami, Haruki. *Hard-Boiled Wonderland and the End of the World.* Translated by Alfred Birnbaum. Tokyo: Kodansha International. 1991.

76. Birnbaum, Alfred. Email interview with author. March 22, 2017.

77. Luke, Elmer. Phone interview with author. May 2, 2019.

78. Birnbaum, Alfred. Email interview with author. April 27, 2019.

79. Murakami, Haruki. "Kikigaki: Murakami Haruki kono jūnen 1979–1988." *Murakami Haruki bukku, Bungakukai shigatsu rinji zōkangō.* Edited by Yutaka Yukawa. Tokyo: Bungeishunju, 1991.

80. Luke, Elmer. Phone interview with author. July 17, 2017.

81. Birnbaum, Alfred. Email interview with author. September 19, 2017.

82. Birnbaum. Alfred. Email interview with author. October 25, 2017.

83. Sterling, Robert. "Down a High-Tech Rabbit Hole." *Washington Post*, August 11, 1991.

84. McGill, Peter. "Dreams of High Skies and Unicorn Skulls." *Observer*, October 6, 1991.

85. Loose, Julian. "Sheeped." *London Review of Books*, January 30, 1992.

86. Loose, Julian. Email interview with author. April 18, 2017.

87. Luke, Elmer. Letter (fax) to Haruki Murakami. March 29, 1991.

88. Franklin, Andrew. Letter (fax) to Haruki Murakami. September 12, 1992.

89. Murakami, Haruki. Letter (fax) to Andrew Franklin. September 12, 1992.

90. Franklin, Andrew. Email correspondence with author. December 23, 2019.

91. Jolis, Gillian. "Proposed Promotion Budget Dance Dance Dance." January 21, 1993.

92. West, Paul. "Stealing Dreams from Unicorns." *New York Times*. September 15, 1991.

93. Luke, Elmer. Letter (fax) to Haruki and Yōko Murakami. October 9, 1991.

94. Luke, Elmer. Phone interview with author. February 28, 2019.

95. Murakami, Haruki. "The Birth of My Kitchen Table Fiction" translated by Ted Goossen. *Literary Hub*. June 25, 2015. lithub.com/haruki-murakami-the-moment-i-became-a-novelist. Last accessed March 12, 2020.

96. Murakami, Haruki. Interview with author. January 24, 2018.

97. Birnbaum, Alfred. Interview with author. March 21, 2017.

4. The Elephant Vanishes and Dance Dance Dance

1. Sela, Maya. "Brave New Literary World." *Haaretz*. February 24, 2009. www.haaretz.com/israel-news/culture/1.5079682. Last accessed March 21, 2020.

2. Murakami's words in the actual foreword are "The only way to find out what the editor had in mind when he made these selections is to ask the man himself."
3. Rubin, Jay. Interview with author. October 27, 2017.
4. Rubin, Jay. Email interview with author. March 3, 2017.
5. Rubin, Jay. Email interview with author. March 3, 2017.
6. Rubin, Jay. Email interview with author. March 3, 2017.
7. McClellan, Edwin. "The Impressionistic Tendency in Some Modern Japanese Writers." *Chicago Review*, vol. 17, no. 4, 1965.
8. Rubin, Jay. Email interview with author. March 3, 2017.
9. Princeton University Library Homepage. "Kunikida Doppo by Jay Rubin." catalog.princeton.edu/catalog/1878024. Last accessed March 12, 2020.
10. Rubin, Jay. Email interview with author. March 3, 2017.
11. Kunikida, Doppo, and Jay Rubin. "Takibi the Bonfire." *Monumenta Nipponica*, vol. 25, no. 1/2 (1970): 197–202.
12. Kunikida, Doppo, and Jay Rubin. "Five Stories by Kunikida Doppo." *Monumenta Nipponica* 27 (3), Sophia University (1972): 273–341.
13. Rubin, Jay. Email interview with author. March 3, 2017.
14. Rubin, Jay. Review of *River Mist and Other Stories* by Kunikida Doppo, translated by David G. Chibbett. *The Journal of Japanese Studies*, vol. 10, no. 1 (Winter 1984): 228–231.
15. Rubin, Jay. *Haruki Murakami and the Music of Words*. London: Vintage, 2005. 348–349.
16. Rubin, Jay. Email interview with author. March 3, 2017.
17. Rubin, Jay. Email interview with author. March 3, 2017.
18. Turney, Alan. Review of *Sanshirō*, a novel by Natsume Sōseki and Jay Rubin. *Monumenta Nipponica*, vol. 33, no. 2 (Summer 1978): 215–216.
19. Rimer, J. Thomas. Review of *Sanshirō* by Natsume Sōseki, translated by Jay Rubin. *The Journal of the Association of Teachers of Japanese*, vol. 13, no. 1 (April 1978): 109.

20. Rubin, Jay. Email interview with author. March 3, 2017.
21. Rubin, Jay. Email interview with author. March 3, 2017.
22. Rubin, Jay. *Murakami Haruki to watashi*. Tokyo Keizai. Kindle version. 2016.
23. Rubin, Jay. Email interview with author. March 3, 2017.
24. Rubin, Jay. *Haruki Murakami and the Music of Words*. London: Vintage, 2005. 352.
25. Rubin, Jay. Email interview with author. March 3, 2017.
26. Rubin, Jay. *Haruki Murakami and the Music of Words*. London: Vintage, 2005. 352.
27. Luke, Elmer. Email interview with author. February 9, 2017.
28. Rubin, Jay. Email interview with author. March 3, 2017.
29. Rubin, Jay. *Murakami Haruki to watashi*. Toyo Keizai, 2016. 16.
30. Fisketjon, Gary, Philip Gabriel, and Jay Rubin. "Translating Murakami: an email roundtable." December 18, 2000, to January 18, 2001. www.randomhouse.com/knopf/authors/murakami/complete.html. Last accessed February 20, 2020.
31. Craft, Kuniko Y. Email interview with author. June 16, 2017.
32. Devereaux, Elizabeth. PW Interviews: "Japan's premier novelist is 'seeking new style.'" *Publishers Weekly*. September 21, 1991.
33. Rubin, Jay. Email interview with author. March 3, 2017.
34. Asher, Linda. Email correspondence with author. March 10, 2020.
35. Asher, Linda. Letter to Elmer Luke. 1991.
36. Luke, Elmer. Letter (fax) to Yōko and Haruki Murakami. April 24, 1992.
37. Gabriel, Philip. Email interview with author. May 6, 2018.
38. Murakami, Haruki. Interview with author. January 24, 2018.
39. Shirai, Tetsu. Interview with author. March 1, 2017.
40. Murakami, Haruki. Interview with author. January 24, 2018.
41. Murakami, Haruki. "Shōsetsuka ni natta koro" in *Shokugyō*

toshite no shōsetsuka. Tokyo: Switch Publishing, 2015. 273. My translation.

42. Murakami, Haruki. "Amerika de Zō no shōmetsu ga shuppan sareta koro" in *Zō no shōmetsu tanpensenshū 1980–1991.* Tokyo: Shinchosha, 2015. 17. My translation.

43. Murakami, Haruki. "Amerika de Zō no shōmetsu ga shuppan sareta koro" in *Zō no shōmetsu tanpensenshū 1980–1991.* Tokyo: Shinchosha, 2015. 17. My translation.

44. Murakami, Haruki. "Shōsetsuka ni natta koro" in *Shokugyō toshite no shōsetsuka.* Tokyo: Switch Publishing, 2015. 273. My translation.

45. Kawakami, Mieko, and Haruki Murakami. *Misuzuku wa tasogare ni tobitatsu.* Tokyo: Shinchosha, 2017.

46. Murakami, Haruki. Interview with author. January 24, 2018.

47. Luke, Elmer. Interview with author. March 25, 2018.

48. Luke, Elmer. Phone interview with author. May 17, 2019.

49. Gallagher, Tess. Email interview with author. March 9, 2019.

50. Eggers, David. "Why Knopf Editor in Chief Sonny Mehta Still Has the Best Job in the World." *Vanity Fair,* October 2015. www.vanityfair.com/culture/2015/09/sonny-mehta-knopf-editor-in-chief. Last accessed February 21, 2020.

51. McFadden, Robert D. "Sonny Mehta, Venerable Knopf Publisher, Is Dead at 77." *New York Times.* December 31, 2019. www.nytimes.com/2019/12/31/books/sonny-mehta-dead.html. Last accessed February 21, 2020.

52. McDowell, Edwin. "Director of Pan Books Is Named Chief at Knopf." *New York Times.* January 20, 1987.

53. McFadden, Robert D. "Sonny Mehta, Venerable Knopf Publisher, Is Dead at 77." *New York Times.* December 31, 2019.

54. Notes from Haruki Murakami office. March 5, 2019.

55. Murakami, Haruki. "Amerika de Zō no shōmetsu ga shuppan

sareta koro" in *Zō no shō metsu tanpensenshū 1980–1991*. Tokyo: Shinchosha, 2015. 17–18.

56. Murakami, Haruki. Interview with author. January 24, 2018.

57. Murakami, Haruki. "Amerika de Zō no shōmetsu ga shuppan sareta koro" in *Zō no shō metsu tanpensenshū 1980–1991*. Tokyo: Shinchosha, 2015. 17–18. My translation.

58. Notes from Haruki Murakami office. March 5, 2019.

59. Mehta, Sonny. Letter to Haruki Murakami. November 5, 1991.

60. Mehta, Sonny. Letter to Haruki Murakami. December 10, 1991.

61. Mehta, Sonny. Letter to Haruki Murakami. January 22, 1992.

62. Cohen, Robert. "New Publishing Star, Sonny Mehta, Talks Profits as Well as Art." *New York Times*. November 13, 1990.

63. Murakami, Haruki. Interview with author. January 24, 2018.

64. Luke, Elmer. Email interview with author. September 19, 2017.

65. Walker, Larry. "Bringing Japanese Literature to the West: The Knopf Translation Program, 1955–76." SWET Newsletter, Number 117/Walker, Larry. "Unbinding the Japanese Novel in English Translation: The Alfred A. Knopf Program, 1955–1977." Doctoral dissertation at University of Helsinki, Faculty of Arts, Department of Modern Languages. 2015.

66. Luke, Elmer. Email interview with author. September 19, 2017.

67. Sapiro, Gisele. "Translation and the Field of Publishing." *Translation Studies* 1:2 (2008). 157.

68. Murakami, Haruki. "Murakami Haruki rongu intabyū." *Kangaeru Hito*. Tokyo: Shinchosha, 2010. 90. My translation.

69. Shirai, Tetsu. Interview with author. March 1, 2017.

70. Asakawa, Minato. Interview with author. May 1, 2018.

71. Levi, Stephanie. Email interview with author. June 15, 2017.

72. Ura, Kuniaki. Interview with author. April 23, 2019.

73. Luke, Elmer. Interview with author. September 1, 2014.

74. Murakami, Haruki. Interview with author. January 24, 2018.

75. Levi, Jonathan. Email interview with author. April 24, 2018.
76. Luke, Elmer. Email interview with author. March 16, 2017.
77. Murakami, Haruki. Interview with author. January 24, 2018.
78. Notes from Haruki Murakami office. March 5, 2019.
79. Luke, Elmer. Phone interview with author. March 7, 2019.
80. Luke, Elmer. Letter (fax) to Jessica Green. April 24, 1992.
81. Pockell, Leslie. Letter (fax) to Elmer Luke. May 7, 1992.
82. Luke, Elmer. Letter (fax) to Haruki Murakami. May 19, 1992.
83. Murakami, Haruki. Interview with author. January 24, 2018.
84. Luke, Elmer. Interview with author. March 16, 2017.
85. "Maxwell E. Perkins Award: Past Recipients." Center for Fiction. centerforfiction.org/grants-awards/maxwell-e-perkins-award /maxwell-e-perkins-award-past-recipients. Last accessed February 21, 2020.
86. EW Staff. "The 101 Most Powerful People in Entertainment." *Entertainment Weekly.* November 1, 1991. ew.com/article /1991/11/01/101-most-powerful-people-entertainment/. Last accessed February 21, 2020.
87. Luke, Elmer. Email interview with author. March 16, 2017.
88. Luke, Elmer. Email interview with author. March 15, 2017.
89. Luke, Elmer. Email interview with author. March 16, 2017.
90. Urban, Amanda. Email correspondence. March 19, 2020.
91. Wolff, Tobias. Email interview with author. July 25, 2017.
92. Murakami, Haruki. Interview with author. January 24, 2018.
93. Notes from Haruki Murakami office. April 12, 2019.
94. Gallagher, Tess. Email interview with author. March 9, 2019.
95. Kellerman, Stewart. "Raymond Carver, Writer and Poet of the Working Poor, Dies at 50." *New York Times.* August 3, 1988.
96. Luke, Elmer. Email correspondence with author. March 22, 2020.
97. Luke, Elmer. Email interview with author. March 16, 2017.
98. Luke, Elmer. Email interview with author. March 16, 2017.

99. Murakami, Haruki. "Kaigai e dete iku. Atarashii furontia" in *Shokugyō to shite no shōsetsuka*. Tokyo: Switch Publishing, 2015. 276.

100. Murakami, Haruki. "Amerika de Zō no shōmetsu ga shuppan sareta koro" in *Zō no shōmetsu tanpensenshū 1980–1991*. Tokyo: Shinchosha, 2015. 18.

101. Luke, Elmer. Email interview with author. January 23, 2018.

102. Luke, Elmer. Email interview with author. March 25, 2017.

103. Luke, Elmer. Letter (fax) to Haruki and Yōko Murakami. June 10, 1992.

104. Urban, Amanda. Letter (fax) to Elmer Luke. June 16, 1992.

105. Luke, Elmer. Letter to Haruki and Yōko Murakami. June 16, 1992.

106. Luke, Elmer. Email interview with author. March 16, 2017.

107. Kawakami, Mieko, and Haruki Murakami. *Mimizuku wa tasogare ni tobitatsu*. Tokyo: Shinchosha, 2017. 306. My translation.

108. Murakami, Haruki. "Murakami Haruki rongu intabyū." *Kangaeru Hito*, Summer 2010, Shinchosha. 93. My translation.

109. Murakami, Haruki. *Shokugyō to shite no shōsetsuka*. Tokyo: Switch Publishing, 2015. 274. My translation.

110. Birnbaum, Alfred. Interview with author. March 21, 2017.

111. Fisketjon, Gary. "A Letter from the Editor of *The Elephant Vanishes*." Haruki Murakami website. www.harukimurakami.com/q_and_a/editors-letter. Last accessed February 20, 2020.

112. Gallagher, Tess. Email interview with author. March 9, 2019.

113. Murakami, Haruki. Interview with author. January 24, 2018.

114. Risen, Clay. "Literary Hideaway." *Nashville Scene*, December 7, 2006.

115. Alter, Alexandra, and John Williams. "Knopf Fires High-Profile Editor over Policy Breach." *New York Times*. May 17, 2019. www.nytimes.com/2019/05/17/books/gary-fisketjon-knopf.html. Last accessed February 20, 2020.

116. Fisketjon, Gary. Email interview with author. March 7, 2017.

Notes

117. Murakami, Haruki. "Amerika de Zō no shōmetsu ga shuppan sareta koro" in *Zō no shōmetsu tanpensenshū 1980–1991*. Tokyo: Shinchosha, 2015. 18–19. My translation.
118. Fisketjon, Gary. Email interview with author. March 7, 2017.
119. Fisketjon, Gary, Philip Gabriel, and Jay Rubin. "Translating Murakami: an email roundtable."
120. Fisketjon, Gary. Email interview with the author. March 7, 2017.
121. Murakami, Haruki. Interview with author. January 24, 2018.
122. Fisketjon, Gary. Email interview with author. February 21, 2018.
123. Murakami, Haruki. "Amerika de Zō no shōmetsu ga shuppan sareta koro" in *Zō no shōmetsu tanpensenshū 1980–1991*. Tokyo: Shinchosha, 2015. 19.
124. "Dokusho no aki ima eigobon ga uretemasu. Nihon no bungaku yakushita mono mo ninki." *Yomiuri Shimbun*, October 25, 1990.
125. Fisketjon, Gary, Philip Gabriel, and Jay Rubin. "Translating Murakami: an email roundtable."
126. Hillenbrand, Margaret. "Murakami Haruki in Greater China: Creative Responses and the Quest for Cosmopolitanism." *Journal of Asian Studies* 68, issue 3 (2009).
127. Fisketjon, Gary, Philip Gabriel, and Jay Rubin. "Translating Murakami: an email roundtable."
128. Murakami, Haruki. Interview with author. January 24, 2018.
129. Murakami, Haruki. "Mekishiko Dairyokō" in *Mother Nature's* and later "Henkyō kinkyō." Tokyo: Shinchosha. Kindle. 2016.
130. Luke, Elmer. Email interview with author. March 16, 2017.
131. Murakami, Haruki. "Amerika de Zō no shōmetsu ga shuppan sareta koro" in *Zō no shōmetsu tanpensenshū 1980–1991*. Tokyo: Shinchosha, 2015. 19. My translation.
132. Luke, Elmer. Letter (fax) to Haruki Murakami. September 18, 1992.
133. Murakami, Haruki. Letter (fax) to Elmer Luke. September 16, 1992.
134. Murakami, Haruki. "Amerika de Zō no shōmetsu ga shuppan

sareta koro" in *Zō no shōmetsu tanpensenshū 1980–1991*. Tokyo. Shinchosha, 2015. 19.

135. Fisketjon, Gary. Email interview with author. March 7, 2017.

136. Birnbaum, Alfred. Interview with author. March 21, 2017.

137. Fisketjon, Gary, Philip Gabriel, and Jay Rubin. "Translating Murakami: an email roundtable."

138. Luke, Elmer. Email interview with author. July 18, 2017.

139. Luke, Elmer. Email interview with author. July 19, 2017.

140. Murakami, Haruki. Interview with author. January 24, 2018.

141. Notes from Haruki Murakami office. March 5, 2019.

142. Murakami, Haruki. "Meikingu obu nejimakidori kuronikuru." *Shinchō*. November 1992. 272.

143. Fisketjon, Gary. Email interview with author. March 30, 2017.

144. Fisketjon, Gary. Email interview with author. March 31, 2017.

145. Rubin, Jay. Letter (fax) to Gary Fisketjon. December 7, 1992.

146. Rubin, Jay. Letter (fax) to Gary Fisketjon. January 3, 1993.

147. Luke, Elmer. Letter (fax) to Haruki Murakami. January 25, 1993.

148. Kidd, Chip. Interview with author. September 4, 2014.

149. Kidd, Chip. Email interview with author. April 23, 2017.

150. Kidd, Chip. Email interview with author. April 23, 2017.

151. Kidd, Chip. Email interview with author. April 23, 2017.

152. Murakami, Haruki. "Chippu Kiddo no shigoto" in Special Issue of *Coyote: Tokyo Literary City*. 2013. 88–89.

153. Kidd, Chip. Email interview with author. April 23, 2017.

154. Murakami, Haruki. "Amerika de Zō no shōmetsu ga shuppan sareta koro" in *Zō no shōmetsu tanpensenshū 1980–1991*. Tokyo: Shinchosha, 2015. 20. My translation.

155. Fisketjon, Gary, Philip Gabriel, and Jay Rubin. "Translating Murakami: an email roundtable."

156. Fisketjon, Gary. Interview with Ryōichi Niimoto for "Eigo de yomu Murakami Haruki." NHK Radio. April/May 2014.

157. Notes from Haruki Murakami office. March 13, 2020.

158. Murakami, Haruki. Interview with author. January 24, 2018.

159. Murakami, Haruki. "Amerika de Zō no shōmetsu ga shuppan sareta koro" in *Zō no shōmetsu tanpensenshū 1980–1991*. Tokyo: Shinchosha, 2015. 20.

160. Mitgang, Herbert. "From Japan, Big Macs and Marlboros in Stories." *New York Times*. May 12, 1993.

161. Murakami, Haruki. "Jikan wo mikata ni tsukeru. Chōhen shōsetsu wo kaku koto" in *Shokugyō toshite no shōsetsuka*. Tokyo: Switch, 2015. 136.

162. Max, D. T. "The Carver Chronicles." *New York Times Magazine*. August 9, 1998. www.nytimes.com/1998/08/09/magazine/the-carver-chronicles.html. Last accessed February 20, 2020.

163. Max, D. T. "Book World: Japanese Stories of Import." *Washington Post*. May 28, 1993.

164. Luke, Elmer. Letter (fax) to Haruki Murakami. March 20, 1991.

165. Murakami, Haruki. Letter (fax) to Elmer Luke. March 20, 1991.

166. Memorandum of an agreement between Kodansha International Ltd. (the Publisher) and Alfred Birnbaum (the Translator) for a translation of Haruki Murakami's Dance Dance Dance (the Work). September 13, 1991.

167. Birnbaum, Alfred. Interview with author. March 21, 2017.

168. Luke, Elmer. Email interview with author. April 7, 2018.

169. Murakami, Haruki. "As Translator, as Novelist: The Translator's Afterword." Translated by Ted Goossen in Allen, Esther, and Susan Bernofsky, ed. *In Translation: Translators on Their Work and What It Means* (English Edition). Columbia University Press, 2013. Kindle edition.

170. Murakami, Haruki. "Honyakusha toshite, shōsetsuka toshite: yakusha atogaki" in *Gurēto Gyattsubī* by F. Scott Fitzgerald, translated by Haruki Murakami. Tokyo: Chuokoronshinsha, 2006. 333.

171. Murakami, Haruki. *Dance Dance Dance*. Translated by Alfred Birnbaum. Vintage International. Kindle version.

172. Birnbaum, Alfred. Interview with author. July 12, 2012.

173. Birnbaum, Alfred. Email interview with author. March 20, 2019.

174. Luke, Elmer. Letter (fax) to Haruki Murakami. January 25, 1993.

175. Luke, Elmer. Letter (fax) to Haruki Murakami. June 25, 1993.

176. Luke, Elmer. Interview with author. July 25, 2012.

177. Murakami, Haruki. Interview with author. January 24, 2018.

178. Murakami, Haruki. Interview with author. January 24, 2018.

179. Jolis, Gillian. "Proposed Promotion Budget Dance Dance Dance." January 21, 1993.

180. Luke, Elmer. Email interview with author. June 5, 2017.

181. Luke, Elmer. Email interview with author. January 22, 2018.

182. "Dance, Dance, Dance." *Publishers Weekly.* October 18, 1993.

183. Harris, Michael. "Some Satire, a Bit of Mystery, a Dash of Philosophy." *Los Angeles Times*, January 24, 1994.

184. Rifkind, Donna. "Another Wild Chase." *New York Times.* January 2, 1994.

185. Mitgang, Herbert. "Looking for America, or Is It Japan?" *New York Times.* January 3, 1994.

186. Birnbaum, Alfred. Interview with author. March 21, 2017.

187. Asakawa, Minato. Interview with author. April 21, 2017.

188. Luke, Elmer. Email interview with author. January 22, 2018.

189. Jolis, Gillian. "Proposed Promotion Budget Dance Dance Dance." January 21, 1993.

190. Laurel, Graeber. "New and Noteworthy Paperbacks." *New York Times.* April 2, 1995.

191. Murakami, Haruki. Interview with author. January 24, 2018.

5. The Wind-Up Bird Chronicle

1. Kelts, Roland. "Lost in Translation?" *The New Yorker.* May 9, 2013. www.newyorker.com/books/page-turner/lost-in-translation. Last accessed March 12, 2020.

2. Gottlieb, Robert. *Avid Reader: A Life.* New York: Farrar, Straus and Giroux, 2016. 237.

3. Murakami, Haruki. "Amerika de Zō no shōmetsu ga shuppan sareta koro" in *Zō no shōmetsu tanpensenshū 1980–1991*. Tokyo: Shinchosha, 2015. 16.

4. Murakami, Haruki. "Hitokui kūgā to hentai eiga to sakka tomu jōnzu" in *Uzumakineko no mitsukekata*. Tokyo: Shinchosha, 1996. 50. My translation.

5. Murakami, Haruki. "Amerika de Zō no shōmetsu ga shuppan sareta koro" in *Zō no shōmetsu tanpensenshū 1980–1991*. Tokyo: Shinchosha, 2015. 24.

6. Dyer, Geoff. "Richard Avedon" in *Otherwise Known as the Human Condition: Selected Essays and Reviews*. Graywolf Press, 2011.

7. Angell, Roger. "The Fadeaway." *New Yorker*. February 9, 2009. www.newyorker.com/magazine/2009/02/09/the-fadeaway. Last accessed February 20, 2020.

8. Updike, John. "Imperishable Maxwell." *New Yorker*. September 8, 2008.

9. Collins, Nancy. "Demi's Big Moment." *Vanity Fair*. August 1991. www.vanityfair.com/style/2018/04/demi-moore-cover-story -august-1991. Last accessed February 20, 2020.

10. Carmody, Deirdre. "Richard Avedon Is Named New Yorker Photographer." *New York Times*. December 10, 1992.

11. Updike, John. *Due Considerations: Essays and Criticism*. New York: Knopf, 2007.

12. Snyder, Stephen. Email exchange with author. January 27, 2020.

13. Carmody, Deirdre. "Tina Brown to Take Over at The New Yorker." *New York Times*. July 1, 1992. Yagoda, Ben. "New Yorker" in *Encyclopedia of American Journalism*, ed. Stephen L. Vaughn. New York: Routledge, 2008. 348.

14. Weintraub, Joanne. "Tina Brown's *New Yorker*." *American Journalism Review*, April 1995. ajrarchive.org/article.asp?id=1692. Last accessed February 21, 2020.

15. Garfield, Simon. "From Student Rag to Literary Riches." *Observer*.

December 30, 2007. www.theguardian.com/books/2007/dec/30 /culture.features. Last accessed February 21, 2020.

16. Murakami, Haruki. "Rongu Intabyū." *Kangaeru Hito.* Summer 2010. 95.

17. Murakami, Haruki. Interview with author. January 24, 2018.

18. Murakami, Haruki. Interview with author. January 24, 2018.

19. Murakami, Haruki. Letter (fax) to Elmer Luke. September 16, 1992.

20. Birnbaum, Alfred. Interview with author. March 21, 2017.

21. Murakami, Haruki. Letter (fax) to Elmer Luke. September 16, 1992.

22. Rubin, Jay. *Haruki Murakami and the Music of Words.* London: Vintage, 2005. 350.

23. Rubin, Jay. *Haruki Murakami and the Music of Words.* London: Vintage, 2005. 348.

24. Murakami, Haruki. Interview with author. January 24, 2018.

25. Birnbaum, Alfred. Email to author. March 22, 2017.

26. Luke, Elmer. Letter (fax) to Haruki Murakami. September 18, 1992.

27. Rubin, Jay. Letter (fax) to Haruki and Yōko Murakami. September 18, 1992.

28. Murakami, Haruki. Letter (fax) to Jay Rubin. September 26, 1992.

29. Rubin, Jay. Letter (fax) to Haruki Murakami. September 27, 1992.

30. Rubin, Jay. Letter (fax) to Haruki Murakami. October 16, 1992.

31. Rubin, Jay. Letter (fax) to Haruki Murakami. October 18, 1922

32. Murakami, Haruki. Interview with author. January 24, 2018.

33. Murakami, Haruki. Interview with author. January 24, 2018.

34. Birnbaum, Alfred. Interview with author. August 13, 2017.

35. Birnbaum, Alfred. Email interview with author. October 3, 2017.

36. Luke, Elmer. Email interview with author. May 25, 2017.

37. Birnbaum, Alfred. Interview with author. January 11, 2016.

38. Luke, Elmer. Email interview with author. September 19, 2017.

39. Luke, Elmer. Email interview with author. April 24/27, 2018.

40. Luke, Elmer. Phone interview with author. October 16, 2016.

41. Venuti, Lawrence. *Scandals of Translation: Towards an Ethics of Difference.* London & New York: Routledge, 2002. 4–5.

42. Nesbitt, Huw. "Jorge Luis Borges's lost translations." *Guardian.* February 19, 2010.

43. Venuti, Lawrence. *Scandals of Translation: Towards an Ethics of Difference.* London & New York: Routledge, 2002. 5–6.

44. Murakami, Haruki. Interview with author. January 24, 2018.

45. Bloom, Lexy. Email exchange with author. March 15, 2019.

46. Birnbaum, Alfred. Interview with author. March 21, 2017.

47. Luke, Elmer. Email interview with author. October 1, 2017.

48. Murakami, Haruki. "Murakami Haruki rongu intabyū" in *Kangaeru Hito.* Summer 2010, Shinchosha. 95.

49. Murakami, Haruki. "Murakami Haruki rongu intabyū" in *Kangaeru Hito.* Summer 2010, Shinchosha. 95.

50. Murakami, Haruki. Interview with author. January 24, 2018.

51. Rubin, Jay. Interview with author. October 27, 2017.

52. Asher, Linda. Email interview with author. November 6, 2017.

53. Rubin, Jay. Interview with author. October 27, 2017.

54. Asher, Linda. Email interview with author. December 10, 2017.

55. Buruma, Ian. "Becoming Japanese." *New Yorker.* December 23, 1996.

56. Rubin, Jay. Edited Draft Translation of "Another Way to Die" by Haruki Murakami. Papers of Jay Rubin at the Lilly Library, Indiana University, Bloomington, Indiana. December 16, 1996.

57. Rubin, Jay. Edited Draft Translation of "Another Way to Die" by Haruki Murakami. Papers of Jay Rubin at the Lilly Library, Indiana University, Bloomington, Indiana. December 18, 1996.

58. Rubin, Jay. Edited Draft Translation of "Another Way to Die" by Haruki Murakami. Papers of Jay Rubin at the Lilly Library, Indiana University, Bloomington, Indiana. December 16, 1996.

59. Rubin, Jay. Edited Draft Translation of "Another Way to Die" by Haruki Murakami. Papers of Jay Rubin at the Lilly Library, Indiana University, Bloomington, Indiana. December 18, 1996.

60. Murakami, Haruki. "Another Way to Die." Translated by Jay Rubin. *New Yorker.* January 20, 1997.

61. Murakami, Haruki. Interview with author. January 24, 2018.

62. Rubin, Jay. Interview with author. October 27, 2017.

63. Draft contracts between Haruki Murakami and Knopf for *The Wind-Up Bird Chronicle* and *South of the Border, West of the Sun.*

64. Rubin, Jay. *Haruki Murakami and the Music of Words.* London: Vintage, 2005. 342.

65. Fisketjon, Gary, Philip Gabriel, and Jay Rubin. "Translating Murakami: an email roundtable."

66. Murakami, Haruki. Interview with author. January 24, 2018.

67. Rubin, Jay. *Haruki Murakami and the Music of Words.* London: Vintage, 2005. 342.

68. Rubin, Jay. *Haruki Murakami and the Music of Words.* London: Vintage. 2005, 342.

69. Rubin, Jay. Letter to Gary Fisketjon and Robert Glover. Papers of Jay Rubin at the Lilly Library, Indiana University, Bloomington, Indiana. April 17, 1997.

70. Rubin, Jay. Letter to Gary Fisketjon. Papers of Jay Rubin at the Lilly Library, Indiana University, Bloomington, Indiana. May 9, 1997.

71. Rubin, Jay. Letter to Robert Glover. Papers of Jay Rubin at the Lilly Library, Indiana University, Bloomington, Indiana. August 18, 1997.

72. Rubin, Jay. Letter to Robert Glover. Papers of Jay Rubin at the Lilly Library, Indiana University, Bloomington, Indiana. August 18, 1997.

73. Luke, Elmer. Interview with author. July 25, 2017.

74. Rubin, Jay. *Haruki Murakami and the Music of Words*. London: Vintage, 2005. 254.

75. Rubin, Jay. *Haruki Murakami and the Music of Words*. London: Vintage, 2005. 342.

76. Fisketjon, Gary. Email interview with author. March 7, 2017.

77. Fisketjon, Gary. Email interview with author. March 7, 2017.

78. Dowell, Erika. Email exchange. June 9, 2018.

79. Murakami, Haruki. Interview with author. January 24, 2018.

80. As of 2004, in an email to Amanda Urban, Rubin states that he is not eager to see an unabridged version of the book published but is in favor of making omitted material available in another form.

81. Kidd, Chip. *Chip Kidd: Book One: Work: 1986–2006*. New York: Rizzoli, 2005.

82. Weiss, Philip. "Forget DeLillo and Pynchon—Murakami's the Guy for Me." *New York Observer*. December 22, 1997.

83. Iyer, Pico. Email interview with author. May 16, 2017.

84. Rubin, Jay. Interview with author. October 27, 2017.

85. Murakami, Haruki. Interview with author. January 24, 2018.

86. Kakutani, Michiko. "The Wind-Up Bird Chronicle: A Nightmarish Trek Through History's Web." *New York Times*. October 31, 1997.

87. James, Jamie. "East Meets West." *New York Times*. November 2, 1997.

88. Kakutani, Michiko. "'The Wind-Up Bird Chronicle': A Nightmarish Trek Through History's Web." *New York Times*. October 31, 1997.

89. Weiss, Philip. "Forget DeLillo and Pynchon—Murakami's the Guy for Me." *New York Observer*. December 22, 1997.

90. Strecher, Matthew. *Haruki Murakami's The Wind-up Bird Chronicle: A Reader's Guide*. London and New York: Continuum, 2002.

91. Murakami, Haruki, and Masashi Matsuye. "Murakami Haruki Kuronikuru" in *Kitaru beki sakkatachi*. Tokyo: Shinchosha, 1998.

92. Fisketjon, Gary. Email interview with author. November 21, 2017.
93. Fisketjon, Gary. Email interview with author. November 21, 2017.
94. Kelts, Roland. Email interview with author. November 10, 2017.
95. Mitchell, David. Email interview with author. March 16, 2018.
96. Díaz, Junot. Email interview with author. November 20, 2017.
97. Iyer, Pico. Email interview with author. May 16, 2017.
98. Birnbaum, Alfred. Email interview with author. November 26/ December 28, 2017.
99. Luke, Elmer. Email interview with author. December 22, 2017.
100. Fisketjon, Gary. Email interview with author. November 21, 2017.
101. Notes from Haruki Murakami office. March 5, 2019.
102. Wroe, Nicholas. "Christopher MacLehose: A Life in Publishing." *Guardian*. December 28, 2012. www.theguardian.com /books/2012/dec/28/christopher-maclehose-life-in-publishing. Last accessed February 21, 2020.
103. MacLehose, Christopher. Email interview with author. December 1, 2017.
104. Fisketjon, Gary. Email interview with author. December 5, 2017.
105. MacLehose, Christopher. Email interview with author. December 5, 2017.
106. "Sakka Murakami Haruki no ninki, ei de jiwari tokusōbon kankō mo." *Asahi Shimbun.* July 16, 2001.
107. MacLehose, Christopher. Email interview with author. December 1, 2017.
108. "Sakka Murakami Haruki no ninki, ei de jiwari tokusōbon kankō mo." *Asahi Shimbun.* July 16, 2001.
109. MacLehose, Christopher. Interview with author. June 17, 2013.
110. MacLehose, Christopher. Email interview with author. December 1, 2017.
111. Baggaley, Paul. Email interview with author. January 5, 2018.
112. Rubin, Jay. Letter to Victoria Miller. Papers of Jay Rubin at the

Lilly Library, Indiana University, Bloomington, Indiana. February 9, 1998.

113. MacLehose, Christopher. Email interview with author. December 1, 2017.

114. Murakami, Haruki. Interview with author. January 24, 2018.

Image Permissions

Image Permissions

DAVID KARASHIMA has translated a range of contemporary Japanese authors into English, including Hitomi Kanehara, Hisaki Matsuura, and Shinji Ishii. He coedited the anthology *March Was Made of Yarn: Writers Respond to the Japanese Earthquake, Tsunami, and Nuclear Meltdown* and is coeditor of Pushkin Press's Contemporary Japanese Novellas series and Strangers Press's Keshiki series. He is an associate professor of creative writing at Waseda University in Tokyo.